Renewing

The Renewal

A Firestorm In
The Catholic Church

Renée Alda Marazon
MAPS for life
Perrysburg, Ohio

Copyright © 2004 by Renée Alda Marazon with exclusive rights to MAPS for life. All rights reserved. No part of this publication can be adapted, reproduced, stored in any retrieval system, or transmitted in any form or by any means electronic, mechanical, photocopying, recording, or otherwise without permission of the author.

Published by   MAPS for life
                 29336 Belmont Lake Rd.
                 Perrysburg, OH 43551
                 Phone/Fax: (419) 661-1945
                 E-Mail: maps@marazon.com
                 Web Site: www.marazon.com

Distributed by   Ministry to Catholic Charismatic Renewal
                 Diocese of Toledo
                 550 Clark Street
                 Toledo, OH 43605
                 Phone: (419) 691-6686

Library of Congress Cataloging-in-Publication Date

Marazon, Renée A.
     Renewing the Renewal: A Firestorm in the Catholic
     Church/Renée A. Marazon—1st edition p. cm.
     ISBN 1-889114-21-9

Printed in the United States of America

Scripture texts in this work are taken from the *New American Bible with Revised New Testament and Revised Psalms* © 1991, 1986, 1970 Confraternity of Christian Doctrine, Washington, D.C. and are used by permission of the copyright owner. All Rights Reserved. No part of the *New American Bible* may be reproduced in any form without permission in writing from the copyright owner.

Contents

Acknowledgements

To the Father whose creative love creates us anew each day with visions, thoughts, ideas, and proclamations of His Greatness! To Jesus in whose name all things are now possible and through whose Precious Blood all are saved. To the Holy Spirit, sanctifier of minds and hearts. To Mary, Mother of Sorrows, through whose intercession we are forever graced.

I wish to thank my husband David for his patience, friendship, and unconditional love

I wish to thank Patricia and Terry Szyperski for lighting a fire under my feet, and for their insights, encouragement, and friendship.

With deepest gratitude to Reverend Jerome Nowakowski, Jill Laytart, Sr. Marie Julie Reineke, SND, and Mark Nehrbas for their review and editorial comments, and to members of the Spiritual Leadership Council of the Ministry to Catholic Charismatic Renewal, Diocese of Toledo for their editorial contributions.

About The Author

Renée A. Marazon has served as the Healing Ministry Coordinator, Ministry to Catholic Charismatic Renewal, Diocese of Toledo, from 1986-1991 and again from 1996 to the present. She has presented workshops at national and local conferences and has ministered in Trinidad and Tobago as well as across the U.S. giving retreats, missions, days of renewal, and seminars on topics related to healing, prayer, the mystics, prophecy, growth in the Spirit, raising children for heaven, and the moral and spiritual development of children and families. She is a gifted teacher and motivational speaker.

She is the author of numerous articles and books. Her most recent publication, *The Catholic Handbook of Child Growth, Development, and Learning* is a powerful resource for families and all who work with children and young adults. The Marazon approach to education, a whole-child focus to planning and assessment, is used by charter schools, public schools, Head Start, family childcare, home school parents, and military child development programs around the world.

Ms. Marazon received her Bachelor of Arts degree from Ursuline College in Pepper Pike, Ohio and a Master's degree from Bowling Green State University. She held a faculty position at Lourdes College in Sylvania Ohio from 1983 to 1997 where she served as Chairperson for the Department of Early Childhood.

In her varying ministry roles, she continually expresses a passion for the child that draws others to see each child as a unique gift from God. Her message is constant—"Look to the child. Check in with the child who is so competent and gifted." Her most important gifts in life are her husband David and her children, Matthew and Stephen, stepchildren, Nicole and Jon, and beautiful grandchildren.

She is passionate about the Church, filled with zeal for life in the Spirit, dedicated to helping others gaze upon the face of Christ and come to know about the Father's great Love, and certain that all can experience God's presence in their lives through listening, speaking, seeing, tasting, and touching the Risen Christ in prayer and in one another.

Forward

In his Apostolic Letter *Novo Millennio Ineunte* (2001), written at the start of the new millennium, John Paul II challenged the entire Church, to "put out into the deep." He did not address his call to any one particular movement or group within the Church. Rather, he directed his challenge to all movements, all groups, and all people in the Church. This fact has great significance for all Catholics and even greater significance for those involved in renewal movements such as the Catholic Charismatic Renewal. As we read his Apostolic Letter, we realize at once that his broad-based challenge requires us to respond to his call both individually and as a renewal movement.

When John Paul II (2001) challenged the Church to go out into the deep, he specifically advised parishes to design new pastoral initiatives that would be rooted in and energized by the Gospel of Jesus Christ. He advised that such initiatives be "adapted to the circumstances of each community." He further counseled that the content of any new pastoral initiatives should be focused on transforming parishes into schools of holiness, schools of prayer, and schools of communion, with emphasis on Sunday Eucharist, Reconciliation, the role of grace, listening to the Word of God, and proclaiming the Word of God to others.

As we ponder the call of the Holy Father to put out into the deep, we are faced with many unknowns. The moment we say, "Yes Lord, I will put out into the deep to catch souls for your Kingdom." our dilemma will most likely be focused on how to get out into the deep, what kind of nets to cast, and once there, where to cast them. *Renewing the Renewal: A Firestorm in the Catholic Church* challenges individual Catholics, prayer groups, and Renewal leaders to put out into the deep—the mainstream of the Catholic Church and once there, to design, produce and cast nets into the deep waters of parish life in order to catch Catholic souls for Christ.

Renewing the Renewal inspires, energizes, and compels those who are living in the Spirit to go as missionaries into the deep—the mainstream of the Catholic Church as it illustrates reasonable plans, attainable goals, and doable methods of how to go into the deep so that the nets we cast ensure a bountiful catch for Christ. Real-life stories lead the way giving step-by-step guidelines and examples of what to do and how to do it. Each chapter includes questions or exercises that encourage prayer and reflection and lead individuals, prayer groups, and the Renewal to take action steps leading to renewal of the mainstream Catholic Church.

Renewing the Renewal is a book of hope, enthusiasm, excitement, and anticipation of how the Holy Spirit will use us individually and use the Renewal to revive, replenish, repair, revitalize, rekindle, rejuvenate, and regenerate the Church. In the process, each of us will be renewed, and so will prayer groups and the Renewal Movement at both the diocesan and national level.

We must put out into the deep. It is time for us to go! If we dare to venture out into the mainstream of the Church, we will see God's love and mercy, and His miracles at work in places we never thought possible. Imagine the firestorm that will let loose on the earth should John Paul II's vision for renewing the Church become a reality!

See I Am Doing A New Thing

Remember not the events of the past,
the things of long ago consider not;
See, I am doing something new!
Now it springs forth ,do you not perceive it?
(Is 43:18-19)

Just as the Holy Doors across this land closed to signal the start of a new millennium, unimaginable trials and challenges were laid on the doorstep of the Catholic Church in America. We were less than two years into the new millennium when our anticipation and enthusiasm for the "New Springtime in the Church" had been tempered with disbelief, sadness, and shame. Catholics have been confused, angry, ashamed, and unsure of how to respond with yet one more media announcement. There have been disagreements and even confrontations cropping up within families and among friends, clergy, and Church leaders. Some have chosen deliberate silence while others have been driven to speak out. All agree these are difficult times in the Church.

At a time when Charismatic Catholics could be called upon to minister to families, clergy, Church leaders, pastoral teams, and whole parish communities, it appears that there are too few prayer groups and too few prayer group members remaining to truly impact the greater Church. In some areas of the country, the number of prayer groups has significantly dwindled and those who still attend prayer meetings are but a fraction of those who attended years ago.

We who remain active in the Renewal yearn for new members, especially the young, to come and experience what we have experienced for so many years, namely the power of the Holy Spirit at work in us and in God's people— teaching, convicting, guiding, revealing, and healing through the very same charisms that were present in the early Church.

As we continue to persevere in living in the Spirit, it is only natural that we should wonder about the future of the Catholic

Charismatic Renewal. We cannot help but think about the past and begin to long for its return. We hunger for a prayer meeting with 100 voices praising the Lord. We yearn for standing room only at Charismatic Masses and healing services and we long for Life in the Spirit Seminars to be at maximum capacity. We pray, fast, and intercede for our annual conference in the hopes that the chairs will all be filled, and more chairs will have to be added to the conference hall.

Despite all of our prayers, none of these things happens. Nonetheless, we continue to tell our stories of the past, hoping it will help us feel better. We want to be comforted in remembering, but instead of being comforted, we oftentimes become sad, frustrated, or worried about the future of the Renewal. We are held captive, confined to our own limited thoughts, enslaved, and at times immobilized by the notion that we must have it again, the way it was back then. We long for the things of the past instead of longing for the Holy One of the present.

We must not despair! Instead, as we read from the prophet Isaiah, we must hope and trust fully in God's plan:

> Remember not the events of the past,
> the things of long ago consider not;
> See, I am doing something new.
> Now it springs forth, do you not perceive it?
> In the desert I make a way, in the wasteland, rivers
> (Is 43:18-20).

Down through the ages, the Lord has always done new things with, in, and through His people. Why would He not be doing so right now? Why should He not be causing rivers to flow where there was once wasteland, unity where there was once division, and wholeness where there was disintegration? Indeed, God does have a plan to bring about reconciliation in place of anger, healing where there was once sickness, and grace where there once was disgrace.

Instead of yearning for, reminiscing about, or brooding over the Renewal of the past, we can be an integral part of this new thing God is doing right now. For this to happen however, we must be more attentive than we have ever been to the Renewal of the present time, to the movement of the Holy Spirit in our present time. If attendance at prayer group and Renewal events is dwindling, is this a sign of the demise of the Renewal? Is the Renewal on the road to extinction?

We know it is not possible for the Renewal to die for it is an instrument of God's Pentecost mission. From the time of its humble beginnings, the Renewal has been a gift to the Church. However, the way it will continue to be a gift in this third millennium, may be quite different from the past. This is precisely why we must be very attentive to how God is calling us into new ministries—ministries that we would not have thought possible ten years ago. In addition, we must also discern where God is leading us to minister—places we might never have imagined.

It is somewhat ironic, a bit of an oxymoron, that we would yearn for the Renewal to be like it was years ago. In so doing, we hinder the renewal of the Renewal. The Renewal must continually grow. For the moment it becomes stagnant, it ceases to be a renewal movement. Therefore, we must not desire the Renewal to be as it was in years past. Rather, we must yearn for it to be better than in years past.

The Renewal must be more powerful—operating more fully under the anointing of the Holy Spirit. It must be more effective in the mainstream Church, nurturing and supporting the spiritual development of everyday Catholics in our parishes. It must be more passionate about promoting life in the Spirit in the mainstream Catholic Church and it must be more creative in the way it presents life in the Spirit to the mainstream Church. Above all, the Renewal must be more holy than it has been in years past. We in the Renewal must be more authentic, not only teaching about the Holy Spirit, but also using the gifts and living in the Spirit.

No one yearns more than God Himself for such a renewed Renewal—one that would put out into the deep to minister in the mainstream of His Church. If we dare to pray for a renewal of the Renewal and if we agree to be a part of renewing the Renewal, we will find ourselves working outside the Renewal and inside the mainstream Church. When this happens, the Church will be consumed in a firestorm, set ablaze by the Holy Spirit.

Take Time To Reflect And Act

Take a few moments to talk about the differences between your current prayer group and your prayer group of the past. Talk about the graces that are present now in your prayer group that were not there in the past. Focus on these graces, taking them into prayer, and asking God what He wants you to know about them. As you spend time in prayer, ask God to show you what "new thing" He is doing with you and/or with your prayer group. Try to clear your mind and your heart, and ask God to send forth His Spirit to enlighten you. Remain in the quiet for several minutes. When you come out of the silence write or talk about what you heard God speak to you. If what you heard demands a response, ask God to guide and direct you. Continue to pray each day, asking God to reveal His heart to you—His love for His Church and His longing for His people to know about and accept the gift of salvation. Each time you pray and write what you hear God speak to you, share it with at least one other person. Pray daily for the gifts of wisdom, discernment, and obedience.

For Renewal Leaders

Plan a gathering of Renewal leaders to pray and talk about the "state of the Renewal" in your diocese. Discuss the differences between the current Renewal movement and that of the past. What new thing is God showing you? What does this mean for your individual members, prayer groups as a whole, and the Renewal? Ask God to reveal His heart to you—His love for His Church and His longing for His people to know about and accept the gift of salvation. Record what God reveals to you. If what you heard demands a response, ask God to guide and direct you. Each time you gather spend time in prayer, write, and discern what you hear God speak. Especially pray for wisdom, discernment, and obedience.

11

Put Out Into The Deep

At the beginning of the new millennium, and at the close of the Great Jubilee during which we celebrated the two thousandth anniversary of the birth of Jesus and a new stage of the Church's journey begins, our hearts ring out with the words of Jesus when one day, after speaking to the crowds from Simon's boat, he invited the Apostle to "put out into the deep" for a catch: "*Duc in altum*" (*Lk* 5:4). Peter and his first companions trusted Christ's words, and cast the nets. "When they had done this, they caught a great number of fish." [*Lk* 5:6] (John Paul II, 2001, p. 7)

We in the Renewal have learned over the years that it is simpler to cast our nets in shallow waters than to do so in deep waters. In other words, we have discovered that it is rather easy to evangelize Catholics who have a hunger and longing for something "more" in their lives. Such Catholics frequently approach us and are themselves approachable. In contrast, it is much more difficult to evangelize Catholics in the mainstream Church who are content where they are in their relationship to God. Their responses to our evangelizing efforts are sometimes, "Thanks, but no thanks."

As a renewal movement, we have never put forth an intentional and systematic effort to evangelize Catholics in the mainstream Church. Some of us occasionally go directly into the mainstream of the Church to witness, preach, or teach others about living in the Spirit, but most of us simply do not go there. Why is this so? Why have we not put out into the deep, unknown, uncharted waters to bring the Renewal into the mainstream Church? Why have we not gone into the deep to cast our nets where the need is so great and the catch is so plentiful, where there are so many souls thirsting for living water flowing from the side of Christ?

To find answers to these questions it may be helpful to evaluate ourselves at both a personal as well as a prayer group or Renewal Movement level, and to do so in response to the challenges put forth by John Paul II in his Apostolic Letter (2001). As we begin this self-examination process, it might be helpful to expand upon the John Paul II's image of "putting out into the deep." Consider for a moment that the boat in the water is the Renewal Movement. When Christ asks us to put out into the deep, is He asking us to chart a new direction for the Renewal? Is He asking us to steer the boat, the Renewal, towards the deep waters. If we take up John Paul II's challenge, we will be required to set a course that leads us away from our prayer groups and local Renewal communities, the familiar, safe, and comfortable places, and instead, leads us out into the deep water—the mainstream Church.

If we follow the signs of the times and look to both the needs of the Renewal and the needs of the Church, we should not be surprised that the Lord would ask those of us in the Charismatic Renewal to go into the mainstream Church. Some of us have been in formation for many years now. The Holy Spirit has formed us well and gifted us beyond our understanding! God has often used us to be His instruments of healing, miracles, prophecy, word of knowledge, wisdom, preaching, and teaching. We know that we did not experience the gifts and power of the Holy Spirit simply for our benefit—for our own sanctification, but we also received these gifts to build up the Church (1 Cor 14:12).

In some areas of the country there are so few Charismatics left to minister within their prayer groups, it seems only logical that we would now be called to go, with our gifts, into the mainstream Church. Even if our prayer groups are thriving, it is still makes perfect sense that God would call us into the mainstream Church. After all, we have over thirty years of formation. We ought to be more than prepared and ready to give witness to God's grace and to share the gifts we have received with those in the mainstream Church. After years of being a movement within the Church, are we ready to be fully integrated into the mainstream Church as a normal and natural part of the everyday life of the Church?

If we are not convinced of our readiness to go into the mainstream Church, perhaps we ought to consider the urgency for us to go. In recent years, many of us have witnessed a gradual decline in the number of prayer groups. The median age of our members appears to be between 50 and 60. Of those who attend Life in the Spirit Seminars, no matter their age, few if any, seem to make a commitment to attend prayer group on a regular basis. While we, the faithful elders in the Renewal have wisdom and leadership abilities, we pray for the young to be with us, that we might teach them and mentor them. Through all of our frustration and longing for the young, we keep asking one another, "Where are all the young people?"

The cause of our frustration and longing may be, in fact, our own doing. The reason is that as we continue to cast our nets near the shoreline and those we catch tend to be closer in age to our own age. This is only natural since the people our own age seem to be the ones most comfortable in approaching us. Likewise, they tend to be the ones we are most comfortable approaching. This phenomenon, gives us a strong rationale for putting out into the deep—for that is where people of all ages and stages in life can be found.

Another reason to put out into the deep is our own belief in the value of the gifts of the Holy Spirit. We frequently discuss among ourselves how critical the gifts of the Holy Spirit have been in our own spiritual formation—gifts such as prayer, spontaneous praise, tongues, worship, healing, preaching, teaching, prophecy, and discernment. Yet it seems that we do not consider these same gifts a necessity for those in the mainstream Church. If we did, we would already have presented our parishes with plans that could incorporate and integrate these gifts, as a natural and normal part of everyday parish life. To the contrary, we have held the charisms of the Holy Spirit to ourselves, reserving them for use in our own personal lives and for use at prayer group and Renewal events.

Why else have we not gone out into the deep? Is it for fear of rejection, persecution, being misunderstood, or being labeled? Is it for fear of offending people? It is only natural for us to want to avoid persecution and rejection. However, as Christians, we are called to a higher standard of living, one in which God's grace is sufficient to overcome our fears (John Paul II (2001). Jesus says, "Blessed are you when people hate you, and when they exclude you, and denounce your name as evil on account of the Son of Man" (Lk 6:22). By His grace, we are able to not only overcome our fears, but also welcome and rejoice in persecution for the sake of His Kingdom!

Why have we not gone out into the deep? Perhaps it is due to our own Catholic upbringing, which taught that each person's faith is a private matter. Some may argue that it is wrong to impose our spirituality on others. Indeed, we ought to be sensitive to each person's unique relationship with the Lord. However, there are many Catholics who have no relationship with the Lord and who might never develop one, were it not for someone stepping out to witness, teach, and talk with them about Jesus—His gift of salvation, and life in His Spirit.

Additionally, some Catholics are very good at "following the rules" to get to heaven, yet they are spiritually dead. They simply go through the motions of "belonging to a religion." Evangelizing such Catholics is not imposing our spirituality on them. It is inviting them to surrender their lifeless lives to Jesus who gives them life to the fullest the. It is inviting them to embrace Jesus' spirituality—that of living in the Spirit—the same Spirit that was poured out at Pentecost when Jesus directed His followers to "...wait for the promise of the Father about which you have heard me speak...in a few days you will be baptized with the holy Spirit" (Acts 1:4). It is the very same Spirit Jesus was referring to when He said, "And [behold] I am sending the promise of my Father upon you; but stay in the city until you are clothed with power from on high" (Lk 24:49).

It is also true that some of us have been taught to guard against "coming on too strong" for fear of offending people. However, we often misinterpret what it means to come on too strong. It may be possible to come on too strong if we are only promoting ourselves, and our life in the Sprit. Such conversations start with "I" and talk about "me." It is not possible to come too strong if we are talking about God the Father's love, His Son Jesus, and the gift of the Holy Spirit.

When we think about coming on too strong, we might want to remember all those we know who were evangelized into other churches because we did not come on strong enough about Jesus and His gift of salvation. Similarly, we may know Catholics, who were so hungry for spiritual food, they were willing to leave the Catholic Church to get it. They did leave and they continue to do today in a gradual but steady stream, willing to be ministered to by other Christian communities, who are not at all afraid to introduce ex-Catholics to the Gospel of Jesus Christ. Our Christian brothers and sisters are also not afraid to tell these same ex-Catholics about the charisms of the Holy Spirit, nor are they afraid to exhort them to use the charisms of the Holy Spirit to grow holy and to build up their church assemblies.

We who are seasoned in the Renewal have grown confident in the gifts of the Holy Spirit at work in us. Yet it seems we are only confident using the gifts in the comfort of our own prayer groups or Renewal events. The thought that we might be called, in this new millennium, to go out into the deep, the mainstream of the Church to proclaiming Jesus, life in His Spirit, and the gifts of the Holy Spirit, may seem far too difficult a task, far too frightening, and even impossible.

Nevertheless, it is not only to benefit the mainstream Church, that we should put out into the deep, but it is also for our own good that we go. For the moment we move out of our comfort zones and go, we will be forced into total dependency on God as we attempt to witness, teach, and preach about life in the Spirit. We will find ourselves in ministry situations that many of us may have never before experienced. Perhaps some of us will not know what to do in these situations. What a great place for us to be—on our knees, begging God to pour out His gifts upon us and guide us every step of the way as we move out into His mainstream Church. Let us not allow fear to keep us from ministries that require our total reliance on God.

Nearly two years ago our Holy Father, John Paul II (2001) told the entire Church to put out into the deep and cast nets for a bountiful catch. This includes all of us as individuals, and as members of prayer groups and the Renewal Movement. Therefore, we must go. It is time to go! As we venture into the mainstream Church, we will see and experience God's mercy and His miracles in places we never thought possible, and in seeing and experiencing, we will be witnesses to a firestorm in His Catholic Church.

Take Time To Reflect And Act

Take a few moments now to ponder what it might mean for you personally or your prayer group to "put out into the deep."

Have you been boating close to the shoreline? Do you know why? What fears do you have about going into the mainstream Church to use your gifts to build up the Church?

Come before the Lord in long periods of silence. When the silence is over ask God to reveal what He means for you when He says, "Put out into the deep."

For Renewal Leaders

Take a few moments now to ponder what it might mean for the Renewal to "put out into the deep."

Has the Renewal been boating close to the shoreline? Do you know why? What fears do you have about going into the mainstream Church to use your gifts to build up the Church?

Come before the Lord in long periods of silence. When the silence is over ask God to reveal what He means for the Renewal when He says, "Put out into the deep."

Dispelling Eight Myths About The
Catholic Charismatic Renewal

I thought of its celebration [Jubilee 2000] as a providential opportunity during which the Church, thirty-five years after the Second Vatican Ecumenical Council...would examine how far she had renewed herself, in order to be able to take up her evangelizing mission with fresh enthusiasm. (John Paul II, 2001, p. 8)

As we reflect on the growth of the Renewal Movement since its early beginnings, we all would agree that it has been a powerful and fruitful gift to our Church. Many Charismatic Catholics currently serve as lectors, Eucharistic ministers, catechists, and members of pastoral teams. Others are involved with programs and movements such as Christ Renews His Parish, Cursillo, Renew, Alpha for Catholics, RCIA, Disciples In Mission, Life Teen, and the Marian Movement. A few have started religious orders for women and men and covenant communities.

Nevertheless, in light of John Paul II's challenge to use the arrival of the new millennium as an opportunity to examine how far the Church has renewed itself since Vatican II, we ought to conduct the very same examination of ourselves, the Renewal Movement and our prayer groups. The start of the third millennium might just be the perfect time to revisit our vision and mission statements, Renewal activities, and the role Charismatic Catholics play in renewing the mainstream Church.

If we take up the challenge to examine ourselves, let it be an honest self-examination that asks these difficult quesitons: Have we been boating too close to shore when it comes to fishing for souls for Christ? Have we only been evangelizing Catholics one-on-one, ministering to those who walk into our daily lives, or those already in our prayer groups or the Renewal? Have we actually been fishing for souls for the Renewal rather than fishing for souls for Christ? Would we be able to recognize the subtle difference?

Most would agree that ministering close to shore has seemed to work for us over the years. At least it seemed to work until recently when John Paul II (2001) asked us to examine the current impact of the Renewal in terms of its mission of evangelization. If we are convinced that the Renewal today is having a significant impact in the mainstream Church, we can be satisfied to continue with business as usual. If however, we wish to take John Paul II's challenge seriously we will probably agree that business as usual will not be an effective approach for renewing the Church in the new millennium.

The degree to which the Renewal will be a gift to the Church in this new millennium will be determined within the framework of the Holy Father's simple yet far-reaching challenge to "put out into the deep" as presented to us in *Novo Millennio Ineunte* (2001). It may be that the extent to which the Renewal puts out into the deep, is the extent to which it will be a viable force influencing the Church in the new millennium. In essence, if we wish to take up our evangelizing mission in the new millennium, we will be required to renew the Renewal. This renewal journey will demand from us a spirit of honesty, open-mindedness, willingness to change, courage, and risk-taking. Above all, it will require us to surrender to the promptings of the Holy Spirit every step of the way.

As we begin to take up the challenge to renew the Renewal, we might first consider eight myths about the Catholic Charismatic Renewal that have the power to impede our efforts. Without reading any further, you might already be thinking, "Ah hah, finally the truth will be told about Catholic Charismatics so that those in the mainstream Church will be able to understand us better and appreciate our gifts."

Unfortunately, those who were hoping for such an awakening will be disappointed. This is because the eight myths I wish to dispel, are not those held by Catholics about Charismatics, but rather those held by Charismatics about themselves—that is to say, the myths that we in the Renewal hold about the Renewal, our prayer groups, our individual ministries, and ourselves, as Catholic Charismatics.

Until we dispel these myths, we may not experience great success in putting out into the deep waters of the mainstream Church. In fact, if we hold onto these myths, we will most likely find ourselves anchored in shallow waters very close to the shoreline. There is a price to pay if we remain anchored in these shallow waters. The worst possible price is that we would be tossed about by the winds and waves pushing us farther away from the mainstream Church and closer to our isolated prayer groups and Renewal Movement. Should this happen, we are likely to find prayer group attendance diminishing further. Those who do remain faithful to the Renewal will continue to show up. However, it is likely they will also continue to grow more frustrated. It is also possible that the few remaining prayer groups and the Renewal will no longer have sufficient energy or resources to sustain the Renewal on a local or national level.

If we dare to consider these myths and work to dispel them, we will surely experience challenges and difficulties. Additionally, if we open our minds and hearts, and say, "Yes" to the Holy Spirit's endless ways of bringing Christ to the world and the world to Christ, we will see great signs and wonders, and we will be witnesses to a firestorm in the Catholic Church.

Not all eight myths will be applicable to every person in the Renewal, every prayer group, or diocesan Renewal across the country. However, as you read each one of the following myths, prayerfully consider its relevance and implications for your present situation. Prayerfully consider if any of these myths speak to you, your prayer group, or the Renewal?

1. The Spirituality Of "Living In The Spirit" Is Simply One Way To Grow In Holiness.

The first myth to dispel is perhaps the most important. When we in the Renewal communicate to others that living in the Spirit is simply one way to grow in holiness, we betray both the mission and the work of the Holy Spirit. We need only to revisit the Gospel of John, Chapters 14-17, and the Pentecost story in the Acts of the Apostles to recognize that living in, through, and with the power of the Holy Spirit is the only way to grow in holiness. The *Catechism of the Catholic Church* (1994) states that life in the Spirit fulfills the very vocation of man (Gen 1:2, 2:7; #1699). It declares that the Holy Spirit animates all creation (#703), awakens our faith (Jn 17:3; #684), enables us to communicate with Christ (1 Cor 12:3; 2 Gal 4:6; #683), grants gifts to all (#2003), is the master and source of prayer (Rom 8:26; #741; #2652), restores us to Divine likeness (#734), reveals God and the Trinity to us (#244; #684; #687), and is the source of all holiness (#740).

Through these statements, the Church reminds us that life in the Spirit is not simply one way to grow in holiness. It is the only way! The Holy Spirit, sent by the Father, is the One who helps us find our way to the Father and life in the Spirit is the only means we have to come to know Jesus, our Bridge to the Father—the Way, the Truth, and the Life, for we know from Jesus Himself that no one comes to the Father except through Him (Jn 14:4).

Life in the Spirit began on Pentecost, the day the Church was born, and life in the Spirit continues up to this very day. Its purpose is to form righteous and holy men and women (CCC, #734, #1699). When the Holy Spirit comes into our lives, first in Baptism, and then Confirmation, Reconciliation, Eucharist, the other Sacraments, the Word, and at numerous times throughout our daily lives, so too comes special graces in the form of spiritual gifts that help us love God and love our neighbor as ourselves. The reality is that life in the Spirit is the only weapon we have to combat the world, the flesh, and the devil and live as Christ taught us to live. It is the one and only means for growing in holiness. To this end, the Church accepts her mission, her obligation, and her authority to bring the faithful into a deeper awareness of the power of the Holy Spirit and the gifts of the Holy Spirit that make us holy and enable us to build up the Body of Christ (CCC #698).

Thus, whether we are at a Renewal event or at Sunday Mass, we in the Renewal are no less the Church and therefore have no less a mission than the one given at Pentecost. This means, at all times, we are required to give witness to and proclaim God's salvation through the power of the Holy Spirit, just as the men and women did at the first Pentecost, in the early days of the Church, and throughout all of history since the year of our Lord. Additionally, since God desires that all be saved, and since salvation is found in the Truth, the missionary mandate of the Church demands that we go out and respond to every person's longing to know God (CCC #851).

What do these mandates mean for each of us individually? What are their implications for our Church today? Our diocese? Our parish? It means we must have serious and extended conversations with our pastoral leaders and ministers, revisiting what Jesus Himself said to His disciples about their mission and about the work of the Holy Spirit as we retell, compare, and contrast the stories of the disciples' lives before and after Pentecost. It means we must let our pastors and pastoral ministers know that the Holy Father (2001), "earnestly exhorts the pastors of the particular churches, with the help of all sectors of God's people, [to] confidently to plan the stages of the journey ahead" (p. 40). It means that each local Church set forth specific detailed plans that include goals, methods, formations, and enrichments of the people (John Paul II, 2001).

What does this mean for us in the Renewal? It means we must tell our stories to our pastors and pastoral leaders, witnessing both before and after we became aware of the power of the Holy Spirit to guide and direct our lives and before and after we began living in the Spirit and ministering through the gifts of the Holy Spirit (CCC #688, 767, 798-801, 951, 1508). We must talk with our pastoral leaders, about the Isaiah gifts of the Holy Spirit—wisdom, understanding, counsel, fortitude, knowledge, piety, and fear of the Lord (CCC# 1831). We must also talk with our leaders about the charisms of the Holy Spirit—tongues, prophecy, words of knowledge, preaching, teaching, healing, miracles, spontaneous prayer, exhortation, worship, administration, hospitality, encouragement, and above all, love (CCC #688, 767, 798-801, 951, 1508).

We cannot talk about one set of gifts—the Isaiah gifts, and exclude the other set of gifts—the charisms of the Holy Spirit. These charisms are given to each person, for personal holiness and to build up the Church (1 Cor 12:4-11). The charisms of the Spirit are critical to the life of the whole Church. Yet some of us in the Renewal have been holding them to ourselves. We reserve their use for our personal lives, prayer group, and Renewal events.

It is time to take the charisms of the Holy Spirit out of our "renewal closets" and confess them to the mainstream Church. The operative word here is "confess" because until now these charisms have been a part of our secret lives in the Spirit. They must come into the light so that those in the mainstream Church can learn about them, see us operating in them, come to understand their value to the Church, and even embrace them for their own spiritual journeys and ministries in the Church. We must model them, teach about them, and help our brothers and sisters in our parishes discern them for their own lives. Once discerned, we must help form our brothers and sisters in their gifts, encouraging and coaching them to use their gifts in the Church and in their everyday lives.

We Charismatic Catholics are the perfect ones to mentor and coach our brothers and sisters in the mainstream Church because of our years of experience and our zeal for living in the Spirit. Additionally, Catholic Charismatics may be the only ones who could talk about and give witness to both living in the Spirit and using the charisms of the Holy Spirit. For this reason, we must tell ourselves and believe in our hearts, "If not us, then who will put out into the deep to confess life in the Spirit and model and teach about the charisms of the Holy Spirit?"

Some among us may be tempted to say, "We cannot take these gifts out of the closet and teach about them or encourage them to be used in the mainstream Church, for if we do we will surely offend people." Once again, we may need to rethink our position. How is it possible to offend people by offering them a deeper awareness of the Holy Spirit at work in their lives? How is it possible to offend people by offering them spiritual gifts that nurture their growth in holiness and build up the Body of Christ? It seems we sometimes have a one-sided approach to offending people, especially since there is often very little concern about offending people with Bingo or beer at church festivals. A "Pentecost" perspective should bring us comfort in knowing that we are in God's plan for salvation—a plan that demands the continual renewal of His Church through the power of the Holy Spirit—the same Spirit that came at Pentecost and gave gifts to men and women.

We, who are in the Renewal, simply know too much about the Holy Spirit, His work, His charisms, and His power, to be silent any longer. We must no longer be timid when evangelizing others into a fuller awareness of their Baptism. We must no longer be timid when it comes to telling Catholics what their Baptism really means—that they can now live in Christ through the power of His Holy Spirit, and grow holy. In an encouraging way, St. Paul reminded Timothy to "...stir into flame the gift of God that you have through the imposition of my hands. For God did not give us a spirit of cowardice but rather of power and love and self-control" (2 Tim 1:6). Paul went so far as to warn the Corinthians not to neglect the gift they had received since it was given to them by prophetic utterance when the council of elders laid hands on them (1 Cor 14:15).

Perhaps we ought to receive Paul's encouragement and his admonition as if he were delivering his speeches to us directly. We do need to be reminded not to neglect the gifts and charisms of the Spirit for with them we too were given courage and fearlessness to proclaim Christ Jesus and the work of the Holy Spirit in our lives. The Holy Spirit and the gifts enable each one of us, and thus the entire Church, to become whole and holy. We know it is impossible to come to know Christ without calling upon His Spirit to guide and teach us, and we know it is impossible to grow in holiness without using the gifts of the Holy Spirit to sanctify and transform us.

If we choose to dispel the myth that living in the Spirit is only one way to grow in holiness, we will be required to change when, where, how, why, and to whom we minister. It will no longer be a matter of "why not let people find God in their own way." Rather, it will be a matter of "letting people find God in their own way with the knowledge that they can call upon His Holy Spirit and use the gifts of His Spirit to draw closer to Him."

This perspective requires those who live in the Spirit to minister in the Spirit in the mainstream Church. This perspective also demands that we, who live in the Spirit, make ourselves available to our parishes to witness, coach, mentor, and teach others to do the same in the mainstream Church.

Here is what might happen if we choose to dispel this first myth. The Holy Spirit may prompt us to ask people if we can pray with them for an outpouring of His Spirit at the start of a pastoral council meeting or with the celebrant and all ministers just prior to start of Mass. The Spirit might prompt us to offer to pray with people in our parish who are sick, anxious, or facing difficult situations in their lives. The Spirit might prompt us to request a time for "listening to God" at the start of every parish meeting. We might even be prompted to teach Eucharistic ministers how to pray with the homebound or how to develop and coordinate a personal prayer ministry at the end of Sunday Mass. When practices such as these become the norm in everyday parish life, Catholics will experience how impossible it is to grow holy without the power and the gifts of the Holy Spirit. They will also discover that any time is a good time to call upon the Holy Spirit—our Comforter, and our Counselor. They will realize that in every situation and in every place, God is waiting to anoint His people with His Spirit.

Life in the Spirit, that is to say, living in the Spirit, is indeed the only path to holiness. The moment we fully embrace Christ as our Lord and Savior and live in His Spirit, we are obligated to witness and share this truth with others, for it is the mission of the Holy Spirit, in each of us and in the Church, to bring Christ to the world and the world to Christ. When this happens, there will be a firestorm in the Catholic Church, drawing others to come to the Father through union with Christ through the power of His Holy Spirit.

2. The Charisms Of The Holy Spirit Are Not For Everyone.

The second myth that needs to be dispelled is the idea that the gifts of the Holy Spirit are not for everyone. If we truly believe this, we are saying in effect, that the Holy Spirit is not for everyone. Why?—because the Holy Spirit cannot be separated from the gifts He brings to the faithful. When He comes, He brings gifts. These gifts serve as the manifestation of the Spirit (1 Cor 12:7). His gifts are a true sign of His Spirit at work in us, leading us to the Truth, drawing us closer to God, and making us holy.

What specifically are the gifts that the Spirit of God brings to us when He comes? St. Paul tells us that when Jesus ascended on high, the Spirit gave gifts to all, "And he gave some as apostles, others as prophets, others as evangelists, others as pastors and teachers" (Eph 4:11). St. Paul speaks about these gifts as special ministries within the Church, saying, "Some people God has designated in the church to be first, apostles; second prophets; third teachers; then mighty deeds; then gifts of healing, assistants, administration, and varieties of tongues" (1 Cor 12:25-30). Paul also speaks of other gifts of the Holy Spirit, reminding us that,

> To each individual the manifestation of the Spirit is given for some benefit. To one is given through the spirit the expression of wisdom; to another the expression of knowledge according to the same Spirit; to another faith by the same Spirit; to another gifts of healing by the one Spirit; to another mighty deeds; to another prophecy; to another discernment of spirits; to another varieties of tongues. But the one and the same Spirit produces all of these, distributing them individually to each person as he wishes. (1 Cor 12:4-11)

It would be impossible to know Christ were it not for His Spirit gifting us with faith, hope, and love. It would be impossible to know Christ without His Spirit gifting us with wisdom, understanding, knowledge, piety, counsel, fortitude, and awe. If would be impossible to know Christ without having the ability to hear God speak to us, drawing us to Him that we might contemplate His great love and mercy, His servitude to the Father, His gift of our salvation. Since the manifestation of the Spirit is given for the common good (1 Cor 12:7), it is not limited only to ordained or special ministers within the Church. Rather St. Paul tells us, every person has a manifestation of the Holy Spirit. Yet, so many Catholics do not know this. They do not know that God's Spirit is manifested in them through His gifts. Nor do they know that these gifts enable them to come to know Christ more intimately, follow Him more steadily, and proclaim Him more confidently to the world.

We, who have been so long in the Renewal, know this is true by our own experiences of these manifestations of the Spirit. We operate in His gifts of tongues, interpretation of tongues, prophecy, discernment, healing, and word of knowledge. We use these gifts to draw closer to God, overcome sinful habits, and hear God's voice for our lives. Additionally, we have experienced God's continual anointing in our work of teaching, preaching, healing, and prophesying, as well as in our work of coaching, mentoring, and encouraging prayer group members to learn about and use the gifts of the Holy Spirit.

We have ministered regularly using these gifts in our own inner circles of charismatic friends, within our prayer groups, and within the Renewal. Yet, we have not taken these gifts into the mainstream Church. St. Paul cautioned the Church at Corinth about this very thing, when he told the people to strive more to build up the Body of Christ with the gifts rather than striving to acquire the gifts for their own personal use. In fact, he specifically told them to use the gifts to "excel" in building up the Church when he said, "Since you strive eagerly for spirits [manifestations of the Spirit] seek to have an abundance of them [gifts] for building up the church (1 Cor 14:12).

It is time for all of us in the Renewal to excel in building up the Body of Christ. To do this "excellent" work, we must leave our comfort zones and go, under the anointing and power of the Holy Spirit. Now is the right time to bring into the mainstream Church the ministries we have held to ourselves for so long. This is not an option for us. It is a mandate that we go. If we do not go and introduce the mainstream Church to life in the Spirit and to the charisms of the Holy Spirit, it will be said of us that we stifled the movement of the Holy Spirit, for we knew and we did not speak out. Are we truly disciples of the Christ? If we are, we must go, and we must build up His Church. If we are not, we will find a reason or perhaps even an excuse not to go.

Over the years, we have heard Catholics and other Christians alike declare that the gifts of the Holy Spirit were meant only for the early Church in order to give birth to the Church. There are scriptural reasons why we know this is simply not true. First, St. Paul is very clear about why we have been given these gifts. It is to equip all of us, the saints, for the work of ministry, for building up the Body of Christ (Eph 4:12). Second, Paul never puts an exact time limit on how long these gifts will be with us. In fact, he does just the opposite, when he says the gifts of the Spirit will be with each of us and with the Church, until we become one in faith and in knowledge of the Son of God (Eph 4:13).

Our mandate to take the charisms of the Holy Spirit into the mainstream Church also comes directly from the *Catechism of the Catholic Church* where we read that the gifts and charisms of the Holy Spirit, whether extraordinary or simple and humble, are given to us to build up the whole Body of Christ. It says, "...charisms are graces of the Holy Spirit which directly or indirectly benefit the Church, ordered as they are to her building up, to the good of men, and to the needs of the world" (#799).

Through Scripture and the *Catechism,* we are assured that the gifts of the Holy Spirit are very relevant for the Church of the third millennium for we know that we are neither one in faith, nor do all have knowledge of Jesus, His Son. This single passage from Ephesians provides the Renewal the strongest rationale yet, for why the gifts of the Holy Spirit and the charisms of the Holy Spirit are so needed and so relevant for the Church today. We must confess with certainty that these gifts will be with us until everyone on the face of the earth knows Jesus, the Christ, and until all are one in Him.

With this knowledge, we can go forth in confidence to minister the Holy Spirit and His gifts in the mainstream of the Church. It is not ours to decide who can know about the gifts and who can receive these gifts. It is ours to witness, share, confess, and proclaim and let God decide how He wills to distribute the gifts (Heb 2:3). In this regard, we are assured of the Church's support for living in the Spirit and operating in the charisms of the Holy Spirit. This is because the Church herself counsels all to accept charisms with gratitude. She refers to the charisms as a wonderfully rich grace that enables God's people to grow in holiness. The Church also sees the charisms as a rich grace that dispenses new energy to God's people equipping them for the task of evangelization.

St. Paul helps us understand another important reason God granted us these gifts. He tells us they were given to us as a remedy for our human weakness and immaturity—so that we would no longer be as children, tossed to and fro and swept away by every wind of doctrine and by the cleverness, craftiness, and deceit of the world (Eph 4:8-15). This then is the question, "Do we need a remedy for our human weakness and immaturity?" If the answer is "no" then we need not continue reading this book for it will not be helpful to the person who sees himself or herself strong and mature in Christ. If however the answer is "yes" then we must not despise these gifts but rather seek after them in order to draw closer to the One who gives them and in order to confess the presence of these gifts in our lives. We are weak and immature in Christ and we need a remedy. "Send us your Spirit, O God and give us your gifts we most need to grow closer to you."

Paul offers us a wealth of information about the charisms of the Holy Spirit. He tells us that each one of us has gifts but that these gifts are all different. He emphasizes that we need each other's gifts in our lives and in our communities. He also teaches us how these gifts can serve as a remedy for our weakness and immaturity by encouraging us to use the gifts we were given for the purpose they were given. For example, the one who has received the gift of prophecy should use it in proportion to his faith. In other words, the gift of prophecy should be used to build up the faith of the people to the degree to which the prophet has enough faith to hear the word spoken and declare it to the assembly. If the prophet is timid with the gift, the body will not be as fully graced as God intended.

The same is true for ministry. Paul says this gift should be used for service. If however, the minister holds back in acts that would truly serve the Body of Christ, the ministry gift will have less of a graced-filled effect on the Body. The teacher should teach under the anointing of the Holy Spirit or otherwise deprive the students of an anointed teaching. The one who has the gift of exhortation should exhort the people or else deprive the people of God's encouragement. The person gifted with the ability to give alms, should do so generously, not holding anything back. The one who rules should do so with care, and the person who performs works of mercy should do so cheerfully.

These charisms of the Holy Spirit are freely given to us by God and as such we must use them both humbly and responsibly for our own holiness, and even more so, to build up the Church. In the *Catechism of the Catholic Church* (1994), we are cautioned that there are two provisions in order for grace to flow from operating in the charisms of the Holy Spirit. First, the charisms must be genuine gifts of the Holy Spirit and second, they must be used under the authentic promptings of the Holy Spirit (# 800).

These two cautions should continually lead us back to the pastors of our parishes, pastoral leaders, and the elders in our Charismatic communities in order that we might ask them to discern our gifts for ministry. It is critical to have our gifts discerned prior to entering ministry work. Additionally, if we operate in gifts of the Holy Spirit, under the constant authority of the Church, we will always have at our disposal, graces flowing from our obedience.

When this protocol is followed, we have the community's discernment that our gifts are genuine and with this assurance, we will have the confidence to use them under the authentic promptings of the Holy Spirit. Rarely are we, as Catholics, invited to discern our gifts of teaching, preaching, prophecy, healing, hospitality, administration, or leadership. It is not common practice in the Church to discern peoples' ministry gifts through a formal discernment process. As a result, many Catholics are never invited to use their gifts, even though they themselves know they have ministry gifts. Sometimes, we hear from ex-Catholics that they are involved in various ministries in their new Churches. They tell us with enthusiasm in their voices that their new Church invited them to learn about the power of the Holy Spirit and their gifts for ministry. Sure enough, our ex-Catholics are soon ministering in their new churches and thriving in their ministries—ministries that God confirmed through personal prayer and the discernment of the community.

From the time of the first Pentecost, the mission of the Holy Spirit has not changed. It is the same mission Jesus defined for us before He ascended to the Father—the mission to go, proclaim the Kingdom of God, and heal. Each one of us must therefore re-define ourselves as missionaries, commissioned by Jesus through the power of the Holy Spirit to share what we know about living in the Spirit with all those we meet. We must go, using whatever means possible to share Christ, proclaim the Father's Kingdom, and heal, through the power of the Holy Spirit.

We must invite all we meet to seek the power of the Holy Spirit for their lives and to seek the charisms to grow in holiness and build up the Body of Christ. For this to happen, prayer groups must move out into the mainstream Church, confessing their life in the Spirit, offering to pray with people, witnessing God's love and mercy, proposing to teach and preach missions and retreats, and modeling life in the Spirit. In essence, Catholic Charismatics must go wherever the Lord tells them to go and they must do whatever He tells them to do.

If we dare to dispel the myth that says the charisms of the Holy Spirit are not for everyone, we will be forced to move out into the mainstream Church to carry on the Pentecost mission of evangelization. However, we will not be baptizing Catholics, as the apostles often did, for they are already baptized. Rather, we will be reminding Catholics to stir into flame the gift that was given to them at their Baptism and Confirmation (Tim 1:6). Paul reminded Timothy that God did not give us a spirit of cowardice but rather one that makes us strong, loving, and wise (2 Tim 1:6-7). Paul wrote this letter to Timothy after he had encouraged and, at the same time, reprimanded Timothy saying, "Do not neglect the gift you have that was conferred on you through the prophetic word with the imposition of hands of the presbyterate. Be diligent in these matters, be absorbed in them, so that your progress may be evident to everyone" (1 Tim 4:14).

If we agree to dispel this myth, we will be required to remind Catholics that when they were baptized and confirmed they received the Holy Spirit and His gifts to grow in holiness and to build up the Church. We will be required to encourage Catholics to pray for a fresh outpouring of the Holy Spirit each day. We will be required to tell Catholics that the Holy Spirit anoints them with His presence and His gifts each time they receive Eucharist; go to Reconciliation; pray the Mass, the Rosary, and the Liturgy of the Hours; or come before the Blessed Sacrament in adoration. Perhaps most important of all, we will be required to encourage Catholics to pray for and discern their gifts and charisms given to them by the Holy Spirit in order that they might use their charisms under the anointing of the Holy Spirit, to build up the Body of Christ—bringing souls to Christ and bringing Christ to others.

Each of us has a mission and a ministry to grow holy and to build up the Body of Christ, that is to say, the members of our family and those of our parishes. When we first learn about the Holy Spirit and the charisms, we may not realize immediately that they are meant for the whole Church. However, soon enough we come to this realization and when we do, we must also realize that we have a part to play in letting those we meet in the Church know we have learned. Once this happens however, we are no longer able to stand before God claiming ignorance about our role and our responsibility in evangelizing—namely bringing Christ and life in His Spirit to the world. The moment we all realize the fullness of our apostolate, there will indeed be a firestorm in the Church!

3. If We Talk, They Will Listen.

The third myth to dispel is the belief that if we talk, they (faithful Catholics in our parishes) will listen. Haven't we all experienced times when we began to evangelize fellow Catholics by telling them about the Holy Spirit when suddenly their eyes begin to wander and they begin to fidget? Have you ever talked with someone in your parish about the gifts of the Holy Spirit when, in the middle of a sentence, the person looks at his or her watch and suddenly remembers he or she had something else to do or somewhere else to be? Perhaps you have noticed, that when you start to tell some folks about Jesus or your life in the Spirit, their postures seem to say, "That's nice" or "I am not really interested in what you are telling me." Then there are those times when fellow parishioners see us coming and they simply turn and walk in the other direction. As if to add insult to injury, some parishioners have even labeled us "craze-o-matics."

It is obvious that these experiences are not very hopeful signs or encouragements that would make us want to continue evangelizing Catholics in the mainstream Church. Still, we do it, one-on-one, hoping that something we say will entice people to come to our prayer group, want to know more about the Holy Spirit, or ask us about the charisms and gifts of the Holy Spirit.

In the early years of the Renewal, talking seemed to be a fruitful way to evangelize the Catholics we met, either in church or at church events. In the early years of the Renewal, as we spread the Good News about Jesus and the Holy Spirit by word of mouth, our prayer groups expanded at a rapid pace. This rapid expansion was the result of our word-of-mouth ministry but we must also remember it was God's work through us. It was His plan. We enjoyed this rate of growth for many years until a downward trend began in some areas of the country.

At first glance, we want to say it is something we are doing. What is different? Today, we probably talk to just as many people as we did years ago but fewer seem to respond to what we say. We can only speculate as to the reasons. Perhaps it is because many more people have heard about the Charismatic Renewal and they associate what we are saying with a group or a movement rather than with a way of living and being. Perhaps people have heard about Charismatics and some of what they have heard frightens them. Perhaps some get the feeling that we are more of a "private club" than a ministry open to all in the Church. Perhaps some do not realize that the Church welcomes and supports the Charismatic Renewal Movement throughout the world.

Whatever the reasons, when we try to share one-on-one about life in the Spirit and the gifts of the Spirit, many Catholics simply do not respond. Is it possible then, that God is asking us to evangelize our brothers and sisters in a different way? John Paul II (2001) asked us to translate the Gospel of Jesus Christ into "pastoral initiatives adapted to the circumstances of each community" using "detailed pastoral plans" with "goals, methods, formation, and enrichment of the people involved" (p. 40). What if instead of immediately sharing about the Holy Spirit, we simply said, "How would you like to go for coffee so we can get to know each other a little better? May I pray with you? May I share a good book with you? Or would you like to read Scripture together?" Imagine what would happen if we began to evangelize by simply being in closer relationship with the people in our parishes. As we grew to know our fellow parishioners, they would begin to ask us about our life in Christ and the power and gifts of His Holy Spirit. Imagine what would happen if our lives were so filled with God's love that others simply wanted to get to know us so that they could learn more about God, His love and mercy and life in His Spirit. If this were to happen, our lives would be the living Gospel of Jesus Christ.

Since our talking is no longer as fruitful in the present as it has been in the past, perhaps it is time to act and love in ways that build up the Body of Christ—our parish communities. If we dare to take up this challenge, we might then be able to say by experience, "When we act in love they listen and become curious about our life in the Spirit."

The moment we agree to dispel this third myth, "If we talk, they will listen." there will be consequences for us. We will be forced to find new ways to evangelize Catholics in our parishes using our actions more and our words less. We will have to learn how to replace talking with listening and loving. This may mean that we will have fewer opportunities to promote the gifts of the Holy Spirit with our words and more opportunities to bring them God's love and mercy through loving acts of kindness and through listening. This also means we will have more opportunities to use the gifts of the Holy Spirit as we listen and love, each one bringing the fire of the

Holy Spirit with us into our parishes, and then watching as God sends forth a firestorm into His Church.

4. If We Invite Them, They Will Come.

The fourth myth to dispel is the notion that if we invite them, they (faithful Catholics in our parishes) will come. Whenever we do find an approachable Catholic, who is willing to listen to our witness and exchange faith stories with us, the first thing we Charismatics tend to do, is invite the person to come to our prayer group or the very next Life in the Spirit Seminar.

Similarly, the moment we realize someone in our parish is searching for a deeper relationship with the Lord, our invitation goes to them to come to prayer group with us, attend a Charismatic conference, or make a Life in the Spirit Seminar. We become excited over the prospect of a person who has just experienced Christ Renews His Parish, believing in our hearts that this person is ready for more—namely Baptism in the Holy Spirit and the Charismatic Renewal Movement.

Over the years, prayer group meetings, conferences, and seminars on the Holy Spirit have indeed generated many blessings, helped people learn about the Holy Spirit, and resulted in many Catholics being baptized in the Holy Spirit. However, considering all the invitations we have given out these past few years, relatively few members of our parishes seem to be responding. The reasons may be varied, schedule conflicts, childcare issues, irregular work schedules, and finances. Some may not be comfortable in large group settings. Others may not be able to get away for an entire weekend retreat. Others simply may be overcommitted.

Whatever the reasons, the fact remains that each year fewer Catholics are responding to our invitations to come with us to Renewal events. With this trend, it seems only natural that we should wonder if ten years from now, there will even be enough people to sustain the Renewal Movement as a vibrant and enduring stream of grace in the Church.

As we ponder the outcome of decreased participation in the Renewal Movement, we are faced with questions that seem to demand answers. "Must a person attend a prayer group or Charismatic event in order to be introduced to life in the Spirit? Do Catholics who have received the sacraments of Baptism and Confirmation need to attend a Charismatic event in order to receive a fresh outpouring of the Holy Spirit? Is it necessary to be at a Charismatic event in order to grow in the Spirit, learn how to live in the Spirit, receive the gifts of the Holy Spirit, or be formed in the gifts of the Holy Spirit?

If we answer "no" to even one of these above questions, we must begin to think differently about the mission and the role of the Charismatic Renewal Movement in the Catholic Church. If we say "no" we must also begin to respond differently when we encounter approachable Catholics in our parishes who are unaware of the power and the gifts of the Holy Spirit. We must discover what they know and ask them what they want to know about Jesus, the Holy Spirit, and the gifts of the Spirit. As we talk with them, we must be discerning and responsive to what they say they needed in order to develop a deeper relationship with God.

Do the approachable Catholics we meet in the mainstream Church want to learn more about the Church? If they do, we offer to find answers with them in the Catechism of the Catholic Church (1994). Do they want to know more about the Father, the Son, and the Holy Spirit? If so, we can introduce them to the Gospels of Matthew, Mark, Luke, and John as well as the Acts and Letters. If we know how to access the Church documents such as encyclicals and apostolic letters (See www.vatican.com) or the writing of the saints and doctors of the Church we find answers together with them.

If they want to know more about Jesus, His work of salvation, His promise of an advocate, we can mediate with them on the Gospels of Jesus. If they want to know about prayer, we can introduce them to various forms of prayer such as vocal, meditative, and prayer with another. If they want to know more about living in grace, the Sacraments, and life in the Spirit, we can reference the Catechism (1994) and share what we learn. Most of all, we can witness to the work of the Holy Spirit in our own lives.

Of course, all of this implies that we ourselves are continually studying our faith—the Scriptures, traditions and teachings of the Church. This also implies that we are able to refer people to resource persons, books, videos, and audiotapes as needed. Whatever, whenever, and however we teach and witness, if we ourselves do so under the anointing of the Holy Spirit, calling upon the gifts of the Holy Spirit, we can be sure that those we evangelize will be on the receiving end of the graces that flow from our teaching and witnessing.

As we move into the deep—the mainstream Church, we must remain focused on coming to know the people who approach us in friendship. We must strive to understand them and love them. We must want to know, understand, and love them more than we want them to know, understand, and love us. For this to happen, we must encourage them to talk about their faith experiences, rather than trying to get them to listen to our experiences. We must also understand what they are saying without pushing our agenda. Finally, we must offer them our unconditional love.

In the process of coming to know, understand, and love the people in our parish who approach us in friendship, we will begin to establish bonds of trust and authentic caring. When this happens, we will be free to talk about God, the Holy Spirit, and the gifts of the Spirit; share our faith; and start to pray with each other. We will also grow together in our friendship in Christ and in our life in the Spirit. Through the power of the Holy Spirit, we will know how to nurture and support each other's faith and we will find the Spirit leading both of us out into the deep, prompting us to go, proclaim the Kingdom, and heal others in our parish.

The moment we agree to dispel this fourth myth, consequences arise for us. Yes, we will continue to invite people to prayer group and Renewal events. However, when they do not respond to our invitations, we must have plan "B" ready to go. We must ask ourselves, "How can I get to know this person better? When can I spend time with this person? What spiritual reading books can we read together? What Scripture passages can we share, Jn 14-17 and Acts 1? Or, what does this person want to know about Jesus, about the power Holy Spirit, or about the gifts of the Spirit?"

There is indeed a gradual, but steady, decline in prayer group attendance in many parts of the country. Of those we invite to our Renewal activities, very few come. Nevertheless, there is great hope before us in this new millennium. The hope is this—the more we give others understanding and love, the more they will wonder about us, ask questions, and be curious about our life in the Spirit and the Charismatic Renewal. In this new millennium, we ought to dispel the myth that if we invite them they come." Instead, we might say, if we invite them and they do not come we always have a plan B. We will listen, understand, and learn about them as they learn about us. The more they learn about us, the more they will learn about Jesus and the Holy Spirit at work in us.

5. Prayer Groups Evangelize The Church.

The fifth myth that ought to be dispelled is the notion that prayer groups evangelize the mainstream Church. For some time now, we have held onto the belief that prayer groups evangelize the mainstream Church. Often times, this is not what happens. It is probably more accurate to say that prayer groups evangelize themselves—supporting and encouraging their own members to grow in Christ through weekly teachings. They also evangelize themselves when they offer days of formation and workshops to help their members grow in their ministry gifts.

Prayer groups typically do not consider it their mission or ministry to plan, design, and offer teachings or spiritual growth experiences to their parishes. Nor do they offer formation workshops to help form parish members in the gifts of leadership, prophecy, healing, evangelization, teaching, preaching, exhorting, prayer, praise and worship, or discernment. As we think about this issue, most of us might be tempted to defend ourselves by saying our parishes never invited us to present spiritual growth experiences, give teachings, or offer days of formation. While this is a true statement, most of us know that our parishes have brought people in from the outside to present the very teachings and formation workshops that we ourselves could have done, considering all of the experience we have had in retreat and conference work, workshops, and days of renewal. However, this has not been the case.

If we are honest with ourselves, we know there is no reason why we should not be developing proposals to present teachings, preach missions, and conduct formation workshops in our home parishes. In order to dispel this fifth myth, prayer groups will have to take up the challenge to put out into the deep—the mainstream Church. However, before they go, they must call upon the Holy Spirit to anoint them with courage and creativity. Prayer group members must come together, pray, and talk about their charisms, natural talents, and skills. They must discern their call to put out into the deep. They must conduct a self-assessment to determine how well they have done thus far, putting out into the deep. They must assess each person's natural talents, skills, and spiritual gifts, keep formal records, and develop a listing of those who are willing to put out into the deep.

Once this discernment is complete, prayer groups will be prepared to plan and design new initiatives that have the potential to promote spiritual growth and a fuller awareness of what it means to live in the Spirit. These plans will then need to be presented to pastors and pastoral teams for consideration. It is very important that prayer groups approach ministry as a "team effort" and continue to meet, pray, discern, and support one another.

When ministering in the mainstream Church, the most important point to remember when using the gifts of the Holy Spirit is to be docile, not flamboyant, subtle not obvious, and humble not proud. Above all, we must be generous, not selfish in praying for and promoting the gifts in our brothers and sisters for indeed, their gifts are our gifts since we are all one body. We must pray to God, asking that He gift others even more than He gifts us and asking that He accomplish more through others than He has accomplished through us.

When prayer group members go into their parishes to minister, they must be concerned first with modeling life in the Spirit and using the charisms when ministering. Modeling preaching, teaching, prayer, spontaneous praise, exhortation, healing, and wisdom will give ministers the opportunity to then talk about these charisms and the Holy Spirit. Using the gifts in ministry and then offering simple explanations of the gifts will probably spark people's interest and curiosity and get them asking questions.

Prayer groups could offer to sponsor Lenten or Advent activities such as an evening of Taize prayer or a mission on a spiritual growth topic such as Christian parenting, recently canonized saints, the mystics, or types of prayer. What would happen if prayer groups were to propose parish retreats, workshops, or days of renewal for teens, parents; Confirmation or First Holy Communion candidates and their families, guardians, and sponsors; bereavement groups; divorced or separated Catholics; or members of Altar-Rosary?

What would happen if, while preaching and teaching, prayer group members operated in the charisms of the Holy Spirit, giving brief explanations? What effect would it have if the explanation referenced Jesus' words, "The Advocate, the holy Spirit that the Father will send in my name—he will teach you everything and remind you of all that I told you" (Jn 14:26)? If these things were to happen, prayer groups could truly say they were evangelizing the Church.

If we agree to dispel this fifth myth in the new millennium, we will actually be agreeing to transform prayer groups into evangelizing ministries in the mainstream of the Church. This carries with it significant consequences for prayer groups and their members. Prayer group leaders will be required to assess their vision and mission statements in relation to the Apostolic Letter (2001) of John Paul II. Prayer groups will be required to plan and design initiatives that enable them to propose ministry activities to their parishes with the expressed purpose of supporting the spiritual needs of their parishes. Prayer groups will be required to coach and mentor prayer group members, raise them up, form them in ministry gifts and in the charisms, and exhort them to go, proclaim, and heal. All will be required to call upon and use the Isaiah gifts of wisdom, understanding, counsel, fortitude, knowledge, piety, and awe. Prayer group members will be required to call upon and use, with sensitivity and discernment, the charisms of the Holy Spirit—teaching, preaching, healing, tongues, prophecy, interpretation of tongues, and word of knowledge. Finally, all will be required to give credit to the Holy Spirit for the gifts they use in ministry. This, in turn, will entice and encourage others to ask for and receive these same gifts so that they too might build up the Body of Christ.

Prayer groups and the Renewal in general have indeed succeeded in evangelizing Charismatic Catholics who participate in prayer meetings, retreats, conferences, and formation days. In this new millennium, we must continue to do so. However, our prayer groups and the Renewal must also take seriously the call to put out into the deep—to minister in the mainstream Church. If prayer groups and the Renewal accept this challenge, they will become support and formation gatherings for their members. Imagine the firestorm that will blaze throughout the Church should prayer groups begin to plan, develop, and implement retreats, missions, days of formation, workshops, and conferences in the mainstream Church.

6. The Mission Of The Renewal Is Baptism In The Holy Spirit Through Life in the Spirit Seminars And Retreats.

The sixth myth that needs to be dispelled is the notion that the primary mission of the Renewal is Baptism in the Holy Spirit through Life in the Spirit Seminars and retreats. Many would agree that the mission of the Renewal is Baptism in the Holy Spirit, in other words, introducing people to life in the Spirit. The means for this to occur are as numerous and varied as anyone might imagine.

We would be in grave error however, to limit our understanding of empowerment in the Holy Spirit to a formal "prayer for Baptism in the Holy Spirit" or to a formal program such as the Life in the Spirit Seminar. Becoming awakened to the power of the Holy Spirit in one's life is determined by God's action in the soul and in the soul awakening to His action. Baptism in the Holy Spirit is not the result of any one program or format that we administer to God's people. Rather, it is the process and experience of being brought into an ever-deeper awareness of God's love and abiding presence with us and within others. We experience Baptism in the Holy Spirit when we encounter the face of the living Christ. Baptism in the Spirit happens as we surrender to God and are immersed in His life. Baptism in the Holy Spirit happens each time God reveals Himself to us.

God baptizes or awakens His people to His Holy Spirit at the most surprising times in their lives. We need only listen to our own witnesses to hear the many beautiful ways God works in His people. His anointing can fall while we are weeping over our sins, in the midst of prayer, when we are giving praise, when we receive Eucharist, experience God's forgiveness, sense our helplessness, hopelessness, and need for God, or at any other moment God chooses to penetrate our souls with His Divine Presence.

When I witness my own conversion story, I relate how I was washed in God's love while kneeling at my bedside. My girlfriend said, "Let's pray!" I was waiting for her to pray a vocal prayer, such as the Our Father, and instead she prayed a spontaneous prayer. I do not remember the prayer because the moment she began to pray, I could feel God's love washing over me. Through the guidance and promptings of the Holy Spirit, I immediately found myself immersed in Scripture, nourished on the Eucharist, and washed clean in the Sacrament of Reconciliation. Several months later, I found my way to a prayer group and a loving community where I learned what had happened to me that night as I knelt at my bedside. Over a period of many years, prayer group members and leaders in the Renewal formed me in the gifts and charisms of the Spirit.

Seminars and prayer formats that promote "Baptism in the Holy Spirit" are indeed one important means through which the people of God are introduced to life in the Spirit. However, we must also agree that these are not the only means. In fact, each one of us individually must consider that one-on-one evangelization and personal prayer with others is another powerful way to bring others into "life in the Spirit."

Finally, prayer groups and the Renewal must also consider proposing workshops, retreats, missions, and days of renewal to their local parishes. The rationale behind such initiatives is rather simple. First, John Paul II (2001) asked that we propose such initiatives to our pastors when he said to pastors, "...with the help of all sectors of God's people, plan the stages of the journey ahead..." (p. 40). Secondly, while we all know and understand that we received the Holy Spirit when we were baptized and confirmed, many in the mainstream Church do not know this for their lives. That is to say, they do not know they can call upon the Holy Spirit and the charisms of the Holy Spirit to grow holy and to build up the Church. This can mean only one of two things—either, they were never taught this truth or they did not "receive" this truth when it was taught to them.

Whatever the reason, most Catholics do not look for or expect spiritual gifts and outward signs of God's presence in their lives, nor do they expect to have within themselves, the gift of His voice, His wisdom, His discernment, and His healing to guide and direct their lives and their ministries in His Church. For these same reasons, many do not know about the outpouring of the Holy Spirit each time they receive the sacraments. Not only do they not know of the Holy Spirit's visitation, they also do not know that each time He comes He brings gifts for their holiness and their use in building up the Church (Eph 4:8).

In this third millennium, prayer groups will surely use some of the very same formats they have always used to teach about living in the Spirit, namely Life in the Spirit Seminars and retreat weekends. However, prayer groups may need to be attentive to new ways to accomplish the Pentecost mission, which bids us "go, proclaim, and heal." In this millennium, there will surely be opportunities to plan and develop new initiatives that nurture and encourage a deeper awareness and openness in people to acknowledge the gift of the Holy Spirit.

There will be opportunities for us to propose spiritual growth experiences to our parishes. We can propose teachings and formation days to formally teach members of our parish about the gifts of the Holy Spirit and life in the Spirit. We can teach and model how the gifts can be used within each traditional Church ministry and organizations such as pastoral council, Altar-Rosary, Christ Renews His Parish, and Eucharistic Ministry formation as well as parish retreats and missions, in which we heighten people's awareness of living in the Spirit. These initiatives may involve us in more traditional parish activities such as annual missions, days of renewal, workshops, retreats, Bible studies, or bringing Eucharist to the homebound.

Several years ago, while giving a weekend retreat, many of those present were "baptized in the Holy Spirit." I had not taught about the Baptism nor had I prayed for it. In fact, the retreat was titled, "Earth, Wind, and Fire." The session on "Earth" dealt with the Father's creative love, "Wind" focused on the Word of God being sent to Earth to redeem and claim God's children for His Kingdom. "Fire" focused on the power and gifts of the Holy Spirit to reveal the Truth. As I was teaching, I became aware of the powerful presence of God in our midst moving the minds and hearts of those gathered and moving my tongue to teach. As I finished teaching, I called for silence and then prayed over the people in the Spirit. Throughout the prayer, those gathered continued to be bathed in the Holy Spirit. Once the prayer was completed, I felt the Lord prompting me to talk about what it means to be washed—bathed—revisited by the Holy Spirit and what it means to live in His Spirit. I was able to do this with little or no effort because God had opened them to see and hear what He was doing through their own experiences.

What would it be like if in place of ministering through a Life in the Spirit Seminar, we were to share our prayer time with other Catholics and during that time, God baptized them in His Spirit—bringing them into a fuller awareness of the graces that flow from their Sacramental Baptism? What would it be like if we were to minister to Catholics in the mainstream Church, and as we did, they were anointed and bathed in the God's Holy Spirit?

The moment we agree to dispel this sixth myth, we can be sure that, once again, there will be consequences. It will be necessary for us to broaden our understanding of the mission of our prayer groups and the Renewal. Once we do this, we will be required to plan, design, and offer our parish spiritual Renewal activities that awaken Catholics to the gifts and charisms of the Holy Spirit.

We must also agree to remain in prayer—that is to say, to pray always. To this end we must agree to contemplate the face of Christ (John Paul II, 2001) in prayer—in praying the Scriptures of His life, death, and resurrection. We must strive to know Him intimately. We must clear our minds of the world's thinking and take on the mind of Christ—studying and responding to the radical nature of His call that beckons us to live in Him through the power of His Holy Spirit.

If we begin our ministry in this way, we will be able to hear how God would have us minister to His people. Furthermore, if we pray always, we will be able to stay in tune with the action of the Holy Spirit as we minister. We will be able to discern God's actions and respond obediently to what He is asking us to do. We will be able to practice the art of listening for His voice. When we hear Him, we will know when and how He desires us to minister in order to promote living in the Spirit as a natural and normal way of life in the mainstream Church. Finally, if we continually contemplate the face of Christ, we will grow daily in our trust of Him and be strengthened in our response to His Pentecost plan to renew the face of the earth.

Let us, in the new millennium, broaden our understanding of the mission of the Renewal. We must not limit our mission to introducing Catholics to life in the Spirit and the gifts of the Holy Spirit. We must also proclaim that our mission is to awaken Catholics to their call—their responsibility to live in the Spirit on a daily basis, awakening them to the gifts and charisms that were poured out in them at their Baptism and Confirmation. We must also say that our mission is to encourage, coach, and mentor Catholics to use the gifts they received for their own holiness and for the good of the Church.

We can set out into the deep by offering spiritual growth experiences to our parish. As we do this, we must be prepared for large groups of Catholics to experience a fresh outpouring of the Holy Spirit. We must also be prepared to offer whatever supports are necessary for those who are so graced, to learn about life in the Spirit through teachings, prayer group meetings, and other means. Are we ready to respond to God's Pentecost actions in the mainstream of the Church? Are we ready for such a firestorm in the Church?

7. Charismatics Left Their Prayer Groups To Serve In Their Parishes, Building Up the Body and Promoting Life In The Spirit.

The seventh myth that must be dispelled is the idea that prayer group members left their prayer groups in order to evangelize in their local parishes. As prayer groups and prayer group members decrease, we in the Renewal try to find comfort in the notion that over the years Charismatics have been leaving our prayer groups in order to promote "life in the Spirit" in mainstream Church ministries. It is probably more accurate to say that Charismatics left prayer groups for a variety of reasons, some good and some not so good.

It is comforting to believe that inactive Charismatics are all evangelizing, witnessing, and bringing the power and the gifts of the Holy Spirit into the mainstream Church, this may not always the case. Some inactive Charismatics may be just that, inactive in using the gifts of the Holy Spirit and inactive in encouraging others to use the gifts. It is true that many inactive Charismatics are in a variety of ministries in the mainstream Church. However, for the most part, they are not intentionally promoting life in the Spirit, nor are they using the charisms of the Holy Spirit as they minister there.

If there were large numbers of ex-Charismatics living in and promoting life in the Spirit as well as using the gifts and charisms of the Spirit, we would see gifts such as healing, preaching, teaching, and shared prayer being used at every level of parish life. If this were true, more parishes would be spiritually rich environments, teeming with prayer, healing, praise, and vibrant worship. Such environments would call upon the gifts and charisms of the Holy Spirit for every liturgy, meeting, and parish function. If indeed, inactive Charismatics had influenced the parish by sharing the gifts and the power of the Holy Spirit, every liturgical celebration and every activity of the parish would be incorporating prayer, praise, worship, exhortation, and prophecy.

If we agree to dispel this seventh myth in the new millennium, we will be agreeing to find ways to gather formerly active Charismatics together and exhort them to operate in the gifts of the Holy Spirit. If we agree to dispel this myth, we will be required to invite inactive Charismatics to come with us into ministry in the mainstream church. Dispelling this myth carries with it significant consequences for those of us who know ex-prayer group and Renewal members. We will be required to develop initiatives that invite inactive Charismatics to gather for the expressed purpose of learning how to integrate the life in the Spirit into everyday parish life. If we agree to dispel this myth, we will be required to coach, mentor, and support inactive Charismatics and invite them back to prayer group to be formed and fed.

What would happen if "former" prayer group and Renewal members knew they were called to be instruments of the Holy Spirit, introducing the gifts and charisms of the Holy Spirit to members of their parish communities? What would happen if prayer groups offered to present workshops on how to use prayer, discernment, or prophecy (listening for God to speak) to ensure that deliberations at parish meetings were guided and directed by the Spirit? What would happen if the prayer group proposed an initiative to pray with the celebrant and ministers prior to the start of each liturgy? Prayer groups would have to reorganize themselves to become schools of formation, preparing their members for evangelization work in their local parishes. Prayer groups would have to redefine their vision and mission statements. Prayer groups would have to become schools of holiness, prayer, and communion (John Paul II, 2001) where members would be supported in growing holy and more deeply in love with God and one another.

What would it be like if they offered personal prayer at the end of every Mass? These and many other activities could be used continually to bring the Baptism of the Holy Spirit into the mainstream Church. Then it would be more accurate to say that former Renewal members have gone into the mainstream Church to evangelize their parishes, which literally means to bring life in the Spirit and to introduce and use the gifts and charisms of the Holy Spirit. Then we could say prayer group members left prayer group to evangelize in the mainstream Church and they are setting a firestorm burning in the Church.

8. The Renewal Is Dying.

The final myth that must be dispelled is the notion that the Renewal is dying. Nothing could be further from the truth. If we make an honest appraisal of the power of the Holy Spirit as the source of our leadership abilities, our ministry gifts, and our vast experiences, we must conclude that the Renewal is just now beginning to mature. In its maturity, it is being forced to put out into the deep—the challenging mission field of the mainstream Church. Once there, the Renewal will be required to expend new energies as it offers its years of experience, depth of formation, and mature gifts to those in the mainstream Church. The mainstream Church is exactly the right mission field, for it is ready for harvesting. It is time to send the workers into the field.

The Renewal is not dying. If it were, we would be forced to conclude that the Pentecost mission was dying and without the Pentecost mission, the Church herself would be dying. This simply is not the situation. God is asking the Renewal to be renewed, to listen for His voice, and be drawn into a deeper understanding of its role in His mainstream church. The Renewal itself is being reformatted to carry out its true missionary mandate—to go, proclaim, and heal. The sooner we acknowledge that God's Renewal is more alive today than it has ever been, the sooner we will be anointed with a zeal and a fire in our souls that will be unquenchable "until we all attain to the unity of faith and knowledge of the Son of God" (Eph 4:13).

When this happens, we will be as the people were at Pentecost, waiting to hear from our leaders, the answer to the question, "What must we do?" When the answers come, we must be prepared to respond. We must go. The missionary mandate of the Renewal tells us to go, proclaim, and heal. This mandate was given to the whole Church the day Jesus appointed the twelve (Mt 10: 6-8; Mk 6:7-13; Lk 9, 1-6) and the seventy-two (Lk 10:1-11), and the moment He commissioned those gathered around Him just prior to His ascension to His Father (Mt. 28:16-20). We in the Renewal have no less a mission than the whole Church.

When He sent the twelve out on mission, He told them to give away everything they had received from Him—every gift, blessing, healing, forgiveness, teaching, preaching, touch, and expression of unconditional love. He said, "Go to the lost sheep...As you go, make this proclamation: The kingdom of heaven is t hand. Cure the sick, raise, the dead, cleanse the lepers, drive out demons. Without cost you have received; without cost you are to give" (Mt. 10:8). This means we can no longer hold the gifts of salvation and unconditional love, the gifts of forgiveness and healing, and the gifts of the Holy Spirit and His charisms to ourselves. We must give as a gift to the whole Church, all of the gifts we have received from God.

This act of giving away everything we have received requires us to follow Christ more closely, listen to Him more carefully, and be with Him and in Him more constantly. To the man who was walking beside Him on the road Jesus said, "Follow me." The would-be follower responded, "'[Lord,] let me first go and bury my father.' But he answered him, 'Let the dead bury their dead. But you, go and proclaim the kingdom of God'" Lk 9:59-60). Some might say, "I already tried to talk to my pastor." or "My parish would never be open to that." or "You don't know how dead my parish really is." Such excuses liken us more to the man walking along the road with Jesus than to the twelve and the seventy-two who went out to proclaim the Kingdom of God. Jesus is telling us in this passages that selfishness and excuses can have no justification in the Kingdom of God.

When Jesus tells the man on the road to go and proclaim the Kingdom of God, He is asking him, and all who would follow Him, to leave the comfort of their homes, change how they are currently living, and move in a completely different direction and once there, proclaim His Father's Kingdom. When He tells us to follow Him, to go and proclaim His Father's Kingdom, He is instructing us to leave the comfort of our prayer groups, change how we are currently ministering, and move out into the mainstream of His Church, and once there, we are to proclaim the Good News of His Father's Kingdom.

Another man, walking along the same road with Jesus, wanted to spend some time at home first and after he said farewell to His family, he would be ready to follow Jesus. To this would-be follower Jesus responded, "No one who puts his hand to the plow and looks back is fit for the kingdom of God." What could Jesus possibly have meant by this? Is it that our prayer groups have been our homes and we have spent far too much time there, being comfortable and resting in the love and security of our brothers and sisters in the Renewal? Are we asking Jesus to wait a while longer, and then we will go? Are we telling Him we need more time with our prayer group communities? For if we are, we can be sure that Jesus is telling us not to look back to see what we have done in the past but rather, to put our hands on the plow—take up the difficult and challenging tasks that lie ahead, and always keep our eyes looking forward into the future. In effect, He wants us to take even greater risks for the Kingdom of God—greater than we have ever taken before.

Since we have had the Kingdom of God proclaimed to us from the beginning of our Renewal experience, it seems only natural that we should be called to this authentic form of discipleship in the third millennium. We have experienced God's healing touch and His signs and wonders. In contrast, so many in the mainstream Church do not yet understand the Father's Kingdom, the meaning of the Cross of Jesus for their lives, and His healing power. This is because so many Catholics do not know about His Holy Spirit—the Advocate, the One who could lead them to the Truth. Likewise, many in the mainstream Church have never experienced God's signs and wonders. Many Catholics are indeed the lost sheep of the house of Israel, not knowing they are lost and not knowing there is so much joy in living in Christ.

If we choose to dispel the eighth myth that says the Renewal is dying, we will be required to re-energize and renew our own hearts, minds, and souls in order to be a part of the renewal of the Renewal and at the same time to be a part of the renewal of the mainstream Church. While it will not look like the Renewal of the past, it will look like a Renewal that has put out into the deep.

We, the elders in the Renewal, have a critical role to play. Once we have agreed to dispel these eight myths we must pray and respond to God's call to plan, design, and implement new millennium initiatives. We must be the ones to exhort and lead prayer groups and Renewal ministries into the mission field of the mainstream Church.

What Then Is To Become of Our Prayer Groups?

If we choose to dispel one or more of the myths about the Charismatic Renewal and if we choose to embrace the call of John Paul II to put out into the deep, the Renewal at the national, diocesan, and prayer group level will need to adapt and develop new formats and initiative in the third millennium. This must happen if we wish to serve as missionaries in the mission field of the mainstream Church. The moment prayer group members decide to go into the mainstream Church to proclaim the Good News, the goals, objectives, methods, and content of Renewal gatherings will need to change. The Renewal and every individual prayer group will need to become a formation school, the place we return to for renewal, refreshment, teachings, workshops, problem solving, discussions, re-learning, re-grouping, and most of all refilling.

The model for using the Renewal in this way is presented to us by Christ Himself. When the seventy-two returned from their first mission, they were jubilant telling of the miracles they had witnessed and rejoicing in God's power working through them. They exclaimed to Jesus, "Lord, even the demons are subject to us in your name!" Jesus used the time immediately following their return to support, encourage, instruct, and teach them saying,

> The seventy[-two] returned rejoicing, and said, "Lord, even the demons are subject to us because of your name."

Jesus said, "I have observed Satan fall like lightning from the sky. Behold, I have given you the power 'to tread upon serpents' and scorpions and upon the full force of the enemy and nothing will harm you. Nevertheless, do not rejoice because the spirits are subject to you, but rejoice because your names are written in heaven." At that very moment he rejoiced [in] the holy Spirit and said, "I give you praise, Father, Lord of heaven and earth, for although you have hidden these things from the wise and the learned you have revealed them to the childlike. Yes, Father, such has been your gracious will. All things have been handed over to me by my Father. No one knows who the Son is except the Father, and who the Father is except the Son and anyone to whom the Son wishes to reveal him." Turning to the disciples in private he said, "Blessed are the eyes that see what you see. For I say to you, many prophets and kings desired to see what you see, but did not see it, and to hear what you hear, but did not hear it." (Lk 10:19-23)

When Jesus tells the disciples, what He saw, He is testifying to their work in His name, agreeing that their work was fruitful and miraculous. When Jesus tells them to rejoice more in the fact that their names were inscribed in heaven than in the signs and wonders they had seen, He was trying to get them to understand above all, that being a child of God was far greater a miracle than performing any miracles in God's name. Also, He was cautioning the disciples about being too prideful and puffed up. He was encouraging them to focus on their real mission.

We also learn in this passage that Jesus had spent a good amount of time with the disciples upon their return, at least long enough to pray with them, thanking His Father for giving them gifts for ministry. Jesus used this same time to teach His disciples about His relationship with His Father—their agreement and their oneness, as well as their anointing of those whom they choose. Finally, in Jesus' prayer for His disciples, He blessed their eyes and their ears for their future ministry work. In effect, Jesus used the time of their return to debrief with them and retrain them in the areas they were weak or lacked understanding.

On a regular basis, we must do as the disciples did, return from ministry and place ourselves in the presence of Jesus and in the Body of Christ—the presence of one another. Our prayer groups are the perfect places to do this, serving as our home base from which we can go out into the deep. They can become schools of formation in leadership and ministry gifts as well as in personal holiness, prayer, and communion with one another. They can become the safe places we go to discuss and analyze our work and to challenge each other's actions and motives in ministry. Our prayer groups can become the places we go to in order to be strengthened by God, where we learn how to surrender our wills to God, allowing Him to develop and form His gifts in us. They can become the mature Christian communities we need in which our gifts can continue to be discerned and developed. Our prayer groups can become places where we intercede for our parish, each other, and each other's ministries.

In a futuristic millennium vision, the prayer group would serve as a formation institute for the parish (See the Chapter titled, "The Renewal and Prayer Groups As Training and Formation Centers"). It would be the place where members of the parish would come to have their ministry gifts discerned and be formed and nurtured in their natural gifts and in the charisms of the Holy Spirit. It would be the place where parish organizations could come to assess their goals and activities in relation to the Pentecost mission—to go, proclaim, and heal. As this happens, our prayer groups would begin to thrive once again but this time with a new millennium mission and vision—with the purpose to continually put out into the deep.

Our Catholic Church is in desperate need of renewal. If it were not John Paul II (2001) would not have used the word "must" when he told ut to "put out into the deep" (p. 23). We ought not to deceive ourselves by denying the present situation in the Church. Some Churches are closing and others, by all account, should be closing. Some Churches with falling attendance are clustering together with one or two priests. Many ex-Catholics fill the seats and the bank accounts of other churches—mostly non-denominational and mostly Pentecostal or evangelical. Many faithful Catholics in the pews are there because of the rules not the Ruler.

Finally, it should come as no surprise that many Catholics on fire for the Lord struggle daily to remain in the Church. They are hungry to receive personal prayer ministry, hear an anointed teaching, be challenged in specific ways to live out the Gospel, and participate in Spirit-filled praise and worship. Their loyalty is split between Mass and the Spirit-filled church down the street as they attend both churches each weekend. They are always, in their own minds, on the verge of leaving the Church, but they keep giving it one more chance to meet their family's spiritual needs for growth and direction in their lives. It seems they are waiting for someone to give them a reason to stay. They know the power of the Eucharist in their lives but it is not enough to allay their fears that their children's spiritual development is not being nurtured by the Church nor by them since they do not feel they are getting adequate teachings on how to raise their children in the faith.

There are so many reasons why the Renewal must put out into the deep. Let us pray to have the courage to step out of our comfort zones and go into the mainstream church to proclaim the Kingdom of God. Let us pray to propose initiatives that introduce mainstream Catholics to life in the Spirit. Let us pray to model what it means to live in the Spirit in the mainstream Church. Let us make bold proclamations of the Truth of Pentecost to our pastors and our pastoral teams. Let us give everyday Catholics in our parish, our witness to the power of the Holy Spirit. Finally, when the history of the Charismatic Renewal is written for the third millennium, let it be said that we left our comfort zones and did not look back. Let it be said that we put out into the deep to proclaim the Kingdom and heal, as Jesus commanded. Let it be said, that because we went, the fire of the Renewal did not go out but instead turned into a firestorm in the mainstream Church.

Is the Catholic Charismatic Renewal Movement ready to set a fire that will turn into a firestorm in the Catholic Church? Is it ready to go, proclaim, and heal? There is no better nor more critical time to do this than now! If we dare to dispel the eight myths about the Charismatic Renewal and put out into the deep, we will know without a doubt that the Renewal is not dying. It is alive and well, enabling the Holy Spirit to do the work He must do—sanctify the people of God and make the

Bride of Christ holy and pleasing to the Father, preparing Her for the second coming of Christ. When these myths are finally dispelled, we will be caught up in a firestorm in the Church where the Holy Spirit will then move to renew the entire face of the earth!

Take Time To Reflect And Act

Take a few moments now to ponder which of the eight myths you most need to dispel, and why.

As you reflect on the myths that you most need to dispel, talk about the implications of doing this, for you individually and for your prayer group or the Renewal as a whole.

What actions might you take to establish your commitment to dispel the myth(s)?

1. The Spirituality Of "Living In The Spirit" Is Simply One Way To Grow In Holiness
2. The Charisms Of The Holy Spirit Are Not For Everyone

3. If We Talk, They Will Listen

4. If We Invite Them, They Will Come

5. Prayer Groups Evangelize The Church

6. The Mission Of The Renewal Is Baptism In The Holy Spirit Through Life in the Spirit Seminars And Retreats

7. Charismatics Left Their Prayer Groups To Serve In Their Parishes, Building Up the Body and Promoting Life In The Spirit

8. The Renewal Is Dying

What Is The Real Pentecost Question?

"I am with you always, to the close of the age" (*Mt* 28:20). This assurance, dear brothers and sisters, has accompanied the Church for two thousand years, and has now been renewed in our hearts by the celebration of the Jubilee. From it we must gain *new impetus in Christian living,* making it the force which inspires our journey of faith. Conscious of the Risen Lord's presence among us, we ask ourselves today the same question put to Peter in Jerusalem immediately after his Pentecost speech: "What must we do?" [*Acts* 2:37] (John Paul II, 2001, p. 39*)*

...we must look ahead, we must "put out into the deep", trusting in Christ's words: *Duc in altum!* What we have done this year cannot justify a sense of complacency, and still less should it lead us to relax our commitment. On the contrary, the experiences we have had should *inspire in us new energy*, and impel us to invest in concrete initiatives the enthusiasm which we have felt. Jesus himself warns us: "No one who puts his hand to the plough and looks back is fit for the kingdom of God" (*Lk* 9:62). In the cause of the Kingdom there is no time for looking back, even less for settling into laziness. Much awaits us, and for this reason, we must set about drawing up an effective post-Jubilee pastoral plan. (John Paul II, 2001, p. 23)

Once we have dispelled the myths about the Renewal, our minds and hearts will be ready to hear John Paul II's (2001) message to us for the new millennium. In his Apostolic Letter *Novo Millennio Ineunte* (2001), he encourages us saying that so much awaits us in the coming years and for this reason, we must set about drawing up an effective post-Jubilee pastoral plan. He writes, "In the cause of the Kingdom, there is no time for looking back and even less time for settling into laziness." He further cautions us not to develop pastoral plans based upon what we have done in the past but rather based upon fresh new initiatives, forward-looking ideas, culturally relevant methods, and risk-taking ventures that would bring souls to Christ. We must anticipate that God will clarify the apostolic steps we must take once we say, "Yes, send me Lord."

The Holy Father tells us there is only one way to set down an effective pastoral plan. It is with the help that comes from God once we profoundly root ourselves in contemplation and prayer. He reminds us that only in contemplation and prayer can we hope to encounter the face of Jesus. He emphasizes that the mission of every baptized Christian will be hopelessly inadequate until we ourselves first contemplate the face of Christ. He expands this thought further saying that our personal growth and formation will be impossible without such contemplation. When we encounter the face of the living Christ and sit with Him in love and in longing, we will come to understand that indeed He is with us and in us always. From this assurance, we will be compelled to ask the same question that was put to Peter after his Pentecost speech, "What must we do" (*Acts* 2:37)?

For so long a time now, individual Charismatics, prayer groups, and Renewal leaders have been asking the same question that was asked of Peter at Pentecost, "What must we do?" However, we were looking to increase participation in our Renewal—namely, what must we do to increase the number of Catholic Charismatics and prayer groups and attendance at prayer group meetings, regional formation days, healing Masses, workshops, and retreats. We were asking what we must do to increase donations so that we can continue to offer renewal programs. We were asking what we must do in order to improve our financial situations so that we can fund our offices. In essence, we were asking, "What must we do to prosper the Renewal?"

We were not asking the authentic Pentecost question, "What must we do to prosper the Kingdom of God in the mainstream Church and on the whole earth, now that the power of the Holy Spirit has set us on fire? What must we do to go, proclaim your Kingdom, and heal so that thousand of souls will be won for the Father's Kingdom as in the early days of the Church?"

Our question was not a bad question it was just not the authentic Pentecost question. Is this perhaps because we have not yet put on a truly Pentecost mind—one that compels us to lift up Jesus for all the world to see and to lift up the power of His Spirit in the mainstream Church in any and every circumstance? Might it also be possible that we forgot to apply, to the Renewal, the teaching of Jesus in Matthew 6:32-34, when He told us to, "seek first the kingdom of God and everything we need will be added to us, to the Renewal, our prayer groups, and our personal lives?

The more we open our eyes and ears to the spiritual challenges facing some of our diocese and local parishes, the more ready we may be to ask the authentic Pentecost question, "What must we do to prosper the name of Jesus and the power of His Holy Spirit in our Church and in the world?" When we awaken to the situations in many of our parishes, we will recognize just how few people of all ages are participating in true spiritual growth activities. While there are some dynamic, Spirit-filled ministries such as "Youth To Youth" and "Life Teen" many teen and young adult ministries tend to be more like social clubs than spiritual growth environments. Spiritual growth and faith development are not always the first and most important goals of a parish activity. At times, peace and justice issues are addressed outside of prayer or acknowledgement of God's presence. In fact, parish experiences that start out spiritually based seem all too quickly to turn into non-spiritual organizations or social clubs.

For example, in some parishes Christ Renews His Parish (CRHP) has gone from being a spiritual support group to a social support group with little or no faith sharing. When this happens, CRHP and other parish ministries begin to look more like "social clubs" rather than gatherings of friends who strive continually, with the power of the Holy Spirit to grow closer to Christ. Other parish organizations such as Altar-Rosary, as well as parish formation activities such as Theology on Tap often lose sight of spiritual goals and objectives and turn into social, fund-raising, or intellectual organizations over time.

The study of religion in many of our Catholic schools is more of an intellectual pursuit than an opportunity to draw closer to God. Throughout the country, our Catholic schools are known for their academic excellence and winning sports programs. Unfortunately, religion is often taught as just another subject with little or no emphasis on the spiritual development or formation of children and their families. Instead, students strive to give teachers right answers in exchange for good grades. One religion teacher reported that of all the religion teachers in her Catholic school, she is the only one who takes her students to chapel for prayer. The teaching of religion as an academic subject is not a bad practice. It helps people understand the teachings and traditions of the Church. However, there is a clear distinction between religion and spirituality. This means we must ensure that the Catholic school, the parish community, and families nurture and support the spiritual development of children first and teach religion as well. Religion will not get our children to heaven. A close intimate relationship with the Lord will get them to heaven.

Of all the challenges facing the Church today, perhaps the most difficult one is how to stop the large numbers of Catholics leaving the Church to become active members of other churches. We must take time to reflect and act on the possible reasons Catholics are leaving the Church. More important than our reflection, however, should be our investigation of the situation. We must have a plan to contact our brothers and sisters who have left the Church and ask them why they left. We may be very surprised to learn the reasons.

In questioning ex-Catholics, many often say the same thing—they left the Church to have their spiritual needs met. They now attend Pentecostal and evangelical churches where they are being ministered to one-on-one and where they are being raised up into various church ministries. Their new churches welcome them and invite them to discern their ordinary and extraordinary gifts. Once discerned, they are formed in the gifts, taught how to use them to build up the Body of Christ. Finally, they are put to work in the church, using their gifts in various ministries such as prayer room, teaching, bible study, parent support groups, children's ministry, teen ministry, and ministry to young adults, the elderly, separated/divorced, singles for the Lord, and so on.

In contrast, it sometimes happens that Catholics, are asked to place their gifts at the service of their parishes in a program such as "tithing time, treasure, and talent." However, sometimes when Catholics respond no one calls upon them to use the gifts they offered the Church. The reasons may vary but the effects remain—gifted Catholics go "unused" in their parishes simply because parish initiatives, that could have made use of their gifts, were never implemented. It seems at times, that the current leaders, preachers, and teachers of a parish almost feel threatened when newcomers join the parish, bringing with them ideas for ministry and gifts of leadership, teaching, preaching, prayer, healing, and so on. When gifted Catholics are not called forth, they become passive members of the parish and the Church loses the benefit of their gifts. If it goes on long enough that they are not called forth, they may find a new parish or leave the Church altogether.

Some dioceses have formed committees to stop the exodus of Catholics leaving the Church for other churches. One such committee of priests was tasked with developing a program that would stop this exodus and bring those who have already left back to the Church. There is no program designed by any human that is capable of accomplishing these two lofty goals. In fact, as John Paul II (2001) tells us, there is only one program for the third millennium. It is the Gospel of Jesus Christ. We must be sure this program is firmly in place in our parishes if we wish to stop the flow of Catholics out of the Church and if we wish to bring ex-Catholics home.

One test to assess whether or not the Gospel of Jesus is firmly in place in a parish might be to discover why Catholics left the particular parish. Once we learn the reasons, we ought to categorize them. Is it for the lack of preaching, teaching, personal ministry, community, worship, or sense of belonging? Is it that our worship and praise is truly dead? Are we unloving, exclusive, and unwelcoming? Is there no personal ministry? Are there no teachings, workshops, or ministries that meet the needs of families (parenting, finances, teens, or caring for elder parents)? Do we fail to discern the gifts of the people? Do we fail to invite them to minister using their gifts? Is it that there is no opportunity for the people to minister or serve in the parish? Is the Word not being preached? If we ask our people these questions, we must listen to their responses and then we must take each response and conduct an honest self-study.

If through self-study we determine these reasons to be valid, then we have two choices. We can either ignore what we have learned, and continue to watch Catholics leave the Church, or we can make the necessary changes. Only then will we have the right to invite ex-Catholics back to our Church for we dare not invite them back if we have not done this work, lest they have nothing to come home to. If we truly desire ex-Catholics to come home, we must be willing to put in the time and hard work to make it happen knowing that our efforts will bear much fruit.

There are other challenges facing the Church in this new millennium. Many Catholics are hungering to know more about their faith, especially how to defend it when confronted by others Christians. They want to know how to defend purgatory, the priesthood, and Eucharist, intercessory prayer to the saints, devotion to Mary, the Scriptural foundations of the Sacraments, and the traditions and the history of the Church. Some want to know how they can best raise their children to grow up Catholic and keep them Catholic. Many Catholics do not know how to read the Bible and still others do not even know they are permitted to read the Bible.

As Charismatics, we are often keenly aware of how God is working in other people because of our own experiences of God working in us. We are often able to discern the most pressing spiritual needs of our fellow parishioners and we tend to notice problems and issues that affect the spiritual growth and development of our parish. These heightened sensitivities make us the perfect ones to gather together with all those who love the Church and propose remedies for what would support and enhance the spiritual life of the parish. Each time we are alerted to other people's concerns for our beloved Church, we must come humbly before the Lord, begging for His mercy, thanking Him for His faithfulness, and praising Him for His immeasurable patience with us all. Once we have done this, we must ask the Pentecost question, "What must we do?"

Together, with others in our parishes and prayer groups, we must ask the Pentecost question and then listen for God's word to us— His remedies and His directives that show us exactly what He wants us to do to renew His Church in the new millennium. We must listen for the "fixes" that would keep Catholics from leaving the Church and cause ex-Catholics to want to come home. We must listen for the types of initiatives that would nurture and enhance the spiritual life of every member of our parish, no matter their age or stage in life.

As we enter into prayer together, contemplating the face of Christ, and asking the Pentecost question we must be ready to write what we hear God say. We must be willing to share what we hear Him say, with others. With the guidance of the Holy Spirit, we must dare to find ways to propose to our pastors and pastoral leaders, innovative initiatives. We must also dare to find ways to put what we hear God speak into action plans. Then, we must trust that God will continue to anoint both us, and our pastoral leaders with eyes to see and ears to hear what He wants for the renewal of our parishes.

Effective pastoral plans, prayer, contemplating the face of Christ, the mission of every Baptized Christian—these phrases incorporated into *Novo Millennio Ineunte* (2001) offer a new perspective to any plans we might bring forth in this new millennium. The plan we hear the Lord speak will not be a magic formula, for there is only one formula, one prescribed way—it is the way of Jesus, the Christ. Jesus must be at the heart of our plan and His Gospel must be the program of any new millennium initiative (John Paul II).

It follows then that the only effective plan we can write, is one in which we commit ourselves to helping others experience Christ, through the Gospel and the living Tradition of the Church. How we do this, as Catholic Charismatics in the mainstream of the Church, will be both exciting and challenging in the new millennium. Will we operate in the charisms of the Holy Spirit? Yes! Will we do so with great care and respect for those around us? Yes! Will we do so with the love and compassion of Jesus? Yes! Will God show us how to do this? Yes! Is it time for us to examine the Renewal, our mission and our vision? Yes! Is it time to sit with the Lord and write an effective pastoral plan for renewing the Renewal? Is it time for us to integrate what life in the Spirit and the charisms of the Holy Spirit more deeply into the mainstream of our local churches? Yes, I believe it is time.

Take Time To Reflect And Act

Take a few moments now to ponder the authentic Pentecost question: "What must I do Lord, to bring about your Kingdom?"

Have you discerned your ministry gifts? Have you prayed with others, talked about, and learned about your ministry gifts?

What ministry gifts do you have? How have you been formed in these gifts? How will you be formed in these gifts?

What do you see as your part in renewing the mainstream Church? What ideas do you have to bring the gifts of the Holy Spirit into specific ministries within the Church? What are your personal responsibilities in this regard? Whom will you influence? How will you do this?

For Renewal Leaders

Set an initiative in place to do informal study of "ex-Catholics" and their issues with the Church. Ask prayer group members to interview ex-Catholic family members and friends to find out why they left the Church. Keep all responses anonymous. Plan a day for sharing the results of the research with prayer group leaders. Form a discussion group. Summarize their issues for leaving the Church. Focus especially on the "pastoral reasons" they left. Invite prayer group leaders to present the results to their pastors and/or pastoral teams for review. Guide prayer groups in designing, organizing, and implementing initiatives that could "fix" the "pastoral" reasons Catholics left parishes. Parishes who implement such initiatives will be ready to invite their ex-Catholics to come "home."

Uncharted Waters

Let us go forward in hope! A new millennium is opening before the Church like a vast ocean upon which we shall venture, relying on the help of Christ. The Son of God, who became incarnate two thousand years ago out of love for humanity, is at work even today: we need discerning eyes to see this and, above all, a generous heart to become the instruments of his work...the Christ whom we have contemplated and loved bids us to set out once more on our journey: "Go therefore and make disciples of all nations, baptizing them in the name of the Father, and of the Son and of the Holy Spirit" (*Mt* 28:19). The missionary mandate accompanies us into the Third Millennium and urges us to share the enthusiasm of the very first Christians: we can count on the power of the same Spirit who was poured out at Pentecost and who impels us still today to start out anew, sustained by the hope "which does not disappoint." [*Rom* 5:5]. (John Paul II, 2001, p. 75)

John Paul II (2001) describes the new millennium as a vast ocean in which we are to venture out into the deep with discerning eyes and generous hearts—there to become God's instruments to make disciples of all nations. He reminds us that we have a missionary mandate to do so which was given to us by Christ Himself. He further instructs us to put out into the deep with the very same enthusiasm of the first Christians. If we want to hesitate even a little, we must resist for he assures us that we can count on the power of the very same Spirit that was poured out on the disciples at Pentecost.

Let us consider for a moment what this passage means when it says we are to be missionaries for Christ, venturing out into the deep to "...make disciples of all nations, baptizing them in the name of the Father, and of the Son and of the holy Spirit" (Mt 28:19). First, the call to be a missionary has several implications. Some people feel the call to become missionaries in foreign countries where people have never heard preached the Gospel of Jesus Christ. Others feel called to be missionaries in their own countries, ministering to those who have not yet heard the Gospel of Jesus Christ. We are all called to be missionaries within our families and we are all called to be missionaries in our home parishes, where some are still living life without the Good News.

When John Paul II (2001) talks about going out into the deep, he is deliberate in telling us the reason—it is to catch souls for Christ by inviting them to follow Jesus, thus making them His disciples. In order for us to go, we ourselves must know the Father, the Son, and the Holy Spirit and the work they do in our own lives, so that when we call others to follow Christ we can witness to them that we, ourselves, follow Him by the power of His Holy Spirit. Moreover, this requires that we be excellent followers of Christ— faithful to His teachings, trusting in His care, and enthusiastic in proclaiming His Kingdom, and persevering in prayer.

The Church has always faced the demanding challenge of incorporating the Gospel into its normal pastoral activity (John Paul II, 2001). However, in this new millennium, the Gospel of Jesus Christ must be rooted even deeper in the hearts and minds of Catholics. This can only happen will happen by calling upon the Holy Spirit to aid us in coming to know Christ more intimately and in coming to know the salvation graces that flow from His Cross. Being rooted in the Gospel and living in the Spirit is required in order to develop a strong protective shield against the temptations of the world, the flesh, and devil at every turn.

Living in the Spirit is not new, yet in this new millennium, it must be continually renewed in every baptized person. Living in the Spirit must be re-told and re-emphasized as the Gospel is incorporated into the normal pastoral activity of each parish. As missionaries to our local parishes, we must continually revisit and reiterate what the Holy Spirit did for the early Church at Pentecost. Above all, we must expect that the Holy Spirit will do the very same work in us and in every baptized Catholic as we go out to the mission fields of our local parishes. We must expect that through our intercession, the Holy Spirit will gift our parish with preachers, teachers, prophets, healers, and leaders.

In these difficult times, we must expect that since Christ is alive in us, our shadow is enough to heal a cripple just as Peter's shadow was. We must believe that preaching under the power of the Holy

Spirit is enough to convert the hearts of thousands. We must anticipate that laying hands on the sick will bring healing to them and to members of their households.

Over the years, we in the Renewal have excelled in translating the Gospel into meaningful initiatives such as Life and Growth in the Spirit seminars, retreats, conferences, days of renewal, formation days, and prayer group ministry. However, for the most part, we have offered these initiatives to our own people—Catholic Charismatics. We have not taken life in the Spirit and the charisms of the Holy Spirit into the deep—the mission fields of the mainstream Church. For example, we know that praying with others is a gift of the Renewal that is a common occurrence at prayer meetings and Renewal events. Praying with others for healing must become a common occurrence in family and parish life as well. We regularly invoke the Holy Spirit to come and anoint our teachers and preachers at prayer group and Renewal activities. We ought to suggest to those who teach in various parish ministries that they too have the duty to invoke the Holy Spirit before they begin to teach us. We might explain that failing to do so could deprive us of teachings that are more deeply anointed by the Holy Spirit.

We believe that when we praise and worship God, He inhabits our praises. We believe that when God inhabits our praises, His grace and healing are poured out upon us. Since we believe this, why don't we inform our parish music ministers of this great news? Shouldn't we share with them what Scripture says about giving praise to God (Ps. 66, 95, 98, 100, 108, & 149) and what the Church documents and letters tell us about praising God and praying the Mass (John Paul II, 1998).

We know that God speaks to His people, giving them guidance and direction for their thoughts, words, and actions. Since we know this, why don't we witness, teach, and call forth gifts of discernment, prophecy, or word of knowledge at the start of parish meetings in order to better hear and know God's plan for our various ministries and activities. Until now, our life in the Spirit has been Renewal focused. However, we can change that, by making life in the Spirit and the charisms of the Holy Spirit pastoral—that is to say, parish focused.

We can do this! By virtue of our Baptism, we have all been gifted and anointed by the Holy Spirit to go as missionaries into the uncharted waters of the mainstream Church. Once there, we are sure to find Catholics living and sometimes even ministering without any knowledge of the Holy Spirit's power to transform their natural gifts into supernatural gifts for their own good and the good of the whole Church. We are to give them the Good News of the Holy Spirit at work in their lives.

We are called to go as missionaries into the uncharted waters of our parishes where some Catholics may not realize that God speaks to them with a prophetic voice in their prayer time. Some may not know that they have the charisms of the Holy Spirit to use to grow holy and to use to build up the Body of Christ. We can go as missionaries into the uncharted waters of our parish, look for, and find Catholics who want to grow in Christ through the power of the Holy Spirit. We can go, knowing that we have not only an invitation to go, but also a mandate to go. We can go, knowing we are mandated to bring members of our parish to Christ. If we dare to go into our own parishes, we will surely set a firestorm ablaze in our parish. If all Catholic Charismatics dare to go into their parishes, they will surely set a firestorm ablaze in the entire Catholic Church and in the world.

Take Time To Reflect And Act

What do you believe John Paul II meant when he said each one of us was called to be a "missionary for Christ?"

How would you defend the missionary mandate to put out into the deep?

What Scripture passages would you reference in talking about the Holy Spirit to Catholics in the mainstream Church?

How would you explain your own life in the Spirit to Catholics in the mainstream Church?

What steps can you take to become a missionary in the mainstream Church?

Transforming Parishes Into Schools Of Holiness, Prayer, And Communion

It is in the local churches that the specific features of a detailed pastoral plan can be identified — goals and methods, formation and enrichment of the people involved, the search for the necessary resources—which will enable the proclamation of Christ to reach people, mold communities, and have a deep and incisive influence in bringing Gospel values to bear in society and culture (p. 40)....I therefore earnestly exhort the Pastors of the particular Churches, with the help of all sectors of God's People, confidently to plan the stages of the journey ahead, harmonizing the choices of each diocesan community with those of neighboring Churches and of the universal Church (p. 40)....What awaits us therefore is an exciting work of pastoral revitalization — a work involving all of us. As guidance and encouragement to everyone, I wish to indicate *certain pastoral priorities* which the experience of the Great Jubilee has, in my view, brought to light. (John Paul II, 2001, p. 41)

As we read in *Novo Millennio Ineunte* (2001), we discover that the work of writing an effective pastoral plan is to be viewed as an exciting revitalization project that involves each one of us. It is rather remarkable to learn that we are all invited to be a part of the planning and implementation process of renewing the Church in the third millennium (John Paul II).

What does this mean for Charismatic Catholics? It means that our Holy Father has personally invited each one of us to approach our pastors and pastoral teams in order to share with them the content of *Novo Millennio Ineunte* (2001). As we ponder this invitation, we must realize it is more than an invitation, it is the Holy Father's permission and his challenge that we go and encourage our pastors and pastoral teams to set forth new initiatives that will support and nurture the spiritual lives of every Catholic sitting in our parish pews.

Through this Apostolic Letter (John Paul II, 2001), leaders and prayer group members alike have been given an opening through which to engage in meaningful dialogues with our pastors and pastoral teams, offering them goals, objectives, resources, methods, and enrichment experiences that will enhance the spiritual growth of our parishioners at every age and in every organization within our parish. The goals and objectives we write must be in line with the vision of John Paul II for the Church in the third millennium. In this regard, he instructs us to keep all of our renewal efforts focused on the Gospel of Jesus Christ as it is proclaimed through the power of His Holy Spirit. The material resources we use must include Scripture as well as the teachings and traditions of the Church. The people who minister must be Catholics who are well formed in faith and well informed about their faith.

The methods we use must be appropriate to the developmental characteristics of those to whom we minister, young and old alike. We must know and understand the cultural, economic, and social needs of our parish members, those who struggle with financial difficulties, family relationships, and parenting. We must provide for the spiritual growth of our young children, teens, young adults, older adults, married, single, religious, ordained, divorced, and widowed so that we reshape our entire parish community, bringing Gospel values to bear in our society and in our culture and leaving no one behind (John Paul II, 2001).

To accomplish this mission of the Church, the Holy Father emphasizes several priorities that must be at the heart of any new initiatives we put forth in the new millennium. These priorities call for a more focused attention on and greater understanding of Sunday Eucharist, Reconciliation, the primacy of grace, listening to the Word, proclaiming the Word, diversity of vocations, and ecumenical commitment. His priorities also put forth the call to holiness, prayer, and communion (John Paul II, 2001). While all of these priorities are critical to the Church's mission in the third millennium, the Holy Father speaks of three other priorities, holiness, prayer, and communion, in a rather unique way. He calls for parishes to become schools of holiness, schools of prayer, and schools of communion. In establishing these three schools within a single parish, all of the other priorities can be addressed.

If we are to succeed in developing our parishes into schools of holiness, prayer, and communion, we must ask God to help us intentionally establish these three priorities in our home parishes. This will not happen, however, without deliberate attention to each one of them. Each priority must be addressed in every renewal activity or experience the parish plans—in writing goals and objectives, designing activities and experiences, and even in selecting methods and materials. Most important of all, we must strive to develop each of these dispositions in ourselves and support them in one another—within our families, communities, prayer groups, and in the Renewal. We must call each other to task on the issues of "unholy" behaviors. We must learn how to pray, and we must practice loving God and one another by putting aside our selfish dispositions.

Such growth will only happen when if parishes agree to be transformed into schools of spiritual growth, development, and learning. A parish's commitment to such lofty goals may depend upon our willingness to approach pour pastors and pastoral leaders to give them a copy of *Novo Millennio Ineunte* (2001) and to highlight and explain these three priorities of holiness, prayer, and communion. We must trust that God will anoint our lips to communicate the contents of the Apostolic Letter and to translate it into common sense language that speaks to the needs of our parishes.

Holiness

First, all pastoral initiatives must be set forth in the context of holiness. Holiness is a continuous grace of Christ that enables the life of every baptized person to be purified and deeply renewed. Holiness remains, more than ever, an urgent pastoral task. The gift of holiness is offered to all the baptized (Eph 5:25-26) and the gift carries with it, the duty to shape the whole of Christian life as St. Paul says, "This is the will of God, your sanctification" (1 Th 4:3) (John Paul II, 2001).

With holiness as the primary focus of all pastoral planning, it is only natural that we would ask, "Can holiness ever be planned?" If holiness could be planned for, what would the education and formation program look like at a parish level? The moment we place pastoral planning under the heading of holiness, the decisions made by the parish will have to embrace a higher standard of worshipping, ministering, and loving. This higher standard will make challenging demands of pastors, pastoral leaders, and all parishioners (John Paul II, 2001).

With the arrival of the new millennium, the Church has the opportunity to propose once again this higher standard of ordinary Christian living (John Paul II, 2001). Imagine a pastoral plan that places primary emphasis on inviting the people of God to seek holiness as their foremost goal in their family, work, community, and parish life. This is not new, but in the new millennium, such a pastoral plan must be presented in fresh language and innovative ideas. It must be presented in the context of a call to action that has already been modeled and taught by Jesus. Holiness must be presented as a radical idea and holiness must be lived in a radical way in the world.

This radical call to holiness is the very same call Jesus made to us on the Mount when he said, "Be perfect as your heavenly Father is perfect" (*Mt* 5:48). Holiness is God's priority for every Christian, every parish, every pastoral leader—His whole Church. However, our response to the call to grow in holiness will not become a reality until we develop an intentional plan of action and set it into motion in our parishes.

As Christians, we must finally refuse to settle for a life of mediocrity marked by weak moral values and ethics (John Paul II, 2001). We must refuse a shallow experience of God and go for a deep encounter with Him. We must seek, ask, and at times even beseech our pastors and pastoral leaders to teach us how to grow in holiness. We must pray and implore them to respond to our requests, for it is so important that we all be supported on our journey to holiness. We must ask our pastors and pastoral leaders to challenge us to grow in holiness. We must tell them we want to know what it means to sell everything, follow Christ, leave father, mother, brother, and sister, not look back, give one's life for another, forgive, give freely to others, love, and be loved.

In order for people to grow in holiness, the parish must become a school of holiness—a training center for teaching Catholics what it means to be holy, how to grow in holiness, and how to support holiness in one another. The methods proposed for a school of holiness must be appropriate to the ages and stages of the parishioners. The ideas generated and planned must be adapted to meet the unique needs of parishioners, their spiritual, emotional, and intellectual needs. The schools must integrate both traditional forms of individual and group support as well as the more recent forms of support offered by associations and movements (John Paul II, 2001). Such movements in the Catholic Church might include lay associate programs for religious orders, Cursillo, Marriage Encounter, Disciples in Mission, Life Teen, and Charismatic Renewal.

Intentionality is the key to developing a school of holiness. With holiness as a parish priority, pastoral leaders will be required to measure every action and activity of parish life in relation to the call to holiness. Does this decision support holiness? In what way does this activity promote holiness? How can we redesign this experience so that it nurtures holiness? What needs to be changed, deleted, or added to this activity in order to ensure that holiness is the primary outcome of what we have planned? These questions will begin to permeate every decision, every initiative, and every action taken by pastoral leaders.

Developing a spirituality of holiness at every level of parish life is not only a great grace it is also a tremendous challenge. It is impossible to grow holy without drawing near to God, and it is impossible to draw near to God without the help of the Advocate, the Holy Spirit. If we are to consider meaningful initiatives that could transform a parish into a school of holiness, we must be prepared to talk about life in the Spirit. In Jn 14:16, Jesus told His disciples, "I will ask the Father, and he will give you another advocate to be with you always, the Spirit of truth...."

In declaring this, Jesus is telling us that He is our first advocate, the one who taught us, modeled for us, encouraged us, and most important of all, redeemed us. He is also telling us that the Holy Spirit, whom His Father would send, is our second help—a help that is needed in order for us to remember all that Jesus did for us while on earth. Why did the Father need to send a helper, the Holy Spirit? Jesus makes it perfectly clear to us when He says, "The Advocate, the holy Spirit that the Father will send in my name—he will teach you everything and remind you of all that [I] told you" (Jn 14:26).

Jesus, now seated at the right hand of the Father, no longer walking in visible human flesh on earth, knew that we would have to be taught and reminded of His work of salvation. He knew we would have had no hope of coming to know the work of His life, death, and resurrection were it not for His promise of a helper. For this reason, He asked His Father for another helper (Jn 14:15). Jesus called this helper, "another" helper making it clear to us that He is our first help, gaining eternal life for us and the Holy Spirit is our second help, the one who reminds us of all that Jesus did and leads us to the Truth (Jn 16:5).

The Holy Spirit comes to us at the moment of our Baptism creating us anew and making us children of God. Once a child of God, the Holy Spirit aids us on our journey to holiness by dwelling within us and pressing the very holiness of God into us. The Holy Spirit is the sanctifier of all people and thus of the Church (CCC #749). For this reason, , we are able to think and act in holy ways and we are able to operate in the gifts and charisms of the Holy Spirit. For this reason, we can draw closer to God and, by His grace, continually prepare our souls to see Him face to face one day and live in union with Him through all eternity (John Paul II, 1986).

If new millennium initiatives are to succeed, they must provide dynamic teachings and regular coaching and mentoring activities to help others live in the Spirit, receive the gifts of the Holy Spirit, and use the gifts of the Holy Spirit. Charismatic Renewal in general and specific prayer groups in particular are in the unique position to offer themselves and their services to their pastors and pastoral teams. We are well organized. We so have many gifted people living under the grace and power of the Holy Spirit. Through the years, those of us in the Renewal have supported, nurtured, coached, and mentored one another along our journeys to wholeness and holiness. For this reason, Charismatics are the perfect ones to support parishes in planning, designing, and implementing experiences that would support and nurture holiness in the life of every individual, every family, every parish ministry and organization.

Now we must be willing to place ourselves and our experiences at the service of our parishes in order to help set up schools of holiness. Our spiritual formation makes us authentic resources and instruments to be used by our parishes in planning, developing, and implementing "schools of holiness." As ones who have been formed in various charisms, we can be called upon to help establish a parish environment that continually invites Catholics to grow in holiness. There are so many ways to help create such an environment—parish missions, retreats, workshops, support groups, journaling, Scripture reading, and spiritual direction to name but a few. There is no limit to what God would tell us to design for our parish if we but sit with Him and make a plan. We can encourage, model, support members on their journey to wholeness and holiness. We can design initiatives that not only nurture holiness but also form ministers who can help others on their journey. Each time we talk to others about our struggles and successes we can be living witnesses to God's abundant graces for those seeking holiness.

Prayer

Another priority for the new millennium is Christian living that is distinguished above all else in the art of prayer. Prayer cannot be taken for granted. We must actually learn, or even relearn how to pray as if the Master Himself were teaching us for the first time. We must be attentive to His teaching and His modeling as He shows us when, where, and how to pray John Paul II, 2001).

It is only in prayer and through the power of the Holy Spirit that we are able to develop intimacy with Christ, remaining in Him as He remains in us (Jn 15:4). Only in prayer, gazing upon the face of our Savior, are we able to uncover the hidden things of the past that hinder us from growing holy in the present. In prayer, we are able to recover our life in Christ and we can be renewed in the power and the gifts of His Spirit. Only in prayer can we come to know the embrace of God's love and mercy. Only in prayer, are we able to abandon ourselves into the hands of God, knowing that He sustains us with His grace and above all, His presence.

John Paul II (2001) says that in this regard, it is essential that we make "teaching Catholics how to pray" a major focus of all pastoral planning in the new millennium. He encourages parishes to do all that is possible to ensure that the parish environment becomes a climate of prayer, for it is in prayer that one finds the eternal Truth, Jesus Christ. When we dare to plunge our parish communities into prayer, we will truly be surrendering ourselves to the deep—for prayer will lead us to deeper faith and deeper, more authentic conversations with God. Prayer opens our hearts to a stream of grace, and this grace enables the word of God to penetrate our souls and transform our minds.

The world is starving for such encounters with Christ, and those who have experienced vocal, meditative, and contemplative prayer have a duty to proclaim to what depths an intimate relationship with Christ can lead. We must continue to progress in our own prayer lives, vocal, meditative, and contemplative, and then we must teach others how to pray and how to progress in prayer. Some may wish to study the great mystics of both East and West to learn and then teach others how to progress in prayer. We can learn and teach others how to move from a genuine dialogue of love to the point of rendering ourselves entirely possessed by the God.

Developing a spirituality of prayer at every level of parish life is both a challenge and a grace. If we in the Renewal are to be among those who establish such a school of prayer, we ourselves must pray and remain committed to prayer. We must not only pray, but we must be lovers of prayer—lovers of intimate union with God, the Father, Son, and Holy Spirit so that when we are called upon to teach what it means to pray always, our lives will give witness to the graces that have penetrated our souls. If we are to be teachers in a parish school of prayer, we must be found among those who encounter Christ, not just in imploring His help, but also in giving Him thanks, praise, and adoration. We must be found among those who encounter Christ through contemplation, listening and ardent devotion, until our hearts fall in love with God (John Paul II, 2001).

In thinking about schools of prayer, we must consider the types of coaching and mentoring activities that would be most helpful in maintaining a spirituality of prayer in a parish. We can teach others about the relationship between prayer and praise. We can coach and mentor others by meditating with them or praying with them for healing. We can ask them to join us for adoration before the Blessed Sacrament. Most important of all, we can offer to integrate teachings and experiences in prayer for every parish function—meetings, missions, retreats, workshops, and even dinner dances and concerts.

As members of prayer groups and diocesan Renewal Movements, we are gifted in prayer. We are drawn to prayers of thanksgiving, praise, worship, and adoration. Our souls are frequently drawn into silent waiting and longing for a visitation from our God. We have years of experience meditating on the word of God and contemplating the face of Jesus and teaching others to do the same. We are gifted in praying with others and leading others to hear God's voice for their lives. We know how to help others image the face of Jesus in prayer.

We, in the Renewal, are the perfect ones to propose ways for our pastoral teams to initiate and expand prayer at all levels of parish life, from communal prayer before meetings to personal prayer ministry at the end of each Mass. We have so much experience to share and we have been well formed in so many types of prayer—vocal, meditative, and contemplative, shared prayer, journaling prayer, and prayers for physical, emotional, spiritual, and inner healing. Who better than Charismatic prayer ministers to propose and plan prayer-related initiatives that will nurture and enhance the spiritual growth of those in our parishes? Who better than Charismatic prayer team and healing ministers to help plan, develop, and implement a spirituality of prayer for parishes?

Communion

Communion is the third priority that must be given deliberate attention by each parish community. Communion is the fruit and demonstration of the love, which springs forth from the heart of the Father. Love is poured out upon us through the Spirit, which Jesus Himself gives to us (Rom 5:5) making us one in heart and one in soul (Acts 4:32). It is in building a communion of love that the Church becomes sacrament—the sign and instrument of God's intimate union with us and our intimate union with Him and with one another. While many things are necessary for the Church's journey through the third millennium, without love, without pure charity, all will be in vain. Paul reminds us of this when he says, even if we speak with the tongues of men and of angels and if we have faith to move mountains, but are without love, all we do is useless and worthless, serving no purpose at all in the Kingdom of God on earth or in heaven (1 Cor 13:2). Love is God's gift to the Church, to the world (John Paul II, 2001).

In practice, what does all this mean? It means that if a parish wishes to design practical plans to promote a spirituality of communion, unconditional love must be the guiding principle of every teaching and every experience given to the people. This means that the ministers of the altar, consecrated persons, and pastoral workers must be trained in what unconditional love "looks like" in the everyday life of the family and the parish. It means that we need continual reminders of how love thinks, how love speaks, and how love acts, as evidenced by the life of Jesus, the Master Lover.

With such a strong focus and clear directive to attain communion, it should make us all wonder just how much our Holy Father can see into our homes and into our parishes. A person needs only to follow behind people walking out of a parish meeting to hear the gossip, insults, and at times, even mean-spiritedness, that rolls off the tongues of our brothers and sisters. There is enough bickering between organizations, pastoral leaders, ministers, and parishioners in general to cause us all to stop and take account of the Gospel message. Does our Holy Father think that we have forgotten how to love one another? Does he think we never learned how to love unconditionally? Is he telling us to re-learn how to love each other?

No matter which is true, John Paul II (2001) is telling us exactly what each of us, both individually and corporately, needs to do in order to characterize our homes and our parishes as places of "holy communion." First, he tells us that each one of us must contemplate the mystery of the Trinity dwelling within. Each of us must be able to see the light of the Trinity shining on the face of our brothers and sisters around us.

A spirituality of communion means that we are able to think of our brothers and sisters as a part of ourselves. This makes us able to share their joys and sufferings, to sense their desires and attend to their needs, to offer them deep and genuine friendship. A spirituality of communion also implies that we see what is positive in others, welcome it, and prize it as a gift from God—a gift to us from God. This is very much the opposite of how we, in our human nature, tend to view others. We most often see their gifts as a threat to our own. Now, we are asked to embrace their gifts as our gifts, their talents as our talents, their strengths as our strengths (John Paul II, 2001).

Additionally, John Paul II (2001) tells us that a spirituality of communion means that we know how to "make room" for our brothers and sisters, bearing "each other's burdens" (Gal 6:2) and resisting selfish temptations which constantly beset us and provoke competition, careerism, distrust, gossip, and jealousy. It seems we must truly go out of our way to minister to one another. We cannot remain closed off and distant from anyone in our community. We must intentionally extend ourselves and truly see Christ Himself in one another. This is all such a radical departure from the competitive message the world sends to us.

Some might want to believe that communion is already present in parish life. However, we ought to reconsider; especially since John Paul II (2001) cautions that we must not deceive ourselves in this regard for unless we follow this spiritual path of authentic "holy" communion with Christ and one another, external structures of communion will serve very little purpose. They would become organizations without a soul, a pretense of communion rather than a means of spiritual growth.

Finally, while it is widely understood and accepted that the Church in the light of the Gospel must interpret social realities, John Paul II (2001) warns us that we must never yield to the temptation to turn Christian communities into mere social agencies. The Church can never forgo her missionary activity among the people, for her primary task is to announce Christ as, "the way and the truth and the life" (Jn 14:6), so that in Him people find their salvation. Our work is incomplete if we feed the poor and do not help them to encounter the face of Christ. Our work is incomplete if we give drink to the thirsty and yet do not invite them to drink from the living water, Jesus. Above all, it is never enough to care for or love others so that we can feel good about ourselves. The only way to reach authentic communion is to fall deeply in love with each person, who is Christ Himself, and allow each person to see and experience Christ in us.

Communion is perhaps the greatest challenge we in the Renewal face, as we offer plans and initiatives to our pastors and pastoral teams. As we ponder meaningful initiatives, we must consider what it might be like to develop a spirituality of communion, that is to say, how people should interact and communicate with one another as well how they must respond and minister to one another. We must discern the best initiatives that would support loving communion among our members. We must think about what types of mentoring and coaching needs would be helpful in maintaining communion. Finally, we ourselves must be in communion with every person we meet for we may be called upon to teach and give witness to what it means to be in communion with Jesus and with those who love Him and those He loves so deeply.

As we accept the grace and the challenge to bring forth initiatives that would create a spirituality of communion in a parish, we ourselves must stand out as true "lovers" of Jesus and true lovers of one another. By our very presence, we must significantly affect the lives of the people in our parish and the varied situations of parish life by modeling our own life in Christ, life in His Spirit, and communion with Him and with others.

Conclusion

Indeed, we are prepared to go forward in hope! This new millennium has opened up a vast ocean and we have been called to put out into the deep of this ocean, relying solely on the help of Christ and the power that flows from His Holy Spirit.

The Risen Jesus accompanies us on our way. He enables us to recognize him, just as His disciples did on the road to Emmaus, in the breaking of the bread (Lk 24:35). May Christ find us attentive and ready to recognize His face and run to our brothers and sisters with the good news: "We have seen the Lord." (Jn 20:25) (John Paul II, 2001).

To put out into the deep, means we must be willing to bring ourselves and the Baptism and gifts of the Holy Spirit into every aspect of parish life. We must be willing to go to people and places in the Church where the Renewal has traditionally never been visible. We must be willing, even eager, to share, teach, and bring the Baptism of the Holy Spirit to every parishioner and parish organization including pastoral council; Altar-Rosary; and ministry to young children, teens, and young adults; ministry to the divorced, single, and grieving; RCIA; religious education; parish school; ministry to the homebound; intercessory prayer; perpetual adoration; musicians and choirs, servers; catechists; and every other parish ministry.

We must put on a "spiritual" mind to ponder the challenges put set forth in *Novo Millennio Ineunte* (2001) for if we were to approach this challenge with our human way of thinking, we would declare it an impossible task to bring the Baptism and gifts of the Holy Spirit into the mainstream of the Church. More than impossible, it would seem irrational, even absurd for us in the Renewal to go into the mainstream Church operating in the charisms of the Holy Spirit within our parishes—but then, that must be exactly how the disciples felt when Jesus said "go out into the deep." Jesus was asking the disciples to take a risk, go where they had never gone and when they got there, to do what they had never thought possible. What He asked them to do, they did. His presence assured them of not only their safety when he declared, "And behold, I am with you always, until the end of the age" (Mt 28:20), but also of their success, when Mark writes, "'These signs will accompany those who believe; in my name they will drive out demons, they will speak new language. They will pick up serpents [with their hands], and if they drink any deadly thing, it will not harm them. They will lay hands on the sick, and they will recover." ...they went forth and preached everywhere, while the Lord worked with them and confirmed the word through accompanying signs'" (Mk 16:17, 20).

He will do the same for us if we trust and go out into the deep. The Advocate, His Holy Spirit will guide us and empower us and He will do miracles such as we have never seen. But we must go, leaving what we have known and done for over 30 years and start doing something different—something new. If we move away from the shore, out from the comfort zone of our prayer groups, we will enjoy a bountiful catch for Christ in the deep waters of His Church. There are Catholic souls out there, just waiting to see, hear, and be touched by Jesus. We are their Jesus, just as they are our Jesus.

Let us not hesitate to invite the Holy Spirit to renew the Renewal. He will show us how to refocus our energy into new missions and the new mission fields of our local churches. If we are willing to listen and obey, we will find ourselves in the deep water—for this is exactly where Christ needs us to be. What these new missions will be like are not yet fully known to us, but they will be revealed to us in time by the Lord Himself. Let us eagerly embrace the call to be missionaries and let us find ourselves in the mission fields of our local parishes. Our mission must be to keep focused on Jesus and the work He commanded us to do—to go, proclaim the Kingdom, and heal the sick.

Take Time To Reflect And Act

What role will you play in helping your parish community respond to the Apostolic Letter of John Paul II, *Novo Millennio Ineunte (2001)*?

Are your pastor and pastoral leaders aware of John Paul II's call to put out into the deep? Submit a proposal to your parish to set up a "study group" to read and then discuss the implications of *Novo Millennio* Ineunte (2001) for your parish—every organization, activity sacramental preparation, retreat, workshop, seminar, and teaching. What initiatives can be initiated in your parish to develop it into a "school of holiness, school of prayer, and school of communion?"

Envision your parish as a school of holiness, prayer, and communion. What does it look like? How could you turn your vision into a reality? What can you take right now to begin to accomplish this? What could you do in the next month, year, and five years to accomplish this?

What Is In The Word "Baptism"?

If we Catholic Charismatics are sincere about responding to the call of John Paul II to put out into the deep, we may wish to reconsider how we communicate our experience of 'life in the Spirit" to those in the mainstream Church. The one expression that we use rather frequently and freely may in then end, significantly hinder our ability to become an integral part of the renewal of the mainstream Church. It is the phrase, "Baptized in the Holy Spirit." This expression took root in the early days of the Renewal, and rightly so. After all, the Catholic Charismatic Renewal was mentored by and modeled after our Pentecostal brothers and sisters. However, there was one major difference between Pentecostal and Catholic Christians. Our Pentecostal brothers and sisters established entire church communities that lived in the power of the Holy Spirit and operated in the charisms of the Holy Spirit. Their churches both accepted and understood the language of "Baptized in the Holy Spirit." Baptism in the Holy Spirit was a part of their core beliefs. Additionally, Pentecostal Christians had no prior experience of a "sacramental baptism."

In stark contrast, the Catholic Church has always had the sacrament of Baptism. Likewise, the Church has always had the words "Baptism" and "baptized" in her traditional and canonical vocabulary as well as in her stated mission of evangelization. Consequently, we as Catholic Charismatics have had a difficult time explaining ourselves to those in the mainstream Church. At times our pastors, deacons, and pastoral leaders question us concerning our language, saying, "What do you mean by baptized in the Holy Spirit? Catholics are already baptized." Indeed, the Church teaches that there is only one Baptism that is needed, water and the Spirit and that is exactly what the sacrament of Baptism does (Jn 3:3-8). For this reason, we may find it difficult to explain Baptism in the Holy Spirit to mainstream Catholics.

If we honestly were to appraise the benefits of this phrase over the years, some might say it has been a language barrier for them. Yet, despite these communication barriers, we continue to approach our Catholic brothers and sisters, telling them about the

Baptism in the Holy Spirit. As long as we continue to use this expression, we may continue to confuse and even turn away our brothers and sisters in the mainstream Church. Similarly, as long as we continue to use "charismatic jargon" when speaking to our pastors and pastoral leaders, they may show concern for our ability to minister in the mainstream Church.

We must consider if we wish to continue with two types of language—one for our charismatic friends and another for everyday life and the mainstream Church. If we are able to slightly altar our charismatic language when we initially encounter Catholics in the mainstream Church, we may find that those to whom we communicate "life in the Spirit" may better understand what we are saying and may even want to learn more and listen more. Later on, as we continue to teach and witness to them about "life in the Spirit, we can give them the "charismatic language" to describe their experiences of being "baptized in the Holy Spirit."

If we truly wish to promote life in the Spirit in the mainstream Church, we must be willing open ourselves up to new ways of communicating "life in the Spirit." There are so many different ways to talk about Baptism in the Holy Spirit so that our pastors and parishioners become more accepting of us and of our messages about the charisms and life in the Spirit. For example, we might say, living in the Spirit, living with a deeper awareness of the power of the Holy Spirit, calling upon the Holy Spirit, or being renewed in the Holy Spirit when we receive the Sacraments. We might talk about coming alive in the Spirit or being washed or refreshed in the Spirit. We might explain how we call upon the Holy Spirit to gift us with what we need to grow holy. We might talk about how the Holy Spirit comes to us in Baptism and Confirmation, and when He comes, He brings gifts to us—gifts of prayer, spontaneous praise, healing, ecstasy, hearing Him speak to us, wisdom, understanding, and so on.

The challenge to find new ways of talking about life in the Spirit, in no way lessens neither the meaning nor the importance of the phrase "Baptized in the Holy Spirit." The theology of "Baptism in the Holy Spirit" is deeply rooted in Scripture and tradition. In St. Luke, we read about John the Baptist's testimony to the people who gathered in the river to be baptized. He told them, "I baptize you with water; but he who is mightier than I is coming,...he will baptize you with the Holy Spirit and with fire (3:16).

Perhaps the clearest understanding we have of the Baptism in the Holy Spirit is depicted in Acts 19. At the beginning of this chapter, Paul posed two questions to the people when he arrived in Ephesus, "Did you receive the Holy Spirit when you believed?" And they said, "No, we have never even heard that there is a Holy Spirit." And he said, "Into what then were you baptized?" They said, "Into John's baptism." And Paul said, "John baptized with the baptism of repentance, telling the people to believe in the one who was to come after him, that is, Jesus." On hearing this, they were baptized in the name of the Lord Jesus. And when Paul had laid his hands upon them, the Holy Spirit came on them; and they spoke with tongues and prophesied There were about twelve of them in all" (1-7). In this passage, we learn that Baptism in the Holy Spirit is an outpouring of the Holy Spirit that comes with truly "hearing" the word and with the laying on of hands.

It is good for us to consider all the ways we can communicate the initial experience of being "baptized in the Holy Spirit" We must be willing to talk about it in whatever ways we can to get our point across to our listeners. In His day, Jesus told stories to get His point across to the people. He spoke to them in the language they understood and accepted. He used the cultural expressions and activities of the day, of the Jewish faith, of the Pharisees, Sadducees, and the Romans to relate God's love and mercy. We should expect that He would want us to minister in His Church in the very same way today, telling our stories in a language that is familiar to Catholics. He would want us to evangelize using simple, understandable language that speaks to their prior experiences and builds upon their prior knowledge.

We must not let anything hinder our missionary work in the mainstream Catholic Church, especially the language we use. For this reason, we must agree to do whatever it takes to talk about, explain, and encourage others to live in the Spirit. If we need to temporarily reserve "charismatic" jargon for prayer group and Renewal events, let us do it. Renewing the Church is far more important than remaining "pure" in how we talk about and witness life in the Spirit.

One of the first, and perhaps most important steps we can take prior to putting out into the deep is to assess our Pentecostal language and begin to change how we talk about "life in the Spirit so that it will be better understood and more readily accepted by our pastors, pastoral leaders, and the laity. This will ensure our initial success and our continued success as missionaries in the mainstream Church. The documents and teachings of the Church and Sacred Scripture provide us with the exact language we need to talk about life in the Spirit. If we are willing to surrender our tongues to the prompting of the Holy Spirit, we may find a cultural shift in our language that is just right for setting a fire that the Holy Spirit can transform into a firestorm in the Church.

Take Time To Reflect And Act

Share how the "charismatic language" has helped or hindered your own personal journey in living in the Spirit.

Share how "charismatic language" has helped or hindered your ministry of evangelization in the mainstream Church.

What specific charismatic expressions or words do you feel might "turn people off" in the mainstream Church or possibly give them a reason not to want to hear about or learn about "life in the Spirit?" How might these expressions be tempered and/or altered to have a more positive effect when talking with others about life in the Spirit?

Sit With Me And Make A Plan

When John Paul II (2001) challenged the Church to examine just how far she had renewed herself in the first 2000 years since the birth of Christ, he invited the Church to assess its fervor and discover a fresh enthusiasm for its spiritual and pastoral responsibilities. Such an examination he said would serve to prepare the Church to take up her evangelizing mission with fresh enthusiasm in the new millennium. It has taken nearly three years for the Renewal Movement, in our diocese to respond in earnestness to our Holy Father's call to renew the Church. Our response has grown out of our own frustrations and fears about the decreasing attendance at Renewal activities and decreasing numbers of prayer groups and prayer group members as well as their increasing fatigue and waning enthusiasm.

Our zeal to have an action-oriented response to the Holy Father's challenge in his Apostolic Letter began to take shape in August 2003, when, at the start of our regular monthly meeting of the 14-person spiritual leadership council, we heard God speak to us in prophecy. That month, like every other month, we had set aside the usual amount of time for opening prayer and praise. Immediately following prayer and praise, there was an extended period of silence to listen for God's word—His direction for the future of the Renewal. As we came out of the silence, the following prophetic word was proclaimed:

> This is my war room. I am your Commander-In-Chief. You are my generals. You are to plan and strategize with me for how it is I wish to wage battle against the evil one who works for the eternal destruction of souls. There is much work to be done. My Church is in shambles. Gather my troops around yourselves. You have leadership skills and sufficient training to lead my troops into battle. (MCCR, 2004)

As soon as this word was proclaimed, our spiritual director urged us to share how the word affected each of us. We sensed that God wanted to do a powerful work through us but we were unsure of what it might be. Several months prior to this meeting, we had felt a call to work with teens at a diocesan level. As a result, we had begun offering our services, in whatever capacity, to our diocesan director of teen and youth ministries.

Prior to receiving this word, we were just beginning to offer our ministry gifts for parish mission work. We had developed brochures with topics that were relevant to every day life issues. Having just completed our first successful parish mission, the pastor offered to recommend us to other pastors and parishes looking for missions that might bring about parish renewal. We were very excited and grateful for his support. We were also keenly aware of the fact that his personal recommendation meant that there was a greater possibility for future missions and other ministries to other parishes in our diocese.

With these two ministries in their beginning stages, we were coming to understand that God was doing something new with the Renewal and with our local church. In reflecting on the prophetic word that night, council members shared their insights as to what this word meant to them. At a personal level, I was deeply moved by this word and sensed that there was something new and different breaking through with the Renewal and within our diocese. For several days after that council meeting, I felt called to take the word into prayer. After several days of prayer, the Lord spoke to me. What He said, I recorded in my journal.

> I am sending you out on mission. Go. Proclaim. Heal. You are to be My missionaries. My Church of Toledo is your mission field. My people are dying. They do not know My voice. They do not know what I have done for them by My Cross and Resurrection. They do not know that they are saved and that they belong to My Father. They do not need to be enslaved by this world. They are restored to new life in Me and they have the power of My Holy Spirit to use to become holy. I will not lose those who have already been claimed for My Father's Kingdom through Baptism. The meaning of their Baptism has not yet been fully revealed to them. Do this work in My Church. You are My missionaries. Go. Proclaim My Father's Kingdom, and heal. This is your mission. Your mission field is My Church. (MCCR, 2004)

As I reread the word, a vision was pressed into my mind. I could see graces flowing into the mainstream Catholic Church as it was being renewed in the new millennium. I could see ordinary Sunday Mass attending Catholics coming into a fuller, deeper awareness of the meaning of their Baptism and Confirmation. I could see the graces of all the Sacraments they had received taking effect in their lives through the power and gifts of the Holy Spirit.

The more I pondered the word, the more I began to perceive that everything we had ever done in the Renewal was now taking on new meaning. The events and experiences of the past 35 years began to hold an even greater significance for us and for the Church. The gifts of the Holy Spirit we had been using, every formation experience we had, every teaching we heard, every workshop, retreat, and conference we attended, everything we learned about, and every thing we learned to do were all coming together in a mission field tapestry. The Renewal in our diocese seemed to be taking on a more defined purpose and more encompassing roles and responsibilities.

I was beginning to realize that the future of the Renewal was not only dependant upon our past formation but more importantly the future of the Renewal was becoming dependent upon our response to do something with our formation in the mainstream Church. The "gift" we were given—life in the Spirit, had to be given away just as Jesus commanded when He commissioned the twelve to go, proclaim the kingdom, and heal (Mt 10:6-8). In his address given to members of the International Catholic Charismatic Renewal, John Paul II (2000) commented that "the Church expects from you [the Renewal] the 'mature' fruits of communion and commitment" (L'Observatore Romano, English ed. 3 June 1998). He further stated, "There is so much need today for mature Christians, conscious of their baptismal identity and of their vocation and mission in the Church and in the world!"

Since its early beginnings, the Renewal has been a stream of grace in the Church. In recent years however, I had begun to wonder how much longer it might continue to be considered a stream of grace given the increasing ages of prayer group members and the decreasing numbers of prayer groups. It seemed logical to think that its influence and impact might lessen as its members aged and declined in numbers.

Now, however, through God's prophetic word to us, and through the two initiatives that were taking shape (teens/young adult workshops and parish missions), I could envision a steady stream of grace flowing into the mainstream Church. I could see the Renewal influencing permanent changes to the "environment" of the mainstream Church. With continuous thought of our gifts and our formation, I began to see a maturity level in the Renewal that I had not recognized until now—a maturity level that would be of great benefit to the mainstream Church in the new millennium.

At the following month's spiritual leadership meeting, we set aside our usual time for prayer and praise, followed by a time of silence to listen for God's word to us. Once again, when our time of prayer had ended, the following prophetic word was proclaimed:

> I have set My angels at the four corners for your protection. You have a safe place in which to operate. Take this time to be entrenched with Me. Listen for My word in silence. Be with Me. Be attentive for we have much work to do in My Church. You have been gifted beyond your imagination. Sit with Me and make a plan. The needs are so great. You must, in this place and in this time, grasp the opportunity. Do not let fear hold you back. My love will set you free. (MCCR, 2004)

The moment this word was spoken, dead silence filled the room. We were stunned by what we heard. After several minutes, we once again began to share what that word meant to us. What was most startling about the word was God's command that we sit with Him and make a plan. The council's usual method of discernment for any new proposals or ministries for the Renewal was quite different from what God was asking of us. We were more accustomed to praying before our meeting that God would anoint our deliberations. Then we would begin the meeting and, whenever necessary, we would stop and brainstorm an idea or formulate a plan, discussing it and then simply bringing it to a majority vote. Of course, we always asked God to bless our work and, at times, we asked Him to confirm our decision by giving us a sign that we were in His will.

This time, however, God seemed to be asking us to do something completely different. God had already opened the door for two new initiatives. Having shown us these two examples of how we might evangelize in the mainstream Church, He was now asking us to sit and make plans with Him. He was asking us to listen for His word, follow His promptings, and act on what He was saying to us in prayer. It was no longer about taking a vote to design "our plan." It was about setting aside time to pray, discern, and design a plan with God as our consultant, advisor, mentor, guide, and counselor—making a plan with Him.

As we pondered His word that we were gifted beyond our own understanding, we knew that we had to delve more deeply into the gifts He had placed in each of us. Yet, as if knowing what a fear-filled reaction we would have to His word, He concluded by telling us not to fear and to let His love set us free from whatever would keep us from sitting with Him and making such plans.

We went back into prayer, this time to ask God to free us from whatever would keep us from acknowledging our gifts and from using them in His Church. We also asked Him to free us from any fear that would hold us back from responding fully. When we came out of prayer, we shared the ministry gifts we were willing to place at the service of the Renewal for mission work in the mainstream Church.

At that point, one of our council members reminded us of the Apostolic Letter (2001) written by Pope John Paul II at the beginning of the new millennium. He reminded us that the Holy Father challenged us to "put out into the deep." I shared more about the letter with the council members. It was fresh on my mind since I had been reading it a few months prior. We shared what we thought "going deeper" meant to us individually and to the mainstream Church.

We ended the council meeting by writing down our gifts and entering what we wrote into the official minutes. We also entered the prophetic word into the minutes as we had done before. This time however, I was much more aware of the word and the responsibility it carried for me personally, as council chairperson and for all of us, as the leaders of our diocesan Renewal Movement. Prior to leaving the meeting that night, we agreed to form an "Ad Hoc" committee" that would meet in a separate session. The role of the committee was to continue to discern God's word, sit with Him, make plans, and report the outcomes to the council.

Ten days later, the ad-hoc committee met to pray, listen, and share what God had been doing since that last council meeting at a personal level, at prayer group level, and at the parish level. The committee then reflected on the word "Sit with me and make a plan." In response to the word, members agreed to make prayer a critical component of any plan we would make. Our plan was to pray for seven days and then make a telephone call to the Vicar of Priests for our diocese. The plan was bold and even bordered on the absurd. I knew that miracles would have to occur in order for the plan to be put into place. I also knew that it was not our plan; it was God's plan and He is a God of miracles. I felt as if we were among the 72 that night who had been commissioned by Christ to go to the ends of the earth, proclaim the Good News, and heal the sick. Jesus told the disciples that signs and wonders would follow their work. Indeed, signs and wonders followed us too!

The chapters which follow give examples of "how to" set out into the deep. The examples include stories of how the ministry worked for us. Each chapter also includes detailed plans, action steps, and the miracles that grew out the ministry. Finally, each chapter provides information that might help other "renewal movements" such as Marriage Encounter, Life Teen, and Cursillo, to initiate similar ministries in their dioceses.

There is one thing we all know for sure after only a few months of going out into the deep. God has confirmed not only His word to us, to sit with Him and make a plan, but also how he had been preparing us for years to put out into the deep—to renew His Church in the new millennium. Get ready for the firestorm.

The remaining pages of this book present ways that Renewal leaders and Catholic Charismatics can put out into the deep to minister in the mainstream Church. Some of the ministries overtly support life in the Spirit by introducing mainstream Catholics to the charisms and life in the Spirit. Other initiatives covertly support life in the Spirit by preaching first about the fall and sin, redemption and Jesus, the promise and the Holy Spirit, and sanctification and life in the Spirit. These ministries presented here illustrate specific ways for prayer groups and the Renewal to go out into the deep to minister in the mainstream Church. It is recommended that these initiatives be adapted or expanded upon as needed.

Take Time To Reflect And Act

Create a quiet space for prayer. Sit in silence and call upon the Holy Spirit to guide your prayer time. Ask God to speak to you—to give you a "word" for your life, your ministry, the Renewal, or the Church. Ask God to give you a word that will help you draw closer to Him. Ask God to give you a word that will convict you of His love. Ask God to give you a word that will guide you in what you must do to grow in holiness, or ask God to give you a word that will guide your ministry. After keeping at least fifteen to twenty minutes of silence, write down what you sense God is saying to you for your life, your prayer group, the Renewal, or the Church.

Keep a journal of what happens during prayer time. After prayer journal what you heard God say either during or after the time of silence.

If God speaks to you personally, share this with one other person. If God speaks to you for your prayer group, the Renewal, or the Church, share it with Renewal or Church leaders. When you share, talk about what it means for you, your prayer group, the Renewal, and the Church.

The *Afterglow Of The Eucharist*
And *The Simple Blessing Prayer*
A Parish Ministry of Evangelization and Healing

In the early days of the Renewal, people regularly offered to pray with one another for whatever needs they had. Our faith was built up as we witnessed God's healing presence in those around us. Our own gift of healing, that of praying with others, blossomed over time. Most of us considered healing prayer an integral part of living in the Spirit. It was also the one ministry that most of us had participated in, both as the ones praying, and as the ones being prayed with for healing.

It is unfortunate that prayer ministry is not as common today around the Renewal as it has been in the past. For example, as prayer group attendance decreases, prayer groups sometimes adopt a less formal format. In lieu of assigned teachings, they have spontaneous sharing and in place of individual personal prayer, they simply end the prayer meeting with group intercessory prayer. Additionally, prayer room ministry is no longer offered at many of our national conferences and annual diocesan conferences. In general, it seems that fewer people than ever are being prayed with at Catholic Charismatic events.

There are no doubt consequences that will develop as prayer room and prayer team ministries dwindle. Without formal prayer room ministries, people may shy away from asking others for prayer. Without prayer teams and people to pray, the gift of healing has less prominence in our lives. Without personal prayer for healing, some people may be deprived of a first-hand experience of God's power to heal. When we fail to pray with one another we deprive God of opportunities to heal us for He tells to ask and we will receive. We also have fewer witnesses to give concerning God's healing power. We miss the opportunity to witness one very important way through which God continues to heal His people even in our modern-day world, namely, through personal prayer. Without such witnessing to God's healing power, we likewise have fewer opportunities to have our faith built up. Finally, when we in the Renewal fail to stop and pray with one another for our personal needs, we are breaking away from one of the most powerful and fruitful traditions in the Renewal—one that has been a part of the Renewal since its earliest beginnings.

Having said this, it is important to acknowledge that it may not be possible to set up prayer room ministries after prayer meetings simply because some prayer groups have too few people attending the meetings and not enough people to serve on healing teams. Likewise, it may not be possible to set up prayer rooms at local, state, and national Charismatic conferences for the same reason or even due to the financial constraints of renting extra space.

Three points of interest demand further consideration. First, there are many Catholic Charismatics, active in the Renewal today, who have years of experience in praying with others. Second, there are still many Charismatics, who are very gifted in praying with others and third, there are Catholic Charismatics who have a powerful gift of healing, one that is truly anointed by the Holy Spirit.

What are we to do with all of this potential grace flowing from our prayer ministries and gifts of healing? Shall we simply let it all die or shall we ask God to transform our gifts into a grace for the mainstream Church—a grace that we ourselves could bring into the mainstream Church under the guidance and anointing of the Holy Spirit?

What would happen if we approached our parish pastoral team and proposed to form, teach, coach, and mentor prayer teams for our parish. We could teach Eucharistic ministers to pray with the sick and homebound right after they give Jesus in communion. We could train CCD teachers to pray with their children in class and children to pray with one another. We could teach families how to pray with their children and children with members of their families. What if we set out for the deep waters, move out of our comfort zones, and establish prayer ministries in the mainstream Catholic Church?

It would seem there is no better time than right now. It seems there are no better ones to do this than Charismatics, for if we reflect upon our years of spiritual formation and our experience in praying with others for healing, we would have to agree that there are few more prepared than Catholic Charismatics, to bring

Christ's ministry of praying with others into the mainstream of the Church. If we dare to initiate such prayer ministries in our local parishes, we might just set a fire ablaze that will turn into a firestorm in the Catholic Church.

Lighting The Fire

In 1983, our diocesan Renewal leadership set up a formal healing ministry. The ministry team underwent extensive formation every year. At the same time, the ministry offered healing retreat weekends, days of renewal, and days of formation. We often brought in well-known speakers and ministers. All of the events we sponsored were rather costly when they involved famous teachers or overnight accommodations.

In order to defray costs, our ministry was forced to charge fees for certain events. However, it always bothered us that people who sought the Lord's healing had to have enough money to pay for it. Healing should be free. It is a gift from God. I often thought that if prayers for healing were a normal and natural part of our family life and our parish community, God's healing would then be free. Parishes would support the formation of prayer teams and healing ministry events and there would be no charge for God's healing love.

Eventually attendance at our healing events fell off. We could no longer afford to offer the retreats and workshops. In fact, there no longer seemed to be a reason for the ministry to continue and so in 1989 we disbanded as a ministry. Many of us sensed that the end of the formal healing ministry was not the end of the ministry altogether. Yet we could not perceive how the ministry could go on in an informal loose structure. We wondered what we were to do with all we had learned about God's healing love through our formation experiences and our experiences in praying with others.

From 1984-1989, I coordinated the healing ministry during which time I personally experienced and observed the fruit of the healing ministry. People were healed physically, emotionally, and spiritually. Miracles happened! A crippled woman danced, the deaf could hear, cancers were healed, and sinners were saved. People gave their lives to Christ. They received and operated in the gifts and charisms of the Holy Spirit. Their minds and hearts were transformed. From my earliest experiences of being prayed with and praying with others, I had always wondered why such a powerful ministry of God's love and mercy had not become a natural and normal part of living as a Catholic.

Oftentimes I would imagine that my parish was a place where praying with others for healing was as natural as praying the Mass or the Rosary. I wondered why such a ministry did not belong to the whole Church. I was convinced personal prayer should be made available to people in every meeting place, every worship space, and every ministry in the Church. Each time I imagined a "prayer ministry" for the whole Church, I could see the grace of God falling on the children in our Catholic schools and CCD classes as they were prayed with and learned to pray with one another.

From the time the healing ministry disbanded right up to the writing of this book, it seems God has been pressing me to understand how critical healing is to His people by giving me opportunities to teach and preach on the subject. Since 1989, I have often been asked to give workshop presentations on the subject of prayer to schoolchildren and their parents/guardians. As an outgrowth of my years of experience in the healing ministry, it was quite natural for me to demonstrate how to pray with another person using a volunteer from the workshop. Additionally, I always followed my demonstration with an opportunity for the adults and children to pray with each other. It has always been a gift and a grace to see how positively children and their parents/guardians responded to the workshop as a whole and to praying with each other.

Whenever I am asked to direct a retreat or present a mission or day of reflection, I frequently feel called to focus on the subject of healing. Of course, whatever I present, I always end each talk with a healing prayer. Whenever someone comments that they are not feeling well I usually ask, "Do you mind if I pray with you for a moment?" As a Eucharistic minister, whenever I visit the homebound and hospitalized, I pray with them for healing, after giving them Eucharist. All of these practices have come to be second nature to me because they have been so much a part of my life since the early days of the Renewal and with my years of experience in the healing ministry.

The fact that I have prayed with people in my family and my parish whenever and wherever possible is a good thing. However, since my ministry was not formally sanctioned by my pastor or pastoral council, it seemed to be just that—my ministry. No pastor or Church authority ever said, "Stop praying with people." but then again, no one officially approved of or even knew that I was praying with the homebound and hospitalized parishioners that I would visit. The reason being, I never told anyone what I was doing.

As I look back over all these years of praying with people for healing, I can honestly say that I have been involved in healing ministry at a personal and diocesan Renewal level—never at the parish level. Until recently, I had never thought to ask permission to teach other Eucharistic ministers in my parish how to pray with others nor had I thought to ask permission to train other parishioners in how to pray healing prayer with others.

Praying with others is meant to be a normal and natural part of the Christian life, but it should also be a "sanctioned" ministry in the parish, similar to that of lectors, Eucharistic ministers, greeters, ushers, intercessors, and so on. Members of the parish should know whom to call when they need prayer or when they need someone to pray with a member of their family.

Since 1989, I had often thought about the idea of a parish prayer ministry but I had never done anything to make it happen. That was a bit unusual for me. I had never hesitated to offer ideas to our leaders in the Renewal nor did I hesitate to design and implement new ministries for our diocesan Renewal Movement. My record of accomplishment at the parish level however was quite different.

As I look back now, I realize it was fear of being rejected and perhaps even fear of being exposed as a passionate Charismatic that kept me from acting on my convictions regarding a parish prayer ministry. Despite the fact that for many years since 1989 the Lord had convicted me about starting such a ministry in my own parish, I never did.

That is, until one day in the fall of 1999, while serving on our parish pastoral council, I approached our pastor and asked permission to propose to the council a personal prayer ministry. The pastor agreed and so at the next meeting I explained in detail, the idea of a personal prayer ministry that could take place at the end of Sunday morning Mass.

As far back as 1988, I had written and published a brochure that described *The Simple Blessing Prayer* (Marazon, 2003, 1988). In preparation for the upcoming parish council meeting, I updated the brochure, putting in more reference to Scripture and adding references from the Catechism of the Catholic Church. I did this in order to provide a rationale for the Afterglow Ministry.

At the start of the presentation, I gave each member a copy of the brochure to review. I explained how to pray *The Simple Blessing Prayer* and then asked one person to volunteer to let me model how the prayer might be prayed. After the demonstration, a few clarifying questions were posed such as how would we announce it, who would pray, how the prayer teams be trained, where would the prayer ministry take place.

To my surprise, the council voted to approve the new ministry for the parish that same night. We then agreed to schedule a formation meeting for parish members willing to serve on a prayer team. We also shared ideas about what to call the new ministry. After some discussion, we agreed that since the prayer would be an extension of the healing power of the Eucharist, the perfect name for the ministry would be the "*Afterglow of the Eucharist.*"

Although we posted news of the new ministry and the formation meeting in the parish bulletin, no one responded. This fact however did not affect the start up of the ministry. Pastoral support continued to be strong, and within a month the ministry was started.

For the first two weeks of the ministry, I was asked to describe the "*Afterglow of the Eucharist*" to our parishioners at the regular Sunday morning Mass. I did this after communion after the closing announcements. I described how each person coming for prayer would be signed with the Cross on the forehead and palms

98

using blessed oil. I emphasized that the oil used was not the Oil the Sick but rather simple blessed oil, a sacramental similar to blessed holy water. I further explained that each person coming for prayer would be asked his/her first name and to state his/her needs for healing, addressing them to Jesus, Himself, by saying, "Jesus, I need you to...."

The focus of *The Simple Blessing Prayer* is always to bring the person to Jesus so that He can minister His healing love. This is why at the very beginning of the prayer the person is asked by the prayer team leader to picture Jesus in his/her mind—perhaps the way Jesus looks is one of his/her favorite pictures. As the prayer begins, the leader asks Jesus to reveal Himself, His love, and His mercy to the person through the power of His Holy Spirit. The prayer is brought to a close after a time of silence. The silence is intended to give the person time to experience the Lord's love and healing touch.

From the third week on, at the closing announcements of each Mass, our pastor, associate pastor, or deacon announced that prayer teams would be available in the front of the Church to pray for whatever needs parishioners might have. The celebrant usually gives a few examples of possible prayer requests by saying, "Come for prayer if you have...an upcoming surgery, a family member who has left the church, a physical, emotional, or spiritual need for healing, an upcoming vacation or business trip, a new baby in the family, the start of the new school year, a medical test, etc".

The Ministry was an immediate success as evidenced by the parishioners who came forward for prayer the very first week it was offered. After more than three years of offering this weekly prayer ministry, our parishioners have come to expect prayer teams to be available for them every Sunday. Some come nearly every week while others come only occasionally. Several non-parishioners have come specifically to our 9:30 a.m. Sunday Mass because they heard about the ministry from others.

One time a man came rushing through the Church doors at the end of Mass, flustered that he had the wrong time for the Mass. Running to the front of the church where we had just finished praying he said, "Thank God you are here. My wife just left me yesterday. She ran off with another man and left me to raise our three children and I don't know what to do. All I could think of was to go to a Church. I saw some cars parked outside and so I came in. God just has to help me!" We prayed and ministered to the man who wept throughout the prayer. If we had not been there after Mass, the Church would have been locked and he would have gone away empty, lost, and distressed. Instead, he felt God's loving arms wrapped around him and words of comfort inviting him to meet with our parish priest or deacon for counsel.

God has visibly touched members of our parish during their prayer experience. There have been physical, emotional, and spiritual healings. Children come, requesting prayers for sports, grades, and even nervousness over an upcoming violin concert. Families stand together and lay hands on one another as we pray for them. Our parish priests, visiting priests, musicians, and pastoral leaders come forward asking for prayer, seeking the Lord's healing touch. Periodically, our priests invite members of the parish to witness how God has touched their lives. They have given witness to and thanks for God's healing touch through the Eucharist, the Afterglow Ministry, and the intercessory prayer chain.

Throughout these past three years, parishioners have come forward asking to be formed so that they can minister at the other weekend Masses that do not have prayer teams. Team members are taught first how to pray as intercessors and then as lead prayers. There are two persons per team. Each team member has been formed in how to pray *The Simple Blessing Prayer.* There are now ten prayer team members who serve in this ministry at the Saturday and Sundays Masses.

One father, coming for prayer for a job, persevered for eight months until God answered His prayers. Each Sunday, the entire family would come for prayer after every Mass. We prayed with the father, while the family members interceded with us and laid hands on him. This family knocked at the door perseveringly, expecting God to come through for them and He did come through in many ways. The family drew closer together through prayer, learned how to pray with each other, and when the job came through, we literally all hugged and cried tears of joy and thanksgiving together. Parishioners have begun to tell their friends that if they come with them to Mass, they can receive personal prayers after Mass. Frequently, people bring their loved ones who are very ill—even in the final stages of cancer, for prayer ministry.

One time, we prayed with a woman who had come to our Sunday Mass celebration because she had heard there was healing prayer after the Mass. She had stage-four cancer. As we prayed with her, we could feel God's power entering her body and we could feel His tremendous love for her being poured out. She suddenly fell back into a team member's arms and she was gently helped to lie down on the floor as she rested in the Spirit. As she rested, the choir members who were practicing nearby, appeared to be concerned for the woman. One team member approached the choir and explained what had happened, assuring them that the woman was fine. Later that day, the prayer team leader placed a courtesy call to our pastor to tell him what had happened. Neither the choir nor the pastor seemed concerned.

Some who pray on prayer teams are Charismatics and they come with prayer team experience. The Afterglow Ministry is intended for the mainstream Church. It will never be accepted if we attempt to make it into a "Charismatic" ministry. Such a willful manipulation of the Afterglow Ministry would probably result in its demise. For this reason, prayer team members who do pray in tongues are asked to do so in silence. Team members are also instructed not to give words of knowledge, visions, or prophecies. Finally, team members are instructed not to pray deliverance, give counsel, or offer advice to anyone. The *Afterglow of the Eucharist* continues to thrive in our parish, as it moves into its third year as a formal parish ministry.

Every Sunday, we are awed by God's presence and the little ways He confirms and shows His approval of this ministry. Often as we are leaving the Church, we wonder who would minister God's love to these people if we were not there. With humility in our hearts, we are led into a deeper commitment to the ministry. We are thankful to our pastor and our pastoral council that they have allowed us to offer this ministry to our parishioners.

The *Afterglow of the Eucharist* is a ministry of proclamation and restoration. The healing power of the Eucharist forms the basis for the Afterglow Ministry. Through this ministry, we can put into action Jesus' command to proclaim and heal, each time we invite people to come forward for personal prayer at the end of weekend Masses. *The Simple Blessing Prayer* is designed to help each person focus on Jesus' healing touch and the graces that flow from the Eucharist. The purpose of praying for healing is to lead those who are hurting physically, emotionally, or spiritually into a deeper, more personal relationship with the Lord.

The Rationale For The Afterglow Ministry

The *Catechism of the Catholic Church* provides a strong rationale for the "*Afterglow of the Eucharist* Ministry." The *Catechism* states that the grace of Christ that flows from the Eucharist is a gift that God makes to us (#1999). The fruits of the sacraments depend upon the disposition of the one who receives them (#1128) and finally, the mission of the Holy Spirit in the liturgy of the Church is to make the gift or grace of communion bear fruit in the Church (#1112). There is no better way to nurture the gift or graces that flow from the Eucharist than to spend extended time in prayer after receiving Eucharist.

While the graces that flow from the Sacrament of Eucharist are abundant, we often do not remain long enough in an awareness of God's presence to allow His grace to penetrate our lives and heal us. In the Doctrine of the Faith, we read, "But if providence ultimately determines the degree and variety of spiritual vitality, our cooperation with graces offered is also a large determining factor. The supernatural life is capable of increase and depth, depending on the frequency and fervor with which the sacraments are received, [and] on devotion to prayer (Harden, 2001). The Afterglow Ministry extends the time of Eucharist and calls upon the graces that flow from the Eucharist to bear fruit in the life of the one being prayed with after Mass.

The Power Of Prayer

Whenever Jesus speaks to us about prayer, he says, "Pray in my name." What does it mean to pray in His name? Jesus—the name above all names—the name that personifies pure love. We must pray in pure love. We are blessed to have such powerful and grace-filled time to pray with another—immediately after we have prayed the Liturgy of the Word and Eucharist—immediately after we have asked for God's forgiveness and that of our neighbors. If we have received Eucharist worthily, it should bear fruit in us almost immediately. I suspect therefore that there could not be a better time to pray in Jesus' name.

When His disciples were in distress he told them that if they remain in Him and His words remain in them, they could ask for whatever they wanted and it would be done for them (Jn 15:17). There are two conditions for asking and for receiving what is asked for in prayer: first that we remain in Him and second that His words remain in us. This means our lives must be surrendered to the Lord as much as possible at all times. We must live in Him—aware of His presence, His love, and His longing for us. We must not only hear Him but we must also obey Him, listening for His voice and doing what He tells us to do. Likewise, to remain in Him we must communicate our love to Him and our true longing for Him. Then if we pray in His name, with His mind and heart on our lips, we can ask for whatever we want and it will be done. We can only imagine that with His Spirit anointing our hearts and our lips to ask for whatever we want that we will indeed be able to pray the perfect prayer for the person—praying for what they most need.

In Jn 14:12-19, we read,

> Amen, amen I say to you, whoever believes in me will do the works that I do and will do greater ones than these because I am going to the Father. And whatever you ask in my name, I will do, so that the Father may be glorified in the Son. If you ask anything in my name, I will do it. If you love me, you will keep my commandments. And I will ask the Father and he will give you another Advocate to be with you always, the Spirit of truth, which the world cannot accept because it neither sees nor knows it. But you know it because it remains with you, and will be in you. I will not leave you orphans; I will come to you.

It is not by coincidence that belief in Jesus, asking in His name, loving Him and keeping His commandments, are bound together as conditions for asking for and receiving what we need in prayer. It is also no coincidence that in this very same passage Jesus tells us that He will pray for us to His Father and His Father will send us another Counselor, to be with us forever—the Spirit of truth, dwelling not only with us but also in us. He closes this passage by telling us that He would not think of leaving us desolate—deserting us. He assures us that He Himself will come to us.

When we hear Jesus say, "Amen, amen, I say to you, whatever you ask the Father in my name he will give you. Until now, you have not asked anything in my name; ask and you will receive, so that your joy may be complete" (Jn 16:23), we must strive to understand more clearly what it means to ask in His name and as we learn what is in "His name" we must change how we think, speak, and act. We are able to do this through the grace of the Advocate—the Holy Spirit who enables us to live everyday with Christ and in Christ, asking in His name, and keeping His commandments. In this way, others will see and know it is God's grace at work in us and our lives will give the glory to His Father.

Persevere In Prayer

Of all the Charismatic ministries we have offered to the mainstream Church, "prayer with another" is perhaps the most powerful, meaningful, and effective ministry. This is because most Catholics acknowledge the power of prayer, especially in times of crisis.

Prayer with another, simply put, is a personalized prayer, a prayer that addresses the needs of the person, as expressed by the person. The pray-er prays for exactly what the person asks, while the person remains silent with hands open to receive all the blessings that God has to give. It is the very same type of prayer Jesus told His disciples to pray whenever they encountered the sick, the dying, the lame, the deaf, and even the dead. When Jesus encountered someone who needed Him, He touched them and often forgave them their sins. He also expressed His love and compassion to them in some intimate way.

The blessing prayer brings at least three people together for prayer, the pray-er, the person being prayed with, and Jesus.

Jesus teaches us about the power of two people praying together in Lk 18:1. The blessing prayer also brings two or more together to pray. Jesus emphasizes the necessity of praying always and not losing heart in Lk 11:5. The Blessing Prayer give the pray-er and the person seeking prayer opportunities to persist in prayer each week. Jesus tells us to ask and we will receive, especially since His Father will give the Holy Spirit to those who ask him (Mk 11:24). For all of these reasons, prayer with another is a powerful means of bringing individuals into a personal relationship with Jesus—bringing them to Jesus and bringing Jesus to them.

Go, Proclaim, And Heal

Let us take a closer look now at Jesus' command to go, proclaim, and heal. Jesus commanded and commissioned the twelve, the seventy-two, those gathered just prior to His ascension to His Father, and all who wished to be called His disciples to do four things. Jesus said, "As you go, make this proclamation. ' The kingdom of heaven is at hand' ….without cost you are to give" (Mt: 10:7-8).

First, He commanded us to "Go." It is clear that Jesus knew most of us would rather cozy up on our sofas and relax in the comfort of our homes. We especially prefer to stay at home if the alternative means taking a risk or going out of our way to do something difficult. No wonder Jesus told us if we want to follow Him, the first thing we must do is GO.

The second command Jesus gave us was "Proclaim the Good News." He was very specific about what we were to say when we got to where we were going. He told us to proclaim the Good News—the reign of God is at hand. He told us to talk with people and state publicly that Kingdom of God is happening right now in our lives. We are in the Kingdom. Everyone, wake up! Experience the Kingdom of God right now through the power of His Holy Spirit!

The third command Jesus gives us is to heal. He not only wants us to go and preach but once there, He has a job for us to do. He wants us to heal in His name. Jesus expects us to lay hands on our brothers and sisters. He expects that when we do, people will be healed. While "we" do not necessarily expect that God will heal through us, "God" expects to heal through us.

The fourth command Jesus gave to His disciples was to take the gift that we received from Him—the gift of going, proclaiming, and healing, and give it away to others so that they too will go, proclaim, heal, and give the gift to others. As soon as Jesus says, "Without cost you received; without cost you are to give." (Mt. 10:8), we realize that Jesus was setting up a mentorship system. He formed His disciples, and through them, He would form others for generations to come, right up to the present day and far into the new millennium.

What is Jesus' promise if we go, proclaim, and heal in His name and give the gifts we received to others? We will do the works He did. We will do even greater ones. We can ask for anything in His name and He will do it (Jn 14:12-14). Therefore, we must ask ourselves, "What is holding us back?" If we dare to say we are followers of Jesus, then we must go, proclaim, and heal and give the same gift we have received to others. We must go if we are to participate in the Church's missionary work of proclamation and restoration. For this is the primary mission of the Church!

Jesus tells us if we are to be His followers, we must GO. Jesus asks us to be risk-takers—stepping out in faith to pray with others. He tells us if we are to be His followers, we must PROCLAIM the Good News. To do this, we must be eager to talk about His work of salvation—inviting others into a deeply personal relationship with Him. He says signs will accompany those who proclaim their belief in Jesus to others—the sick will recover. When we GO, PROCLAIM, and HEAL, Jesus promises that we will do what He did and even greater things because He has gone to the Father. He tells us we will be empowered by His Holy Spirit to do this work and that He will be with us always.

The *Afterglow of the Eucharist* fulfills the four-part command that Jesus gives to His followers. When we go, proclaim, and heal, Jesus promises to be with us. The true grace of the Afterglow Ministry is that Jesus' presence with us is so much more vivid and real because we have just received Him. For this reason, there is no better time to proclaim the Kingdom to others and to heal than immediately following their communion with Jesus.

Prayer with another is clearly distinguishable from personal prayer, communal prayer, and intercessory prayer. Praying with others is not about praying for ourselves or for others. Rather, it is praying with others; enabling them to experience God's healing presence. As we think about this ministry and ponder our commitment to it, we must ask ourselves, "If not us, then who?"

The Simple Blessing Prayer

The Simple Blessing Prayer offers people a powerful prayer experience. Its power comes from Holy Scripture as Christ reminds us, "Again, [amen,] I say to you, if two of you agree on earth about anything for which they are to pray, it shall be granted to them by my heavenly Father. For where two or three are gathered together in my name, there am I in the midst of them" (Mt 18:19-20). We are also reminded in Matthew that God is always ready to give us good things, Again, "If you then, who are wicked, know how to give good gifts to your children, how much more will your heavenly Father give good things to those who ask him" (Mt 7:11). The focus of *The Simple Blessing Prayer* is to bring each person to Jesus so that He can minister His healing love. In this prayer, we always ask Jesus to reveal Himself, His love, and His mercy to the person through the power of His Holy Spirit. *The Simple Blessing Prayer* is prayed by a team of two to three persons. The prayer team consists of a prayer leader and one or two intercessors. The prayer leader is the only one to pray the blessing prayer aloud. The intercessors pray silently.

Prayer team members who have had experience in praying with others will probably be more comfortable praying spontaneously. If so, prayer ministers are still encouraged to follow the guidelines presented on the card until the prayer format becomes second nature. The primary goal of the prayer is to draw the person closer to Jesus through a personal experience of Him and His healing touch. In order to do this, each component of *The Simple Blessing Prayer* should be included in the prayer. The following steps of *The Simple Blessing Prayer* will serve to guide beginning prayer team ministers. Each step is described in detail. Additionally, a rationale is given for each step.

The Simple Blessing Prayer Guidelines

1. **Ask the person** his or her name. Then ask, "_____ (name), what do you want Jesus to do for you?" Listen carefully to what is said because this is exactly what you would pray for the person.

   When we present ourselves to Jesus and ask for His help, we are taking responsibility for our own relationship with Him. We are going to Him ourselves. There is no one asking Him for favors on our behalf. The power in asking is in the words of Jesus Himself, "Ask and you shall receive."

2. **Bless the person** making the sign of the cross on the forehead, and the palms of both hands, saying, "I anoint you for healing in the name of the Father, and of the Son, and of the Holy Spirit, Amen." and using holy water or blessed oil to make the sign of the cross.

   Sacramental Blessings
   A sacramental blessing or the action of giving a person a blessing is described in the *Catechism of the Catholic Church* (1994) as the highest form of a sacramental. "Among sacramentals, blessings come first. Every blessing praises God and prays for his gifts....This is why the Church imparts blessings by invoking the name of Jesus, usually while making the sign of the cross of Christ" (#1671). In other words, *The Simple Blessing Prayer* itself is of greater importance than the blessed oils or holy water used during the prayer. This is even more reason that we must agree to pray with others, blessing them with the sign of the cross, at every opportunity, with or without blessed oil or holy water.

   The Use of Blessed Oil
   Blessed objects, such as oil, water, palms, or ashes serve as reminders of our Savior and His salvation. They give no grace of their own power, but they stir our hearts as visible signs of God presence. Concerning the use of blessed oil in prayer ministry, there is the ancient custom in the early Church of lay people using blessed oil when praying for the sick. The Church encourages this custom to continue today,

so long as a clear distinction is made between the sacrament of the sick and sacramental use of blessed oil and so long as the local bishop approves of the custom for his diocese (U.S. Bishop's Ad Hoc Committee on the Catholic Charismatic Renewal, Sam Jacobs, 2000).

Oil is rich in biblical meaning. It is a sign of abundance and joy. It is thought to be cleansing. It makes the body limber and flexible and is a sign of healing, soothing to wounds. Finally it radiates the skin and brings out its beauty and at the same time it strengthens the body. Oil is therefore a powerful symbol to use to fulfill the soul's need of God's abundance, His joy, cleansing, and healing, radiating His love, beauty, and strength through the window of the soul radiating out to the world.

Sacramentals
The combination of blessing a person, signing the person with the Cross, using blessed oil, and laying hands on the person, all the while asking for the graces of the Eucharist to be poured out in fullness to the person, is a powerful combination of sacramentals that work to sanctify the person—drawing the person closer to God. Such practice, done by the laity, is based on the Church's belief that every baptized person enters into the priesthood of Christ and is called to be a blessing and to bless others. As such, the *Catechism* tells us that the laity may preside at certain blessings (#1668-1669).

3. **Encourage the person** to be open to receive all that God wants to give. Invite the person to open his/her hands. Support the person by placing your open hands under the person's open hands. This gentle touch is both a support and a sign of God's touch and love for the person. If the person's family has gathered around the person for the prayer, invite the family to lay hands on the person as well.

4. **Encourage the person** to close his/her eyes and see an image of Jesus with him or her (It may to helpful to ask if he or she has a favorite picture or painting of Jesus). If so, ask the person to bring this image to mind at the start of the prayer. Helping a person image Jesus, perhaps for the first time, will

be a source of many graces in the person's life, in prayer with others, in prayer alone, and in times of trouble.

5. **Pray** in adoration (blessing), petition, intercession, thanksgiving, and praise. Begin the prayer by blessing God for His goodness and for creating this person. Pray for exactly what the person asks of Jesus using the person's own words. Then pray in intercession for the person using your own words. Ask Jesus to bless the person in body, mind, and spirit. Pray that the graces of the Eucharist flow into the person, bringing God's healing love and mercy. Pray in thanksgiving for what God has already done in this person and for what He will do in the future. Praise God for His faithfulness, mercy, and love.

6. **Close the prayer** by praying, "Glory be to the Father, and to the Son...Amen."

7. **Invite the person** to go to Jesus with his/her needs every day, seeing an image of Him and feeling His gentle touch. If the family has gathered around the person for the prayer, invite all of them to pray with the person at home, in the same way. Give the person or family a copy of *The Simple Blessing Prayer* to pray with each other throughout the week. You may wish to extend your arms to offer a hug to the person if appropriate.

The Simple Blessing Prayer Card

A Simple Blessing Prayer Card serves as a guide for ministers to reference when they first begin to pray with others for healing. One side of the card describes *The Simple Blessing Prayer Guidelines*—seven steps to praying *The Simple Blessing Prayer*.

The Simple Blessing Prayer Guidelines

Ask the person his or her name. Then ask, "_____ (name), what do you want Jesus to do for you?" Listen carefully to what is said because this is exactly what you will pray for the person.

Bless the person, making the sign of the cross on the forehead, and both hands, saying, "I anoint you for healing in the name of the Father, and of the Son, and of the Holy Spirit, Amen." You may use holy water or blessed oil as you make the sign of the cross. The oil is not the oil of the sick.

Encourage the person to be open to receive all that God wants to give, by inviting the person to open his/her hands. Support the person by placing your open hands under the person's open hands.

Encourage the person to close his or her eyes and see an image of Jesus with him or her. (It may to helpful to ask if he or she has a favorite picture or painting of Jesus).

Pray in adoration (blessing), petition, intercession, thanksgiving, and praise. Begin the prayer by blessing God for His goodness and for creating this person. Pray for exactly what the person asks of Jesus using the person's own words. Then pray in intercession for the person using your own words. Ask Jesus to bless the person in body, mind, spirit. Pray that the graces of the Eucharist flow into the person, bringing God's healing love and mercy. Pray in thanksgiving for what God has already done in this person and for what He will do in the future. Praise God for His faithfulness, mercy, and love.

Close the prayer by praying, "Glory be to the Father, and to the Son...Amen."

Invite the person to go to Jesus with his or her needs every day, seeing an image of Him, feeling His touch.

© 2003 -1989 Renée A. Marazon, 419-661-1477

The other side of the card has an actual healing prayer called the *Blessing Prayer for Healing*.

The Blessing Prayer for Healing

The Blessing Prayer for Healing is a prayer that is prayed by and for family members, friends, or anyone needing prayer--at any time of day, in any place, and in any situation.

O Great and Glorious God, You alone are Holy and mighty is the work of your hand. You have created _____ in your image and likeness and You know and care for his/her every need and concern. We come before You now, calling upon the healing power of the Precious Blood of Your Son Jesus Christ, pleading for His Mercy and grace to touch the body, mind, and soul of _____. Having no one else to turn to, and in total surrender to You Jesus, _____ places him/herself in Your loving arms. Most tender loving Jesus, reveal Yourself to him/her (pause). Let your mercy and forgiveness flow into his/her life. Heal in him/her what most needs to be healed at this time. Fill him/her with the Light of Your Divine presence. Let Your Holy Spirit, breathe new life into him/her, releasing Your peace and joy. Empower your servant with the gifts of your Holy Spirit—especially the gifts your servant most needs to grow holy and to build up your Church. Above all, grace Your servant with the gift of holy longing that he/she will desire to be in Your presence all the days of his/her life. We ask this in Your Name and through the power of Your Holy Spirit. AMEN

The Prayer Ministers

Prayer ministers are ordinary members of the parish who feel called to pray with others, proclaiming the Kingdom is at hand and bringing Jesus' healing touch to others. The ministry is open to parish members of all ages and from all walks of life.

What Is In A Name?

As the one to be prayed with approaches, the prayer team gives a warm welcome. The prayer leader asks the person, "What is your name?" Use the person's name throughout the prayer. This affirms that the Lord knows each one intimately and calls each by name (Isaiah 43:1). Touch is a natural means of sharing love and showing care for another. Through our touch, God has a concrete way to reach out to a person. Ask the person, "What do you want Jesus to do for you?" This helps the person speak directly to

Jesus, telling Him what he or she needs, just as the blind man did when Jesus said, "What do you want me to do for you?" The blind man responded, "Sir that I might see" (Lk 18:41).

Encountering Christ

Before starting to pray, ask the person if he or she has a special image of Jesus in a picture, a painting, or a sculpture—Christ crucified, knocking on the door, embracing or holding, etc. If not, look around the Church or the room you are in and help the person to find a visual image. Ask the person to hold this image in his/her mind as you begin to pray.

Gentle Touch!

Then the leader asks, "Is it all right for team members to gently place their hands on your shoulders?" This shows reverence for the person's body and space. Touch should always be light. Team members must never use pressure or push the person in any way.

Resting In The Spirit

Sometimes during the prayer, the person may "Rest in the Spirit." You will know this because the person will not want to open his/her eyes and may seem a bit unsteady. When this happens, support and steady the person with your hands that are already placed under the person's hands. While the person rests, the prayer ministers may pray silently. It is important to remember that God is in charge! When the person opens his/her eyes, you may wish to explain that sometimes while God is touching the depth of a soul, a person may actually rest in His peace. This is called resting in the Spirit. If the person appears to be disoriented, escort the person to a pew or a chair.

Hovering

If it happens that the person prayed with rests in the Spirit and falls back, gently lay the person on the floor. You will also need to explain what has happened to those looking on so as not to frighten them. Ministers should not hover over the person resting but simply be available to help the person get up off the floor.

The Humility And The Unity Of The Team

Prior to the start of the Mass the prayer ministers should gather in the sacristy to pray in intercession for all those who come for prayer. Ministers should encourage the Mass presider and all those who will minister during the Mass to join them for prayer. At the conclusion of the prayer ministry, all team members should pray a short prayer together in thanksgiving for all who came and for God's faithful presence in the ministry.

Confidentiality

Prayer team ministers are bound to hold in confidence whatever occurs during prayer with another. Ministers must be dedicated to daily prayer, frequent reception of the Sacraments, and daily reading of Holy Scripture.

Counseling Or Giving Advice

Counseling or giving advice is not the function of a prayer minister. It is the responsibility of the prayer minister to have faith for, and pray with another for healing. These alone are the prayer minister's only responsibilities. The prayer minister is not responsible for whether or not the person is healed. God is the healer. The outcome of the prayer is God's to know and God's to proclaim through the person. It is always in God's plan to touch and heal His people according to His perfect and loving plan for each person.

Prayer Tongues

Many times those who feel called to the Afterglow Ministry have been or are currently active in the Catholic Charismatic Renewal Movement. This means that many prayer ministers pray in tongues. However, since the Afterglow Ministry is intended for the mainstream Church, praying aloud in tongues may not be acceptable—especially when the ministry is first getting started in a parish. The focus and concern must always be on guiding others to experience Jesus' love and mercy and His healing touch, through *The Simple Blessing Prayer*. Tongues may distract people, inhibit their openness, and interfere in their ability to surrender to Jesus' healing touch. We as ministers must always remember that our ministry to others is not about us. It is about Jesus and those to whom we minister. If we keep this in mind we will be able to guard against the sin of pride. If ministers do feel called to pray in tongues, they are encouraged to do so in silence.

Deliverance Prayer/Exorcism

Deliverance prayer or the practice of naming, calling upon, petitioning, summoning, or commanding evil spirits to take their leave from a person or from any area of a person's life should never be done during *The Simple Blessing Prayer*. Concerning the practice of praying deliverance prayer or prayers of exorcism, prayer ministers must always come under the authority of their local bishops (Marazon, 1998).

Words of knowledge or Prophecy

Words of Knowledge or prophecy must never be given to persons coming for prayer. These gifts are properly ordered when they can be discerned by word-gift discernment teams. Since this is not possible for prayer ministry, these two gifts of the Holy Spirit may not be used.

A Listening Heart

Prayer ministers offer the gift of a listening heart to each person coming for prayer. This means that they listen carefully to the person's needs and pray for these needs. Prayer ministers should not use this ministry time to witness or talk about themselves.

The Prayer Team Leader Prays

If there is more than one person on the team, only one minister is designated to be the prayer leader, the one who prays aloud. The other ministers serve as intercessors. The intercessor may pray silently before, during, or after the prayer.

Referrals

Sometimes when praying with a person, it appears that, the person needs follow-up with a priest in order to receive the grace and strength afforded by the Sacrament of Reconciliation. Other times it may be appropriate to refer a person to a medical doctor or licensed counselor. Do not hesitate to refer the person to the appropriate persons for additional ministry.

Getting Started With The *Afterglow of the Eucharist* Ministry

These simple steps may be helpful in setting up the "*Afterglow of the Eucharist*" ministry in your parish:

1. **Pastoral Support:** Contact the pastor and pastoral leaders to seek their approval for the Afterglow Ministry. Set an appointment to explain and demonstrate *The Simple Blessing Prayer.*

2. **Prayer Team Formation**—once approved:
    a. Designate a Ministry Coordinator.
    b. Announce the formation of prayer teams (bulletin and Mass announcements).
    c. Conduct a formation workshop. There may only be one or two at first but others will come as they experience the graces of this ministry.
    d. Ask the pastor to commission the prayer ministers. It is preferable if it is witnessed by the assembly. Some pastors bless the prayer team ministers each week at the end of Mass.

3. **Mass Announcements:** As soon as prayer teams are formed, make formal announcements in the parish.
    a. Bulletin Announcement: Weekly at first and then at least monthly.
    b. Signs posted at entrance to the Church (Prayer Teams are available after each Mass).
    c. Mass Announcements for the first two weeks: Celebrant and Ministry Coordinator describe the new ministry.
    d. Weekly Mass Announcements: Celebrant announces that prayer teams are present to pray for their needs—healing, jobs, depression, pending surgeries, family members, grief, etc.

4. **The Afterglow Ministry:** Each team consists of at least two persons—one leads the prayer. The other prays in

intercession. After the recessional, the prayer team members come forward to the front of church. They turn and face the people, waiting for people to come forward for prayer.

5. ***The Simple Blessing Prayer***: As each person approaches a team, *The Simple Blessing Prayer* is prayed. If family or friends come forward to support the person coming for prayer, invite each one to place their hands on the person during the prayer.

Bulletin Announcement

You will not want to miss this opportunity to receive personal prayer and deepen the graces of Holy Communion immediately following the 10:30 a.m. Sunday Mass beginning on _____.
Our needs are so great in these times of uncertainty, sickness, disease, family struggles, financial difficulties, parenting issues, trials of every sort, problems at work and school, as well as emotional and spiritual struggles. Whether for yourself or a loved one, our Father is aware of all our needs. He longs to meet them and heal us so that our lives can be lived more fully in Him. When we say, "Lord, I am not worthy to receive you, but only say the word and I shall be healed" we are placing ourselves and our lives into His merciful care. Once there, we hear Jesus say to us, "...whatever you ask in my name, I will do, so that the Father may be glorified in the Son. If you ask anything of me in my name, I will do it" (Jn 14:13). We must stop and soak up God's love and strengthening power that comes to us through the Precious Body and Blood of His Son, Jesus. We must come before Him and ask that we might receive what we most need. After Mass, simply come forward to one of the prayer teams. Tell them your name and what you are asking Jesus to do for you. At that point, you will be anointed with blessed oil. This is not to be confused with the Oil of the Sick. One prayer minister will pray with you for your needs. This ministry has been active at several parishes throughout our Diocese including Good Shepherd, Toledo, St. Charles, Airport Hwy, and St. John, Point Place. Our God is a God of miracles and healing.

Outcomes And Outgrowths Of The Afterglow Ministry

As I look back over the years at our formation and the many experiences we had in praying with others for healing, it seems that everything we did in our formal ministry prepared us for God's plan to bring healing prayer into the mainstream of the Church. It appears to be just the beginning of a vital new thing God is doing. It has much broader implications for the mainstream of the Church, implications that God will surely reveal in His time. For now we must, "Remember not the events of the past, the things of long ago consider not. See I am doing something new. Now it springs forth, do you not perceive it?" (Is 43:18-19), says the Lord as He urges us to listen and respond, to not grow tired or weary, but rather to persevere in living in His Spirit and responding to His call.

There are possible outcomes and outgrowths of the *Afterglow of the Eucharist* ministry. These are that:

- People will experience God's love and His healing touch.
- People will be healed and proclaim the Kingdom of God.
- Parishioners will offer to pray with one another as a normal part of Christian living.
- Families will pray with one another when they are hurting, angry, happy, or frustrated.
- Intercessory Prayer ministers will pray for peoples' needs over the phone.
- Ministers to the homebound will pray with those they visit once they have given Communion.
- School staff will pray with each other and with the children they teach.
- Schoolchildren will pray with one another.
- Those who minister will pray with each other prior to the start of liturgical celebrations.
- Leaders and committee members of parish organizations and ministries will pray with each other prior to the start of each meeting and whenever they meet someone in need.
- Members of the parish will seek out personal prayer ministers whenever necessary.

- The parish community will become comfortable with personal prayer for healing.

- The parish will be open to experiencing other forms of prayer with each other, forms such as contemplative, meditative, and vocal prayer.

- The parish will become a "school of prayer" (John Paul II, 2001)

Prayer after Sunday Mass is definitely a movement of the Holy Spirit. This is easily discerned by the fact that so many diverse parishes across the country began the ministry without ever consulting with or even knowing about each other. Some parishes have been offering healing prayer after Sunday Mass for years. Others began only recently. Some parishes write or call saying that they heard about or read about the ministry and started it in their parish. As calls come in from across the country, we will continue to promote this ministry with zeal and perseverance for it is caught up into a firestorm that seems to be moving by the power of the Holy Spirit, into the mainstream Church. The time is urgent. God's people are starving—begging for understanding in their lives and love in their souls. The *Afterglow of the Eucharist* brings Jesus to them, who is, Himself, understanding and love. Our prayer is that this ministry will grow as a Pentecost mission—spreading as a firestorm in the Catholic Church.

Take Time To Reflect And Act

Form a discussion group. Discuss how the *Afterglow of the Eucharist* ministry could promote schools of holiness, prayer, and communion in your parish or throughout your diocese.

Develop and present a rationale for the *Afterglow of the Eucharist* ministry to your pastor and pastoral team. Also develop and present a plan of action to your pastor and pastoral team. Illustrate in the plan how the *Afterglow of the Eucharist* ministry can enhance the parish's mission and vision. Include a rationale, benefits, goals, objectives, methods, and resources that will be needed to implement the *Afterglow of the Eucharist* ministry. Reassure the pastor that this ministry will not make additional demands on his time. Once the ministry is approved by your pastoral leaders, discern and assign the roles and responsibilities of various prayer group members. Provide detailed information about the planning, formation, and implementation stages of the *Afterglow of the Eucharist* ministry.

For the Renewal

Develop and present a rationale for the *Afterglow of the Eucharist* ministry to your diocese. Also develop and present a plan of action to your diocese. Illustrate in the plan how the *Afterglow of the Eucharist* ministry can enhance the diocese mission of evangelization and keep Catholics from "falling away" to other churches. Reassure the diocesan pastoral leaders that this ministry does not make additional demands on a pastor's time. Request permission to present the *Afterglow of the Eucharist* ministry at a diocesan workshop or pastoral retreat. Once the ministry is approved by diocesan pastoral leaders, discern and then assign roles and responsibilities to various prayer group members. Design the planning, formation, and implementation stages for starting up the ministry in local parishes. Develop coaching, mentoring, and consulting activities that will be used to ensure the success of the *Afterglow of the Eucharist* ministry.

On The Road Again For The Lord
Catholic CharismaticMasses and Healing Services
Introducing Catholics to Life in the Spirit through the Liturgy of the Word and the Liturgy of the Eucharist

Several years ago while driving to an out-of-town business meeting with the spiritual director of our Renewal, Fr. Jerome Nowakowski, we began to talk about the state of the Renewal in our diocese. We shared about the occasional Charismatic Masses that were offered throughout the year and how, although they were called "Charismatic Masses" they had become rather lifeless. There was very little praise, and the little there was seemed to be weak at best with only a few lifting their hands in praise to God. We also commented that very few prayed and sang in tongues and when they did, it was for only a brief period.

We shared our thoughts as to why the Renewal was in such a poor state. We put the blame on ourselves. People were not encouraged to pray in tongues and praise God spontaneously. They were not exhorted to raise their hands nor were they urged to sing out in praise. As we continued driving and conversing, a vision came to mind. I imagined a Charismatic Mass that did not start until the people who came were spiritually prepared to celebrate the Mass. The vision began to unfold in detail. I could see one person standing in the front of the Church encouraging people to sing out and praise God.

I envisioned assigning this person the title of Mass Coordinator (MC) and giving this person the responsibility to not only coordinate preparations before the Mass, but also prepare the people for the Mass. The MC would ensure that all of the necessary ministries were in place for the Mass. These included music, lectors, petitions, offertory gifts, Eucharistic ministers, discernment team for prophetic word, and prayer teams. The responsibilities of the MC would be to coordinate preparations for the Mass and oversee the smooth flow of the Mass. Fifteen minutes prior to the start of Mass, the MC would encourage and exhort the people to give exuberant praise and worship to God.

The MC would tell the people why they needed to give such praise and worship to God, quoting from the Psalms and other Scripture passages. I also envisioned a Mass that would not start until our hearts were sufficiently surrendered to the sanctifying power of the Holy Spirit. To support this effort, the MC would talk about Jesus' gift of His Holy Spirit, which He asked His Father to send to us after He ascended, His Spirit that would move us to worship in Spirit and Truth. I imagined the MC exhorting the people to worship God with their whole being, singing and praising in tongues and raising their hands.

We tossed around these ideas for some time and concluded that if we truly wanted to evangelize people and draw them into a deeper relationship with the Lord through Charismatic Masses, we needed to change how we were praying the Mass and how we were leading the people to pray the Mass. In other words, we needed to change what we were doing. We knew that we needed to speak of the charisms of the Holy Spirit as belonging to every baptized Catholic. Before Mass began, we needed to instruct the people about the gifts that would be in operation during the Mass.

We needed to tell the people that these were the same gifts given to the Disciples and used by them in the early Church. We needed to invite and encourage all those present to be open to operate in these gifts, especially the gifts of spontaneous praise and worship, listening to the Word, listening for the Word of God in times of silence, prophecy, and the lifting of holy hands in praise and adoration of our God.

First, however, we needed to know how many were attending a Charismatic Mass for the first time. Once we knew this, we needed to talk about charismatic style praise and worship, and we needed to invite newcomers to participate with us in charismatic style praise and worship. We could do this best by lengthening the amount of time we spent explaining the charisms of the Holy Spirit. For example, we could continue to define spontaneous praise and worship, singing in the Spirit, and tongues as we always had done, but we could also teach the people how to praise and worship spontaneously and how to sing in the Spirit and pray in tongues. We could do this during an actual practice session before Mass. We knew this would take more time. However, we also knew that if we could do this, we would no longer be relegating newcomers to the role of observer. Instead, all who came to the Mass would be invited to actively pray the Mass expressing spontaneous praise and worship to God throughout the Mass.

As we talked, we admitted that we never intentionally wanted to hold newcomers back from fully participating in our Charismatic Masses. We assumed that newcomers would catch on to the style of charismatic praise and worship throughout the Mass. We also trusted that God would take care of the newcomers—any curiosities, fears, or confusions that might emerge from what they observed, since God had brought them to the Mass.

Through this conversation, we realized how wrong we had been all these years. We needed to intentionally help newcomers receive and operate in the gifts of the Holy Spirit, and we needed to do this prior to the start of the Mass. We realized that God intended for us to evangelize newcomers to our charismatic events. We are the only ones who can help people feel comfortable with what is happening around them.

We must do this by giving newcomers detailed information about the charisms and charismatic style praise and worship and by giving them opportunities to practice and operate in the charisms prior to the start as well as during Charismatic events. Such charisms include spontaneous praise and worship, listening to the Word, listening to the Word of God, prophecy, resting in the Spirit, and yes, even the gift of tongues.

Furthermore, God intends for us to evangelize not only newcomers, but also all who gather to praise and worship Him. Everyone is well aware of the fact that some Charismatics who have been actively involved in the Renewal for years have never received the gift of tongues, spontaneous praise, hearing God's voice (prophecy), and other gifts of the Spirit.

God desires to give His people spiritual gifts for their growth in holiness and for building up His Church. It is hard imagine that people would not wish to receive the gifts of the Holy Spirit. It may be more true that they simply need a bit of personal encouragement and possibly even instructions on how to open up to receive the gifts of the Holy Spirit and how to operate in them.

For this reason, we must commit to encourage and nurture the charisms of the Holy Spirit in newcomers as well as in those who have been involved in the Renewal for years.

Through our discussion that day, we were beginning to set aside our old ways of thinking and ministering, and coming more in line with Jesus' way of thinking and ministering. Jesus was always sensitive to people's comfort levels when he ministered to them. He often told stories to help people understand what He was teaching. He wanted people to know who He was and what His unconditional love was like, so He often told stories. He used similes and metaphors to help people understand His Father's kingdom and when they could not understand His first explanation, He would find two or three other ways to get His point across. He stopped His preaching to feed people when they were hungry and He was careful to send them away before dark. Jesus was sensitive to people's physical needs and comfort. He offered them remedies to counter stresses in their everyday lives, and He instructed people on how to pray to His Father. Above all, He modeled praising, glorifying, and praying to His Father in heaven. Having no prayer book in hand, He always prayed to His Father from His heart.

We agreed that it was indeed the responsibility of the leaders and sponsors of Charismatic events to ensure that all who come feel welcome, included, and comfortable praising and worshipping God. We realized that failure to do so would surely interfere in people's ability to actively pray and benefit from the graces that flow from full participation in Charismatic praise and worship experiences.

We also agreed that since one of the most powerful evangelizing tools was the Liturgy of the Word, it needed to be proclaimed and preached under the anointing of the Holy Spirit. We talked about relating Scripture to everyday life and to the call to holiness. We talked about the fact that the Word requires a response as a sign that it took root in fertile ground. For all of these reasons, we decided that the celebrant should pray a "surrender" prayer related to the Word, over the people at the end of the homily or at the end of the Mass, just before the final blessing.

Finally, we agreed that we ought to help people hear God's voice for their lives. The perfect time to do this would be after Communion through a brief meditation followed by time of silence for listening. We would teach the people how to hear God's voice for their lives, and we would encourage them to use their prophetic gifts to build up the Body of Christ.

The long hours of driving ended and so ended our conversation on how to better evangelize God's people through our Charismatic Masses and healing services. Over the next three months, our visions would remain on both of our hearts and minds, as a prayer and a desire.

At the start of the new year, Fr. Jerry telephoned to say, "We're going to start monthly Charismatic Masses at Good Shepherd (our parish), and I want you to do what we talked about—exhort the people and instruct them before Mass. Let us do everything we discussed and then see what God does with all of it. Take the time you need to prepare the people for worship and full participation in the Mass. Additionally, we are going to take these Masses on the road. We will send letters to pastors and ask them to invite us to come to their parish to celebrate a Charismatic Mass. We will let them know, in the letter, just how beneficial a Charismatic Mass and healing service will be to their people—especially how it will nurture their spiritual lives." We both felt confident that we would receive at least a few invitations from the letters we sent.

The new Charismatic Mass and healing service format, with instructions and practice time, began in January 1998. It was the first of six years of monthly Charismatic Masses and healing services that would be offered on the last Saturday of the month at our home parish. The Mass Coordinator was designated to coordinate all of the necessary ministries. Everyone who was given a ministry assignment for the Mass and healing service gathered for prayers and a blessing in the sacristy, thirty minutes prior to the start of the Mass.

The Mass was advertised to start at 7:30 p.m. However, praise and worship began at 7:15 p.m. Closer to 7:30 p.m. the MC explained the charisms, encouraged the people to give praise and worship to God, and welcomed everyone. The people were asked to respond with a show of hands to the following questions, "How many are attending Mass at this parish for the first time? How many are attending a Charismatic Mass for the first time?"

Many of those present at this first monthly Mass had been to a Charismatic Mass before. Nevertheless, since many had been timid in operating in the gifts of the Holy Spirit, all were introduced to spontaneous praise and worship. Everyone was asked to imagine that a well-known performer or athlete had just come down the center isle of the Church. The people were asked to respond as they normally would at a concert or sports event when the main start came out on stage. With encouragement, the people gathered began to clap and shout, using spontaneous words of welcome and cheer. Then the MC said, "If this is how you would welcome a mere human being, who has God-given talents and gifts, how would you welcome God's own presence with us tonight? Let us all welcome God with us right now." The roof seemed to come off the House of God. The praise was spontaneous and sincere, led by the Spirit Himself.

After praising God for several minutes, the MC asked the people to close their eyes to experience God's presence deep within themselves and all around them in their brothers and sisters. The MC exhorted the people to thank God and to talk to Him about their love for Him using spontaneous words from their hearts. As all praised God, the music ministry began to lead us in more worship and praise.

The vision was becoming a reality. The praise and worship was powerful. This extended time of praise and worship prepared the people to surrender themselves to all that God wanted to do in and through them. We were beginning to experience what it meant to praise and worship God with our whole being—some were doing it for the first time. Others had not done it for a long time.

With hearts softened and surrendered, the people were now ready to hear about the other charisms of the Holy Spirit—healing, prophecy, resting in the Spirit, and tongues. The MC described each charism in detail and gave real life examples of each gift and how it could benefit our lives and the lives of those we love. In talking about the gift of tongues, the MC commented that it would be impossible to receive this gift without opening one's mouth and surrendering the movement of one's tongue to the Holy Spirit who would search our hearts and express what was in our hearts using His own language (Rom 8:26-27). The MC also read from Acts 10: 45-46 about how the Gentiles praised God in tongues as they heard about Jesus. "The circumcised believers who had accompanied Peter were astounded that the gift of the Holy Spirit should have been poured out on the Gentiles also, for they could hear them speaking in tongues and glorifying God (Acts 10:45-46).

Once the gift of tongues was explained, the music ministry led the people in more praise and worship, allowing those who wished to surrender to the gift to do so. People were not only encouraged to surrender their tongues to the Lord, but also their hearts, minds, and voices in praise and honor of our God. As hands opened to praise God, He poured out His Holy Spirit. As this happened, we knew that we were prepared to pray the Mass. All of our senses now anticipated the actions of the Mass.

This very first Mass left us with excitement and expectation for what God wanted to do with, not only the last Saturday of the month Masses, but also with our traveling Mass and healing service ministry we were about to begin—the "On The Road Again For The Lord Ministry."

For the last six years, at least two times each month, a diocesan Renewal team travels to a rural, urban, or suburban parishes in our diocese to offer a Charismatic Mass and healing service. The purpose of this ministry is to introduce mainstream Catholics to Charismatic Masses and healing services, teach and model life in the Spirit, and give people an opportunity to experience God's love and mercy at a very personal level. Wherever we go, we expect to be ministering to both new and familiar faces. Each time we minister, we see a miraculous transformation of those faces even before the Mass begins.

The amount of time spent preparing the people to celebrate the Mass varies from parish to parish. It depends only on the movement of God's Spirit. The opening song resounds. The celebrant clarifies each prayer and action of the Mass beginning with the Penitential Rite and moving through to the Liturgy of the Word. After the homily, the celebrant calls for silence and then closes the silence with a prayer over the people asking that the Liturgy of the Word take root in their lives. Awe and reverence build as we approach the Feast of the Lamb. At the elevation of Jesus' Body and Blood, we raise our voices in adoration. We come to the table and receive Jesus as the celebrant draws our attention to His true presence in the Eucharist.

After Communion, the MC gives a brief teaching on how to deepen the graces of the Eucharist by listening for God's voice in our lives. The people are given three minutes of silence so that all present can practice listening for God's voice. When the silence time ends, the people are invited to proclaim what they heard God speak to them. They are reminded that the gift of prophecy allows them to hear a word from God, and the gift of discernment helps them to know if they are being called to proclaim the word they heard God speak. Each prophecy is further discerned prior to its delivery as the MC reviews each prophecy prior to giving approval to it to be proclaimed.

Following the time of prophecy, the celebrant prays the closing prayer and gives the final blessing. When the Mass ends, the healing service begins. The prayer team ministers are called forward to their stations and the people are invited to come forward for prayer. Using *The Simple Blessing Prayer*, the people are prayed with for the exact need they express (See *Afterglow of the Eucharist*).

Abundant graces flow from every Mass celebrated, for both the team and the people who come. On our journey home from each Mass, we often reflect on the numbers of people who were present that night. Sometimes it is 25; other times it is as many as 200. If we should catch ourselves reminiscing with a sad longing for the over-crowded Masses of 20 years ago, we stop and remember God's consistent and reassuring word to us, "See, I am doing something new. Now it springs forth, do you not perceive it?" (Is 43:18-19). Very soon, we recover our joy. We rejoice, we pray, and we obey, and every other week we go on the road again for the Lord.

Several times soon after we have ministered in a parish, the pastor has called to reserve another date for a Mass as soon as possible. Reservations for a Mass must now be made four to six months ahead. Some pastors ask us to set up a monthly Mass for their parish. Regretfully, we are unable to do so because of our commitment to the entire diocese.

Prayer groups may not necessarily be increasing their numbers through this traveling Charismatic ministry, but the new people we meet often witness that they have encountered the face of Christ in a new and profound way. They tell us how Jesus healed them, how their faith has been strengthened, and how they have learned to listen for God's voice in their lives. We know that God is touching His people deeply through this ministry.

Each time we gather for Mass, we know what the new and old faces desire as they gather in the Church, for their desire is our desire. They long for a closer relationship with Jesus. They want to surrender their lives to Him more deeply. They want to hear Him and touch Him and be touched by Him. They want to love Him and they want to experience His love.

We know how to bring Jesus to others, and we know how to bring others to Jesus through the power of the Holy Spirit at work as we pray the Mass. The way we minister, preach, teach, exhort, encourage, and support people in prayer and praise needs to become a natural and normal part of our daily and Sunday Mass experience. However, as we wait for this to happen, we in the Renewal must continue to introduce and exhort people to praise and worship in the Spirit, listen for God's voice, and experience His healing touch in the Word and in the Eucharist.

The remainder of this chapter illustrates how the Renewal can establish traveling Charismatic Mass and healing service ministries. A timeline, job descriptions, and schedule are offered for consideration.

Timeline For Starting A Traveling Ministry

The first essential step in setting up a traveling ministry is to contact the parishes in your diocese through a letter of introduction. The letter, sent by the liaison or his/her representatiave to the Renewal should contain a request to the pastor to schedule a Charismatic Mass and healing service. The letter of introduction should explain the request in detail so that pastors can take it to their pastoral councils if they so desire. It is more likely that a pastor will consider the request if there is a follow-up phone call. The follow-up phone call also gives the pastor and pastoral team the opportunity to formulate clarifying questions and voice their concerns prior to receiving the follow-up call. Additionally, the follow-up phone gives the Renewal liaison an opportunity to develop a personal rapport with the pastors throughout the diocese.

During the follow-up phone call, the Renewal ministry liaison can also ask the pastor how the Renewal could better serve the needs of the parish. Through follow-up phone calls communication lines are established between the Renewal office and the diocesan parishes. This means that if a pastor or pastoral team is not able to schedule a Mass at the time of the follow-up phone call, there exists the possibility that the parish will consider sponsoring a Mass at some other time in the future. It also means that the Renewal representative will be able to talk about the spiritual needs of the parish in future phone conversations. It is recommended that the ministry representative send a confirmation letter once the Mass is officially scheduled. The liaison may also wish to send brochures and fliers that describe the Mass and healing service, provide detailed information about the roles and responsibilities of the parish and the Renewal office, and provide information about other types of ministries the Renewal can offer the parish.

The actual letter of introduction, requesting permission to schedule a Mass and healing service at a parish, might include the following:

- Brief description of the Charismatic Renewal, its organization, and its mission.
- Statement of intent to offer a Charismatic Mass and healing service.
- Reassurance to the pastor and pastoral team that the traveling ministry is able to take responsibility for the celebrant, altar server, music, and prayer teams and, if needed, lectors, Eucharistic ministers, gift bearers, and ushers.

- Several dates for the Mass and Healing service, from which to choose.
- Follow-up phone calls within two weeks of sending letters in order to speak personally with each pastor to discuss the proposal letter.
- Letter of confirmation including details of the various ministries' roles and responsibilities, once the Mass date is set.
- Communication with the pastor to relate how critical it is for the Mass and healing service be advertised in local and area parish bulletins, local newspapers, and local community service announcements.
- Invitation to the pastor and parish members to serve in the following ministries of the Mass if they so choose:
  o Lectors
  o Eucharistic Ministers
  o Altar Servers
  o Greeters
  o Ushers
  o Gift bearers
- Invitation to the local prayer group to assist in coordinating the Mass and healing service and provide ministers for various ministries. The Renewal Representative contacts prayer group leaders directly.
- Invitation to the parish music ministry to sing/play with the traveling team music ministry.
- Invitation to parish ministers or pastoral teams to serve on prayer teams. Formation for prayer team ministry takes place on-site 45 minutes prior to the start of the Mass.

It is the responsibility of the Renewal office to contact the parish three weeks prior to the Mass, to remind them to place announcements in local and area parish bulletins and make announcements at the end of all Sunday Masses.

Traveling Ministry Core Team

The Renewal ministry liaison or director is responsible for scheduling the Mass and setting up a core team for each Mass. A core team consists of at least four people—the Celebrant, Renewal Representative, Mass Coordinator (MC), and Music/Worship Leader. Whenever possible, it is recommended that there be one or more additional musicians/singers. The director should set up at least two permanent core teams as well as substitutes for the core team members. For example, core teams can be set up to cover certain geographical areas of the diocese.

As soon as a Mass is scheduled, it is important to assign a core team to coordinate the Mass. One week before the Mass, the Renewal ministry representative should call the core team to remind each person about the upcoming Mass and to coordinate the necessary materials, song books, and carpool plans.

The Celebrant

It is strongly recommended that the celebrant be a Charismatic priest, that is to say, one who operates in the gifts of the Holy Spirit, or a priest who is accepting of the charismatic gifts and willing to encourage their use throughout the Mass. It is especially important for newcomers to know that the celebrant approves of the charisms of the Holy Spirit. There is no better way to show approval of the gifts than for the celebrant to operate in them and encourage the people gathered to do the same.

The celebrant chooses the Mass readings of the day or selects readings that he deems appropriate for meeting the needs of the people. The celebrant is given as much assistance as possible by the members of the core team and the parish so that he can use his time to prepare himself to celebrate the Mass. The following is a summary of the celebrant's responsibilities:

- Selects the Readings
- Writes the Petitions (This is optional. The petitions may be written by the Mass Coordinator or given spontaneously
- Prepares the homily

- Decides if the Gloria and the Lord's Prayer will be recited or sung
- Serves as a prayer team leader if desired

The Renewal Representative

The Renewal representative can be the director of the diocesan Renewal or someone designated by the director. The Renewal representative is responsible for setting up a resource table, announcing up-coming events, meeting with prayer group leaders, and welcoming the people. The Renewal representative welcomes the people individually prior to the start of the Mass. The representative also networks with prayer group leaders from the surrounding area prior to the start of the Mass or after the healing service in order to give encouragement to the leaders and personally invite them to upcoming diocesan events. The representative remains available to assume ministry responsibilities as needed throughout the Mass. The following is a summary of the Renewal representative's responsibilities:

- Introduces the team to the local parish priest, deacon, and prayer group representatives
- Sets up an information table
- Greets the people
- Distributes Renewal literature, brochures, prayer cards
- Invites people to sign petition book
- Makes closing announcements
- Prays on team if needed
- Takes responsibility for the Offertory collection at the end of Mass

The Music Ministry Coordinator

The role of the music ministry coordinator is to coordinate and lead praise and worship during the Mass and healing service. The music ministry coordinator selects the music for the pre-Mass praise and worship time, for the Mass itself, and for the healing service. The music minister is responsible for coordinating both the Renewal and the parish music ministers. The music coordinator is also responsible for consulting with the Mass coordinator and the celebrant to ensure that the music enhances and responds to the readings.

It is strongly recommended that music for the Mass and healing service be chose spontaneously rather than planned in advance. This ensures that the music used is led by the Holy Spirit, and that it does what God desires it to do in His people. The following is a summary of the music ministry coordinator's responsibilities:

- Sets up sound and instruments
- Determines Mass parts to be recited/sung prior to the start of Mass
- Selects music spontaneously for Pre-Mass, Mass, and healing service
- Leads pre-Mass warm-up
- Briefs parish musicians/singers if present
- Leads worship and praise during the Mass
- Is led by the Holy Spirit in selecting music
- Listens for the message in the homily to guide music selection for the Presentation of the Gifts
- Ministers throughout the healing service

The Mass Coordinator

The role of the Mass Coordinator (MC) is to ensure that the necessary ministers and ministries are in place for the Mass and healing service. The MC communicates closely with the celebrant, music ministry coordinator, and the Renewal representative. The MC also ensures that all preparation activities are completed prior to the start of the Mass. To aid in these tasks, the MC most often uses a checklist (See Sample Checklist p. 140). The checklist ensures the following activities and ministries are in place: Altar Preparations; Music Ministers; Gloria; Lectors; Responsorial Psalm; Petitions; Gift Bearers; Our Father; Ushers; Eucharistic Ministers; Prayer Teams; Communion Meditation; Prophetic Word; and Calling Forth Prayer Teams.

The MC must be attentive and responsive to the movement of the Holy Spirit when teaching the people about the Holy Spirit as well as when teaching and encouraging the people to receive and operate in the charisms of the Holy Spirit. The MC must also respond to the needs of the core team, members of the parish, ministers for the Mass and healing service, and those who come to pray the Mass. The following is a summary of the MC's responsibilities:

- Consults with celebrant
- Ensures that altar preparations are complete: bread, wine, cups, microphones, candles, etc.
- Coordinates Ministries: Music, Server, Lector, Petitions, Ushers, Eucharistic ministers
- Organizes the Mass Team Prayer Session in the sacristy twenty minutes prior to the start of Mass
- Welcomes the people
- Teaches about the Gifts of the Holy Spirit
- Prays for Empowerment In the Holy Spirit
- Gives a Communion meditation leading to silence and prophecy
- Discerns Word Gifts as people approach microphone
- Coordinates and calls the Prayer Teams to come forward

Prayer Group Representatives

If the local or area prayer group has been invited to assist with Mass preparations and various ministries, it is recommended that the MC meet with them 45 minutes prior to the start of the Mass. At this same time, the MC should review *The Simple Blessing Prayer* format. All prayer team members who serve at Charismatic functions throughout the diocese should follow *The Simple Blessing Prayer* this format. However, the format differs slightly from *The Simple Blessing Prayer* used for parish ministry. The main difference for Charismatic events is that the prayer team leader is encouraged to pray in tongues aloud after praying for the person's prayer request, while at the same time, the intercessors are encouraged to pray in tongues silently.

Those who are new to prayer ministry can serve as intercessors following the same guidelines as outlined in *The Simple Blessing*

Prayer. Prayer group leaders should be encouraged to invite their members to serve on prayer teams. If people from the parish or prayer group wish to serve on prayer teams, they will need to arrive in time for the formation session (45 minutes prior to the start of Mass).

Prophetic Word Gift Ministry

After Communion, the people are asked to be seated for 3 minutes of silence. At that time, everyone is encouraged to listen for God's voice. The MC says, "Ask God anything and listen for His response. How do you know if it is God, who is speaking to you? The response will be the most unconditional loving response that could possibly be given to you." After the silence, people are invited to proclaim the prophetic word, through the following invitation, "Perhaps a Scripture passage came to you or a word, phrase, or even several sentences. If so, you are invited to come forward to the microphone to proclaim what you heard in the silence of your mind. If you believe what you heard will be a blessing to others, build them up, or encourage them, please come forward to share it with all of us gathered here as the Body of Christ."

As people come forward, the MC discerns the messages they feel called to proclaim. If it is discerned to be a word from God, the people are invited to the microphone to proclaim the word. If they wish to talk about their witness, a story, an experience, or something they read earlier that day, they are redirected by being encouraged to "pray right now to receive a message that God would want to speak to His people gathered here." In so doing, the people learn that what they wanted to proclaim may not have been a prophecy, yet God would use what was on their hearts to bring forth a simple prophetic word. This encouragement serves as a "formation" experience.

After the prophetic word is proclaimed, the MC summarizes the messages and then faces the celebrant as a signal that the time of prophecy is over. The celebrant gives the final blessing. The people gathered sing a closing song. The healing service follows.

The Healing Service

As soon as the recessional song is over, the MC invites the prayer team members to come forward to their assigned areas for ministry. Prayer teams consist of three persons. The person who is the prayer team leader is the one who prays the healing prayer aloud. The other two prayer team members serve as silent intercessors or attendants. If the celebrant chooses to be on a prayer team, he should be invited to be the prayer leader and his team should be stationed in the center aisle. Ushers are asked to help guide people to the prayer teams. As mentioned in the previous chapter, prayer ministers do not give counsel, words of knowledge, visions, or any other unsolicited words. They also do not pray deliverance prayer. If a person rests in the Spirit, team members do not hover. Rather, they respect the person by leaving the person alone with God. The team goes on to pray with the next person in line. The ushers should be attentive to those resting in the Spirit to help them get up and to escort them back to their seats.

The following charts depict a possible Mass and Healing Service bulletin announcement, schedule, guidelines, checklist, and opening announcements.

Charismatic Mass and Healing Service
Will be celebrated on _____
_____ will be the Celebrant
Music will be provided by Ministry to
Catholic Charismatic Renewal "Servants in Song."

Come – be refreshed and renewed by the power of Christ's love.

Come   if you need prayer or bring a friend who needs prayer.

Come – if you desire a fuller prayer life, a more loving relationship with God and closer fellowship with other Christians.

Praise and Worship 7:00 p.m.
Mass begins at 7:30 p.m.

Sample Mass and Healing Service Schedule

6:30 pm	The Team arrives. Preparations are made, using the Mass checklist.
7:00 pm	All Mass and Healing Service ministers gather in sacristy for anointing. The ministers call out their names [to the Lord] one at a time as they are prayed over and anointed for ministry. By calling out their names they are indicating that they are present and available to minister in the name of the Lord.
7:15 pm	Praise and Worship begins in preparation for the Mass. Welcome; exhortation to praise, and explanation of charisms are given.
7:45 pm	Mass begins.
9:10 pm	Mass ends and Healing Service begins.
10:00 pm	Healing Service ends. Fellowship is optional.

Charismatic Mass and Healing Service Guidelines

The Charismatic Mass and Healing Service Checklist should include the following demographic information: *Name and Address of the Parish, Pastor's Name, Telephone Number, Contact Person's Name and Telephone Number.* Record the following reminder across the top of the checklist. *Pre-Mass Prayer Session: Celebrant, deacon, servers, lectors, distributors, ushers, prayer teams, musicians, and ministry coordinators gather for a time of prayer and anointing prior to the start of the Mass.*

The Mass Coordinator (MC) welcomes the people, describes charismatic-style worship and the charisms of the Holy Spirit, and exhorts the people to praise and worship God. The following points are covered:

a. **Welcome:** Welcome all and ask who is present for the 1st time at this parish? At a Charismatic Mass?
b. **Identify Prayer Group Leaders:** Ask leaders to please stand to identify themselves and make themselves available after the Mass for those who are interested.
c. **Introduction to Charismatic worship and Gifts:** Spontaneous Praise and Worship (reference psalms); Talk about Blessed Oil; Gifts of Holy Spirit: Tongues; Prophecy; Healing; Resting in the Spirit;
d. **Offertory:** Please make checks payable to_____. Your generosity supports the ministry (retreats, workshops, conferences, national speakers) and helps us send priests and religious to spiritual growth retreats and teaching conferences.
e. **Why have we gathered here?** --to love and praise Jesus.

Charismatic Mass and Healing Service Checklist

Who is Responsible	What is the Activity	Description of Activity
Parish	Mass and Healing Service announcements prior to event	For parish and surrounding parishes, put in bulletin and make Sunday Mass announcements at least two weeks prior to the Mass.
Renewal	Renewal Representative (RR) sets up Information Table	Set up Renewal literature, tapes, free materials, and books.
Renewal	Mass Coordinator (MC)	Give welcome (see above).
Renewal	Prayer Team Coordinator (PTC)	Renewal Healing Ministry Representative: forms prayer teams.
Renewal	Main Celebrant and Parish Priest/Deacon	Celebrant is: Con-celebrant is: Deacon is:
Renewal	Handicap: Those who are wheel chair bound who must leave early may request prayer prior to start of Mass or after Communion.	Ask if this is needed.
	Altar Preparations	__ candles __microphones (ambo & wireless) __ cross bearer __ Book of Gospels ___ wine __ bread __ offertory baskets
Renewal	Praise and Worship Leader Music Ministers	__ Renewal Music Ministers __ Parish Music Ministers
Renewal	Gloria	_____ Sung _____ Recited
	Lector: A Lector has been designated for the Reading (s)	1st Reading proclaimed by _____ 2nd Reading proclaimed by _____
	Responsorial Psalm	_____ Sung _____ Recited by
	Petitions	_____ Sung _____ Recited by
Renewal	Our Father	_____ Sung _____ Recited
	Ushers –for Offertory, Communion, and Healing Ministry	
	Gift bearers	1. _____ 2 _____
	Eucharistic Ministers	1. Main Celebrant 2 _____
	Two hosts and two cups if less than 100	3 _____ 4 _____
	Two hosts and four cups if more than 100	5 _____ 6 _____
Renewal	PTC organizes Prayer Teams: 1 team per 25 people. 3 pray-ers per team: 1 leader and 2 intercessors. Priests and deacons are invited to lead a team. There is at least one intercessor per team who must know how to & be strong enough to "catch." If not, PTC teaches ministers how to pray "The Simple Blessing Prayer"	1_____ 2_____ 3_____ 1_____ 2_____ 3_____ 1_____ 2_____ 3_____ 1_____ 2_____ 3_____ 1_____ 2_____ 3_____
Renewal	Mass Coordinator gives a Communion Meditation; invites and discerns the Prophetic Word:	MC calls for 3 minutes of silence. After silence, the MC calls for prophetic word. The MC discerns each word prior to it being given.
Renewal	Renewal Rep gives Closing Announcements: Upcoming Events; Books, Free Materials, and Tapes in information area.	Literature about Renewal; Renewal newsletters with schedule of activities
Renewal	Mass Coordinator calls prayer teams forward after the Closing Song.	MC calls teams forward
Parish	Refreshments may be offered.	Optional
	Other	

Sample Opening Announcement

Welcome! _____ Parish welcomes you here to celebrate this Catholic Charismatic Mass and Healing Service. _____ (name of ministry) is sponsoring this Mass and your local prayer group is hosting it (optional).

We invite you to pray with us and participate fully in praising and worshiping God. We invite you to thank our Lord for what He has done for us – with your singing and audible praise. We invite you to be present to God, simply being quiet before Him and listening to Him speak to us. We invite you to be sensitive to the Holy Spirit moving us through this celebration. We invite you to pray and worship with your whole being.

In the Vatican II Documents, we read that the Spirit dwells in the Church and in the hearts of the faithful, as in a temple. In us, He prays and bears witness to our adoption as children of our most high God and Father. He bestows upon the faithful varied charismatic gifts. These gifts of the Holy Spirit have been continuously evident in our Church since the very first Pentecost.

In Vatican II we read – "the Holy Spirit...gives the faithful special gifts...There arises for each of the faithful the right and duty of exercising them in the Church and in the world..."

Some of these Gifts of the Holy Spirit will be evident during this Mass. You may hear singing in tongues, praying in tongues, yielding to a prayer language that is inspired by the Holy Spirit – who searches our hearts and intercedes for us according to the will of Our Father...for we do not know how to pray as we ought (Rom 8:27). Demonstrate and praise in tongues with music ministry accompaniment.

Other gifts may be inspired reading of Scripture, contemporary words spoken to us in God's Name – the gift of prophecy. Still other gifts manifested may be words of knowledge and healing.

After Eucharist, there will be three minutes of silence to listen for God's word in our hearts. If you sense that the word you received is to be proclaimed to the assembly, you are invited to come forward to the microphone for discernment of your word and an invitation to proclaim it.

After Mass, we invite you to come forward for an anointing with blessed oil. This is not the Oil of the Sick. It is a sacramental much like holy water. Do not hesitate to bring your needs before the Lord, and allow Him to touch you and minister to you.

There will be many signs of God's presence among us throughout this Mass. There may be tears, proclamations of praise, adoration, tingling sensations, heat, or other sensations. Resting in the Spirit, feeling weak-kneed and wanting to sit or lay down may occur for some present. This is nothing to be concerned about. Resting in the Spirit is a gift from God – the gift of ecstasy—belonging for centuries only to the mystics and saints—but today—it is God's gift to His Church. If it does occur, surrender yourself completely. Ushers will be available to help you sit down or lay down. Whatever you do or do not experience you can be sure of one thing--when you leave here, God will have touched you in a profound way and because of this you will not be the same person as when you arrived.

The offertory collection tonight is for this ministry. We have no other means of support other than your generosity. Please be generous! If you are writing a check, please make it payable to _____.

Let us continue now to praise the Lord and prepare our hearts. When our hearts are properly disposed to celebrate the Mass, we will begin. The Holy Spirit will move us to just the right place and so...We wait. We sing. We praise. We pray. We adore. We worship you, Lord, right now!

A Brief Description Of One "On the Road Again For The Lord" Ministry Team, Diocese Of Toledo, Ohio.

Twice each month, for the past five years, the Diocese of Toledo, Ministry to Catholic Charismatic Renwal (MCCR) has been introducing Charismatic Masses and Healing Services to the farthest reaches of the Diocese. The "On the Road Again" team desires to reach Catholics of all ages who have yet to experience a Charismatic Mass and healing service with the gifts of the Holy Spirit in full operation.

MCCR, like other Renewal ministries, always responds to prayer groups and pastors who initiate requests for Charismatic Masses at local parishes. However, prior to the "On The Road Again" ministry, there was no intentional effort being made to bring Charismatic Masses to parishes without prayer groups. As we prayed about the MCCR mission and vision statements, we as leaders, realized that we had to be proactive in introducing Catholics to life in the Spirit. That being said, we knew that parishes without prayer groups would never initiate contact with our ministry. Additionally, the dramatic decline in prayer groups prompted MCCR to send written invitations to every pastor in the Diocese. Each letter was followed up with a personal phone call to the pastor detailing the Mass and healing service, discussing the needs of the parish, and considering the fruit such a ministry might bear in their parishes.

Many parishes responded to the first round of letters and follow-up calls. Once their initial Masses were scheduled they were put on a call back list. From this list and from on-going new contacts, Masses are scheduled three to four months ahead. Parishes send us to dinner at their area restaurants Mass. welcome at times with dinner

For the past two years, our *On the Road Again for the Lord* traveling team has been invited to minister in other dioceses. No matter where we go, we are showered with grace-filled surprises as those to whom we minister tell how deeply they are touched by God's healing love. The power of the Holy Spirit is becomes a real and personal expereince for so many Catholics. Many are awakened to His love and His mercy. Many hear His voice for the very first time. Many feel His real presence deep within their souls. Many rest in His love and all are healed in the way they most need healing as they encounter the living Christ. His grace is all inclusive.

Take Time To Reflect And Act

For Renewal Leaders

Form discussion groups. Discuss how the *On the Road Again for the Lord* ministry could promote schools of holiness, prayer, and communion in individual parishes and throughout your diocese.

Develop and present a rationale for an *On the Road Again for the Lord* ministry for the Renewal. Write a proposal to present to Renewal leaders. Include a rationale, benefits, goals, objectives, methods, and resources that will be needed to implement the *On the Road Again for the Lord* ministry. Include the details of formation, implementation, and evaluation of the ministry. Develop plans for coaching and mentoring as well as consulting with those who will minister in the *On the Road Again for the Lord* ministry.

Pray For Me 'Cause I Can't Pray

Oh the power of prayer! If there is one ministry we excel in as Catholics and as Charismatics, it is that of prayer. We have intercessory prayer chains, prayer request books, prayer request forms, Mass petitions, telephone requests for prayer, emails asking for our prayers, and even handwritten letters from people we know asking us to pray for them. All of our intercessory petitions are welcomed, encouraged, and greatly honored by God. It is at the core of our belief and practice of our Catholic faith to pray for others. Intercessory prayer is a powerful ministry indeed.

While intercessory prayer ministry is an excellent ministry for bringing people's needs before the Lord, personal prayer ministry can only add to its excellence. This is because personal prayer ministry not only brings people's needs before the Lord, but also has the potential to bring peoples' hearts to Christ and bring Christ into peoples' hearts. This extension ministry of intercessory prayer is called "praying with others." As presented in the chapter on the *Afterglow of the Eucharist*, praying with another is a ministry that fulfills Jesus' threefold command to go, proclaim the Kingdom of God, and heal.

Today, people's needs are just as great as the needs of the people during the time of Jesus. Yet Jesus did not instruct those in the crowd to pray for one another. Instead, Jesus gave the gift of His personal presence to each person who sought Him out. Even to the children who the disciples thought were bothering Him. Jesus gave His embrace, His words, His touch, His encouragement, His mercy, and His love directly to those in need. With this image of Jesus ministering personally to each person He encountered, our healing ministry has made a commitment to help ordinary Catholics encounter the very same hugging, embracing, touching, and loving Jesus in and through personal prayer.

Our commitment is to help people present their needs and the needs of others directly to Jesus Himself. *The Simple Blessing Prayer* is the ideal prayer to use to accomplish this encounter with the living Christ. The *Blessing Prayer* enables people to encounter Christ for themselves and ask Him themselves to meet their greatest needs, whether for themselves or for others.

Whenever people ask us to pray for a situation in their lives or to pray for them or someone they know, we ought to be saying, "Yes I will pray for you in the future. However, would you permit me to pray with you right now as well?" Our children, siblings, extended family members, friends, co-workers, and even acquaintances know that we Charismatics love to pray and love to pray with people. Imagine how powerfully God will use us if we are open to saying, "Let's pray right now." to everyone who asks us for prayer. We can be sure that the Holy Spirit praying in us and through, us will produce much fruit for the Kingdom of God.

In addition to praying for people, we will be able to pray with the people we meet and talk to throughout our day. It will become second nature for us to stop and pray when we meet people who are hurting, when we pass by an accident, receive a phone call about a death or tragedy, or just feel the need to thank God for His mercy, His faithfulness, His gifts, His Divine Providence, and so on.

Most of us would agree that intercessory prayers or prayers for others are the most frequent requests we receive when people approach our prayer teams asking for prayer. This is especially true for our personal prayer ministry after Sunday Mass, the *Afterglow of the Eucharist*. People come forward asking for prayers for members of their families. Parents ask for prayers for their children, children for siblings, and spouses for one another. They ask for prayers for their family members who are dying, suffering from chronic illness, depressed, handicapped, grieving, divorcing, separating, no longer on speaking terms, away from the Church, un-churched, angry, bitter, resentful, holding grudges, etc.

One Sunday morning, during the *Afterglow of the Eucharist*, a parishioner came forward asking for prayers for her sons who were bickering and had not been on cordial speaking terms for over ten years. She came with an old photo depicting her sons at a time when they were best friends. She longed for their relationship to be restored. As we began the prayer, we asked the mother to place the photo of her sons in the palms of her hands and then to move her hands close to her heart, placing the photo of her sons there. Then we asked Jesus to breathe His Healing Spirit into this mother and her sons. We prayed that His Spirit would soften their hearts and in so doing draw the sons closer together and closer to Him. We asked the mother to visualize Jesus touching her sons, softening their hearts, and filling them with His love for one another. As we ended the prayer, we suggested the mother continue this same prayer for her sons every day. We further suggested that she pray that God bring her sons together, thus giving her an opportunity to pray a simple prayer with her sons holding hands.

This mother prayed with this image of Jesus touching and healing her sons for three months. One day, when her sons happened to visit her, all at the same time, she recognized this as an answer to her prayer and immediately asked God to help her pray with her sons. She asked them if she could pray with them holding hands in a circle. To her surprise, they all agreed. She prayed aloud the prayer that she saw Jesus touching and healing them and giving them His gift of forgiveness for one another.

That following Sunday, this mother came forward to the *Afterglow* prayer team after Mass. This time, she came asking for prayers of thanksgiving for her sons had reconciled, and she had a new photo as proof of God's healing love. Proudly she showed us the photo saying, "See, this is how God heals families! We are all back together again and Jesus did it!"

Through this mother's personal weekly encounter with Jesus, seeing Him healing her sons and gifting them with forgiving hearts, her faith was strengthened and confirmed and her family was restored in both giving and receiving the gift of forgiveness.

Imagine if Catholic families learned early on in their parenting years how to pray with one another—parents with children, children with children, and parents with one another. Families would witness God's healing touch in their lives on a daily basis. Their witness in turn would build up other families and encourage them to become families of prayer. This in turn would move out into the parish and build up the entire Church to become a community of prayer.

Years ago, when my son was in eighth grade, he injured his thigh during football practice. Fearful he would not be able to play in the game, he told me about his two-day old injury the night before the game. He asked if I would pray over him. I blessed him, laid hands on his injury, and prayed for healing. When he woke up the next morning, the swelling was gone. There was no sign of injury and there was no remnant of pain. God healed him in His sleep. The most important aspect of this experience was my son's awareness of God's healing love for him. He knew without a doubt that God healed him while he slept.

Whenever we are stressed, worried, anxious, tired, or in physical pain, we must be able to find ourselves in the presence of people who will pray with us. We must be the ones to pray with others as well. Whenever someone calls with bad news, sad news, or glad news, we must be ready to pray with the caller. When we are in a store and the clerk tells us of a concern, a health problem, or a stressful situation, there is no better time than right then and there to stop and say, "Can I pray with you a moment and ask for God's healing touch on your life?" In a storm, on the way to work, in the midst of a family conflict, when the children are quarreling, when parents or siblings are out of control, there is no better time for someone to stop and say, "Let's pray."

Everyone, no matter how young or how old, can learn to pray with another, even young preschoolers. Some may say it is not my gift and they will be right. It is the Holy Spirit's gift to us, given to each of us by virtue of our Baptism. Others may say my pastor will not support this type of ministry. This again, is not a reason for not pursuing a prayer ministry for a parish. We must ask God to give us the words, the passion, and the opportunity to introduce praying with others to our pastors and pastoral leaders. We must approach them with good solid information about the format and content of the blessing prayer. Then we must wait for God to create the opening for us. He will do it. We need only be willing and patient to move in His time.

Praying with one another must become as natural an activity as grace before meals and bedtime kisses. Every person has the capacity to pray with another person. God's grace is always at work prompting us to minister to our brothers and sisters in need. We only need to trust that His Spirit will gift us with the courage to say, "Let's pray." and guide us in the words to pray. Praying with another will eventually become second nature for us provided we are willing to practice praying with another as often as possible. However, until such time as praying with another becomes second nature, we will have to step out in faith, like children eager to try something new, and just do it. Bringing Jesus to others and bringing others to Jesus through prayer is the Pentecost mandate that is given to all of us.

Those who are comfortable praying with others have a two-sided responsibility. First, they must continue praying with others, and second, they must teach others how to pray with others. Such veteran pray-ers must be eager to introduce, demonstrate, model, practice, encourage, and witness praying with another at every opportunity. They must be eager to teach priests, deacons, religious sisters, brothers, associates of communities, third order religious, ministers, teachers, preachers, parents, guardians, sponsors, extended family members, young adults, teens, pre-teens, and young children how to pray with one another at work, home, church, and play.

Pastors and pastoral leaders must be the ones to invite people to stop and pray with one another during meetings when there is need for discernment or in the midst of disagreements and dissentions. Ministers of the Mass can pray with one another for an anointing of the Holy Spirit prior to the start of Mass. Eucharistic ministers can pray the *Blessing Prayer* with those to whom they bring Communion—the homebound, hospitalized, and those in nursing homes and rehabilitation centers. Deacons and priests can pray over engaged couples and teach them how to pray with each other, in times of joy and sorrow and in times of agreement and disagreement. Priests, deacons, and pastoral ministers can pray with those they prepare for Baptism, and they can teach them how to pray with and pray over their babies and children. Families who are grieving can be prayed with by pastoral ministers. Schoolchildren, sports teams, and RCIA candidates can all learn how to pray with one another. Every ministry in the parish can incorporate prayer with others so that the parish becomes known in the community and in the diocese as both a school and a community of prayer.

When this happens Catholics will come to realize that they have a place where they can be ministered to at a deeply personal level, growing closer to Christ and closer to one another. When this happens we, who are commissioned to evangelize others, will have an exciting ministry to talk about with ex-Catholics, inviting them to come home and become a part of and be ministered to by a loving, praying community.

Members of our Catholic communities, who are not ministered to personally by fellow Catholics may, in the end, find themselves being ministered to by our brothers and sisters from other faiths. Let us not allow one more Catholic to leave our beloved Church saying, "No one ministered to me or my family on a personal level. These other people prayed with us. Then they invited us to come to their church, and so we did."

When prayer with another is taught to all and prayed by all, becoming a natural, normal part of parish life, our parishes will become intimate communities of love. We will get to know those we pray with—their names, their needs, and their gifts. This in turn will keep them and us committed to each other, sharing our joys and our sorrows, our strengths and our weaknesses and our gifts, as we live life together in His Spirit.

We are all broken, disjointed, and fractured, and we are all in need of ministers who are not only willing to pray with us but who are also willing to teach us to how to pray with each other. Prayer with another must become a legacy—a life in the Spirit that we pass on to future generations—our children and our children's children so that they will be more holy than we are. Let us be assured of one most important fact—we could not possibly want this more for our children than their Heavenly Father does.

Take Time To Reflect And Act

Form a discussion group and share ways that your prayer group or the Renewal can work to promote the gift of prayer within families, parishes, workplaces, and in the community.

Develop a "Praying with Another' workshop proposal to present to your pastor and/or pastoral leaders. Include a rationale, purpose, objectives, teaching methods, content, and follow-up to the prayer workshop.

Design individual separate initiatives that introduce and teach *The Simple Blessing Prayer* to every aspect of your parish community and parish life including pastoral leaders, teachers, catechists, Eucharistic ministers, lectors, organizations, and ministries.

Design "Holy Family Events" during which you teach children and parents how to pray with each other. Give real life examples of when and where to pray with one another in the family so that prayer becomes a normal and natural part of family life. For example: at bedtime, meals, special holidays, special events; when family members leave the house or come home; visiting family members who are sick, in the hospital, in nursing homes; preparing to take a test; anxious about a test or medical procedure; or feeling a little sad; nervous, angry, frustrated, hurt, out-of-control. Anytime is great time to offer to pray with a member of your family, no matter their age or stage of development.

Confirmation: Is It A Sacrament Of Sanctification Or A Sacrament Of Exit It Is Your Call

I once heard a youth minister refer to Confirmation as the sacrament of exit from the Catholic Church. As painful as it was to hear this said about such a powerful and necessary Sacrament, this statement is probably an accurate description of the Confirmation for some of our young adults and their parents, guardians, and sponsors. Unfortunately, this statement may say more about the teachers and preachers who prepare children for the sacraments than it does about their parents, guardians, and sponsors.

Do pastoral leaders hold parents, guardians, and sponsors responsible for their children's spiritual growth and development? If so, have the pastor and pastoral team told them they are responsible? Have they taught parents, guardians, and sponsors how to fulfill their responsibilities? Are they nurturing the faith development and spiritual growth of parents, guardians, and sponsors so that they are able to fulfill their responsibilities?

When children are baptized, their parents and godparents promise to nurture the faith of their children. During their preparation classes for Baptism, parents, guardians, and godparents are told they must make a commitment to teach their children about God—His love and mercy, His Son Jesus, and His Holy Spirit. The adults are also encouraged to model their own love for God and love for one another. Some parents and sponsors have the inner resources to fulfill this commitment. Others are fortunate enough to have coaches and mentors along the way, who teach and model how to nurture their children's faith in God and love for Him and one another. Too many others, however, struggle with how to nurture their children's faith simply because they themselves may lack the inner resources to do so or perhaps they do not have good role models, mentors, coaches, preachers, or teachers who encourage and help them along the way. If indeed Confirmation is becoming a sacrament of exit for our youth, we their pastoral leaders—teachers, preachers, coaches, and mentors as well as their parents, guardians, and sponsors may be responsible. All of us together may have failed to support families and one another in raising our children in the Catholic faith.

Our first tendency may be to defend our efforts to teach our children about God. We may want to blame the world for hindering our children's spiritual growth and development. It would be logical to blame television, movies, videos, computer games, public education, single parent homes, divorce, and so on. However, not one of these things caused our children to grow up without a personal relationship with Jesus. It is our own failure to intentionally teach our children about Jesus, His gift of salvation, His love, and His call to grow holy that has kept them from knowing and confirming Jesus as their Lord and Savior. What has hindered our children's growth in holiness is our own failure to intentionally model holy living to them. What prevents our children from growing holy is our failure to encourage them to think and act in holy ways.

In this new millennium, parishes must begin to take an honest inventory of the spiritual strengths and weaknesses of their families so that they can fill in the gaps when and as needed. Parishes must design initiatives that will nurture the spiritual growth and development of families from the time their children are baptized until they are confirmed and even beyond Confirmation. Parishes must develop creative ways to nurture the spiritual lives of parents so that parents can in turn, nurture their children's spiritual lives.

Confirmation must not be the sacrament of exit for our children and their parents. It must become known as the sacrament of opportunity for parents to confirm Jesus as their Lord and Savior and to teach, model for, and encourage their children to do the same. Confirmation must also become known as the sacrament of opportunity for parishes to assess how well they have done in ensuring that both parents and their children know Jesus as their personal Lord and Savior, and know the One who longs to sanctify them—the Holy Spirit.

Confirmation is the Sacrament of our children's formal declaration that they "confirm" Jesus as their personal Lord and Savior for the first time in their lives. For some, it will be their initial introduction to come to know Christ and the beginning of their journey in holiness. For others it will reinforce their belief in Christ and it will give them the opportunity to witness it before their family and the Church.

The following story represents one parish's journey to meet the needs of parents, sponsors, and children preparing for the sacrament of Confirmation. This story is by no means a comprehensive solution to the dilemma facing parishes today with regards to children and families growing together in faith. Rather, it is one way a parish can make Confirmation a sacrament of opportunity to nurture the spiritual growth and development of parents, sponsors, and children.

For the past several years, the Renewal in our diocese has been invited by parishes to organize and present retreats to Confirmation candidates and their parents and sponsors. The format used allowed for the adults and children to gather together in a "general session" for the opening talk, separate for two talks, and then come back together for a final general session talk and prayer experience. The opening general session talk was very brief and was focused on Confirmation in general terms, the definition and description of the Sacrament, as presented in the Catechism.

The first talk for parents, guardians, and sponsors was focused on the role and responsibility of parents and sponsors to come to know Christ in a deeply personal way so they could support and nurture their children's relationship with Him. The emphasis was on the parent's role to discipline or rather "disciple" their children. Disciple, the root word of discipline, literally means, "to ask another to follow in one's footsteps. In the context of this definition, parents and sponsors were asked to consider in what ways they were asking their children to follow in their footsteps. The question also posed to the adults was, "In whose footsteps are you following?" —in other words, "who is discipling you as you disciple your children?" The answer of course needed to be Jesus. An extensive discussion followed. The discussion was focused on what it means to be a follower of Jesus, who this man Jesus was, why He died, and what His death had to do with each one of us. The adult session ended with a simple prayer of surrender to Jesus, acceptance of Jesus as our Lord and Savior, and a commitment to become a disciple of Jesus so that we, in turn, might disciple our children in His ways.

This candidate sessions integrated contemporary music, skits, short teachings, peer witnesses, and self-expression through art and dance. The first talk for the Confirmation candidates focused on coming to know Jesus as their personal Savior. The talk ended with a prayer experience in which the children could encounter Christ through an image of Him in their mind. This is called imagery prayer. The prayer was followed by small group sharing. The sessions closed with a simple prayer for healing and an outpouring of the Holy Spirit.

The second talks were also given separately for adults and children. However, both talks were focused on living in and through the power of the Holy Spirit and on identifying and operating in the gifts, charisms, and fruits of the Holy Spirit. Personal witnesses were given to illustrate God's love and mercy, and the power of His Spirit to transform and heal. The candidates added poetry, skits, artwork, and their own creativity to what they experienced in the session. After the second session, the adults and children were given some prayer time to "hear" God speak to them and to share what they heard in prayer. These sessions were also brought to a close with a simple prayer for healing and renewal in the Spirit.

Throughout the day, the adults and candidates were given opportunities to praise and worship God spontaneously. When it was time for the closing session, the adults and children were gathered together in one large room. The closing talk emphasized the temptations of the world, the flesh, and the devil to steal minds and hearts away from God. As such, each adult and candidate needed to confirm Jesus as Lord and Savior on a daily basis. Examples of "teen temptations" were presented including frank talk about drugs, sex, pornography, alcohol, and the occult. The discussion on the occult especially captured the attention of all gathered.

Children nodded when they were asked about their knowledge of and/or experimentation with spells, tarot cards, witchcraft, satanic worship, Ouiji or spirit boards, channeling, palm reading, fortune telling, psychics, séances, curses, astrology, spells, and magic.

Parents also seemed to wake up to the realities of what is present in the world tempting their children and trying to steal their souls away from God. Parents seemed to realize that they had a duty to protect their children from such dangerous practices and without the power of the Holy Spirit, neither they, nor their children could win the battle against the devil. When a hush came over the room there was no doubt that God was working in everyone gathered there—adults and children alike.

In order to bring the retreat to a close, a close, a prayer was prayed over the adults and the children to invite them to reject Satan, all His works, and all His temptations and to accept Jesus as the Christ, the Lord of all. All present were invited to surrender their lives to Jesus in a more conscious and fuller way than they had ever done before.

The timing seemed to be perfect to follow up healing prayer with a demonstration of how to pray with each other in times of trouble and in times of joy. One of the candidates volunteered to be "prayed with." The adults and candidates were invited to watch and listen as *The Simple Blessing Prayer* was prayed with the volunteer.

Following the demonstration, the parents, sponsors, and children were asked to form into groups to pray with one another. As each group finished praying, they were invited to go to the chapel to spend time together before the Blessed Sacrament. Parents, candidates, and their sponsors left the retreat after their time of adoration.

As a follow-up to this retreat experience, parents were asked to form a parent support group at least 30 days after Confirmation. The Candidates would continue their journey together as they integrated into the parish youth group.

It is critical to the spiritual growth of families that pastoral leaders and religious educators provide follow-up experiences that nurture and support living in the Spirit as it related to parenting and teens. Families and youth should be used to facilitate support groups for future confirmation families and candidates. Follow-up days of renewal should be on the schedule and given to parents and sponsors before they leave the Confirmation retreat. Sample follow-up topics might include the Isaiah gifts, the fruits, and the charisms of the Holy Spirit including teaching, preaching, healing, wisdom, words of knowledge, prophecy, tongues, spontaneous praise and worship, and praying the Mass in the Spirit.

The Making Of A Confirmation Outreach Ministry

Since receiving the first invitation to present a Confirmation retreat, the Renewal office has received numerous other invitations. These invitations prompted Renewal leaders to begin to form a Confirmation Outreach Ministry to parishes in our diocese. The diocesan Renewal ministry designed a brochure to help market and advertise the Confirmation retreats to other parishes.

Each time the Confirmation Outreach Ministry schedules planning meetings for a parish retreat, we invite representatives of the parish to come to the meeting. Youth minister, religious education director and teachers, as well as the pastor sit with us and help us to learn how we can best meet the physical, emotional, and most of all, the spiritual needs of the Confirmation candidates, their parents and sponsors. It is critical for the outreach team to know if, when, and how the retreat candidates and adults developed a personal relationship with Jesus. This information influences the content, emphasis, and flow of the Confirmation retreat and the type and amount of follow-up the candidates and their families will need after Confirmation Day.

The ultimate goal of the Confirmation Outreach team is to offer the parish more than a one-time, shot-in-the-arm, Confirmation retreat. The team must be willing provide on-going support, consultation, and encouragement to the parish over an extended period if the parish so desires. In either case, follow-up must be done either by the team or by the parish in order to ensure that Confirmation becomes a sacrament of sanctification rather than a sacrament of exit. This ensures that as a Confirmation candidate is sanctified by the Holy Spirit, so too are the family, the sponsor, and the parish community.

Take Time To Reflect And Act

Describe the spiritual growth of families in your parish? In your diocese?

Does your parish community inform parents that they are responsible for their children's spiritual growth and development? Do parents, guardians, godparents, and sponsors know they are responsible? Does your parish have a plan in place to encourage and teach parents, guardians, godparents, and sponsors how to nurture their own spiritual growth and development so that they can fulfill their responsibilities to do the same for their children? If not, what can you, your prayer group, or the Renewal do to help parishes design initiatives that educate parents on their responsibilities? How can your diocese, parish, prayer group, or Renewal better meet the spiritual needs of families? What initiatives can you propose, bring to your pastor and pastoral team, and offer to implement in your parish?

Form a discussion group. Discuss how your prayer group or the Renewal might promote retreats for First Communion/First Reconciliation and Confirmation candidates and their parents and sponsors.

The Sacramental Preparation of Parents, Guardians, Sponsors, and Godparents

For the past four years, I have been invited by several parishes throughout our diocese to present parenting workshops for parents, guardians, and teachers in preparation for their children receiving their First Holy Communion and receiving the Sacrament of Confirmation. Parents and guardians sign a pledge to attend the required parenting classes or workshops. The workshop I present is focused on the guidance and discipline of children as it relates to their growth, development, and learning. The first activity of the workshop invites parents and guardians to write down the beliefs, dispositions, attitudes, values, spirituality, faith, and morals they want their children to exhibit by the time they are eighteen years old.

Once this exercise is over, the topic of guidance and discipline becomes the focus of the workshop. The adults are surprised to learn that the word "discipline" has its root in the word "disciple." According to Webster, to disciple means to ask someone to follow in one's footsteps. This means whatever parents, guardians, and teachers are expressing through their words and actions, they are also asking their children to express as they follow in their footsteps.

This heightened awareness of how we adults influence children's growth, development, and learning is a sobering experience for most parents and teachers. The questions that must be answered by all of us are, "Who is discipling me? In whose footsteps am I walking? And who should be discipling me?" The response to each of these questions must be Jesus, of course. Yet we often do not parent under the guidance, discipline, and power of our Risen Lord Jesus. Rather, we parent under our own power by raising our children the way we were raised, or the way we see others raise their children.

This parenting perspective is what leads those gathered into a discussion about the power of the Word of God—Jesus Himself to disciple us. We begin to talk about the power of the Holy Spirit to transform our sinful words and actions into holy words and actions, when we follow the Gospel of Jesus. The moment we begin to follow Him, we are able to disciple (discipline) our children with confidence, asking them to follow in our footsteps.

This workshop format is a deeply moving experience for parents, guardians, and teachers. Once the adults realize the power they have to form the hearts and minds of their children through modeling, they often want to take on shame and guilt for how they have failed to do this in the past. This is why it is so important for the workshop leader to pray a healing prayer over families that they not take on guilt or shame, but rather, that they receive God's mercy and forgiveness and, if necessary, ask their children to forgive them for modeling inappropriate actions and words to them.

Commitment and resolve to follow in the footsteps of Jesus need the support of other parents. Therefore, pastoral leaders are strongly encouraged to form Christian support groups for parents and guardians that are rooted in the Catholic faith, the Catechism, and the traditions of the Church. The workshop presenter commits to help the adults of the parish get the support group started and recommends materials that will nurture their efforts to raise their children in the Catholic faith through the guidance of the Holy Spirit.

Take Time To Reflect And Act

Form a discussion group to talk about how your prayer group or the Renewal can form "Parenting Education Teams" to minister to parents and guardians of children who are preparing to receive the sacraments of First Holy Communion or Confirmation.

Help your parish form a support group for parents that is spiritually based and rooted in Scripture, the Catechism, and the traditions of the Church.

Preparing Children For Heaven:
Is This Really How We Want
Our Children To Pray The Mass?

Since Vatican II, the Church has placed greater emphasis on our experience of communion with Christ and with one another when we pray the Mass. The movements of the Mass focus on Christ in our midst—in each one of us, in the Word, and in Eucharist. Whenever my husband and I vacation or travel on business we have the privilege of attending Mass at a variety of Catholic parishes—rural, urban, suburban, and even military. What is most striking about our experiences is the overall sense of "community" one does or does not receive while attending Mass at various parishes throughout the country.

One's initial sense of community seems to be defined and determined by the degree of people's participation in the Mass. The more people sing and pray, the more apt we are to sing and pray. The more joy and enthusiasm people express, the more joyful and enthusiastic we tend to be. The more attentive and responsive people are the more attentive and responsive we are.

When John Paul II (2001) asks us to examine just how far the Church had renewed herself in the first 2000 years since the birth of Christ, he invited the Church to assess its fervor and discover a fresh enthusiasm for its spiritual and pastoral responsibilities. There is no greater need for fervor and fresh enthusiasm for the Church's spiritual and pastoral responsibilities than that which we express as we pray Mass—our roles, responsibilities, behaviors, dispositions, attitudes, values, and beliefs about the Mass.

Let us stop for a moment and reflect on what children learn from us and from those around us as we pray the Mass. Our children are listening to us and they are watching us. We communicate our expectations for our children's actions and words before, during, and after Mass by what we ourselves do or don't do. If we sing, they sing. If we smile, they smile. If we pray, they pray. If we gesture, they gesture.

If we accept this fact, the next step we must take is to assess our own Mass behaviors, dispositions, attitudes, values, and beliefs. What exactly are our children watching us do and hearing us communicate before, during, and after Mass that is teaching and guiding their current and future behaviors and dispositions at Mass? As we take an honest inventory of ourselves—from getting ready for Mass to leaving the parking lot at the end of Mass, we must decide if our own behaviors, dispositions, attitudes, values, and beliefs are indeed the ones we want our children to embrace and pass on to their children and their children's children for generations to come.

To assist with this honest inventory it might be helpful to take apart every movement of the Mass and then reassemble each movement with behaviors, dispositions, attitudes, values, and beliefs we wish to pass on to our children for generations to come. The following movements of the Mass depict possible behaviors that we would not wish to pass on to our children. These sections also include what we can do and what our children can do to change how we both pray the Mass.

Celebrate The Feast

The first set of actions and words to examine are those we express in the privacy of our homes as we prepare ourselves and our families to celebrate Mass. The moment we say to our children, with frustration in our voices, "Hurry up and get dressed. We have to go to Mass." we are suggesting that Mass is an obligation and possibly even drudgery rather than feast, a celebration. We ought to have our "party" voice turned on when we ask our children to hurry and get dressed. "C'mon, hurry we don't want to miss the procession and we want time to visit with Jesus before Mass!" Each time we communicate to our children that attending Mass is something we must do rather than something we want to do, we may be giving our children a reason to object to going to Mass and a reason to misbehave during Mass. Yes, Mass is a Sunday obligation by Church Law. However, if we are living in the Spirit, we will think about Mass with a longing, a hunger for God, and great expectation of what He will do in us. If we believe and value the Mass as a feast, a celebration with our God and in honor of our God, we will prepare ourselves for it with excitement in our voices and yes, even with care for how we present ourselves, physically, spiritually, and emotionally.

What can you do? Whenever you talk with your child about the Mass, do it with excitement and enthusiasm in your voice. Look up and review the Mass readings before Mass starts. Anticipate the blessings and graces that will flow from Mass and Eucharist. Talk with your child about what you want Jesus to do for you and for your family through the grace of the Mass. Model and teach your child to dress with respect and in a way that honors God.

What can your child do? Dress appropriately for Mass. Bring along a children's Bible or prayer book to read.

Remember Your Baptism

Our initial entrance into the Church presents us with the opportunity to remember that we belong to the Father, the Son, and the Holy Spirit. We remember by putting our fingers into the holy water and blessing ourselves with the symbolic waters of our Baptism. The act of signing ourselves with the Cross of Jesus immediately places God's blessing upon us and our children. Furthermore, as we say the blessing, "In the name of the Father..." we have an opportunity to proclaim our belief in the Trinity. This belief and gesture is a powerful witness of our faith, which we can repeat often throughout the day, teaching and modeling for our children. The more we become aware of the graces that flow from blessing ourselves with holy water and the sign of the Cross, the more we will model and teach, and encourage our children to do the same each time they enter the Church. The excitement we express in signing ourselves with holy water says more to our children than any words we speak. If we ignore the holy water font and fail to sign ourselves with the Cross of Jesus, so will our children.

What can you do? Bless yourself with holy water each time you enter a Church. Encourage your child to do the same. Put holy water in your home and bless yourself and your family with it frequently, making the sign of the Cross aloud with your child.

What can your child do? Bless himself/herself with holy water each time he/she enters a Church.

Respect And Honor God

As we approach the altar of sacrifice, it is fitting that we show reverence for we are called to have a conscious awareness of the holiness and greatness of this altar. When we ourselves model how to reverence the altar of sacrifice and genuflect in adoration to Jesus in the Tabernacle, we are teaching our children to give honor and reverence to God. Additionally, gestures of reverence give our children an opportunity to use their whole body and be actively engaged in the celebration of the Mass from the very beginning when we enter Church.

What can you do? Reverence the altar or genuflect to the Tabernacle each time you enter Church. Model and teach your child to reverence the altar or genuflect to the tabernacle each time he/she enters Church.

What can your child do? Reverence the altar and/or genuflect to the Tabernacle.

Ponder Tradition and History

Once we enter the pew, it is good to encourage our children to think about Jesus who is present in the Tabernacle. We can offer children mental images to ponder by asking them to look at the stained glass windows, the Stations of the Cross, the symbols on or near the altar, frescoes, paintings, artwork, candles, and statues. As they do, we can ask them to think about God and say a prayer to Him. We must take the time to teach our children how to look at these religious symbols and use them to think about God's love. They will not be able to do this without our intervention. If we arrive at Mass early enough, we can encourage our children to walk around the Church looking for particular symbols and praying. This is a good way to keep a child's attention both before and during Mass. The time before Mass is the perfect time to look around and ponder the religious symbols with our eyes and use our minds to mediate on their meaning for our lives.

What can you do? Model and teach your child to spend quiet time before Mass looking at the symbols that are present in the Church (Stations of the Cross, statues, walls, paintings, and icons) and meditating on their meaning. Teach your child how to visit the symbols and think about God and pray a simple prayer. Arrive early at Mass and teach your child to walk around the Church looking at the symbols and praying. Give your child one symbol, such as the Cross, to look for and see how many places he or she can find it.

What can your child do? Spend quiet time before Mass looking at the symbols that are present in the Church— meditating on their message. Walk around the Church looking at the religious symbols. Pray a simple prayer to God.

Sing And Participate

When the opening song is announced everyone in the family should have his/her own songbook in hand, ready to turn to the song number that is announced. All of the adults at Mass should continually be urged to sing out in praise to God, especially because the children are watching and following in our footsteps. If we know that our God inhabits our praises, we will be more likely to sing out, inviting God to touch us with His Divine Presence. The opening song tends to set the tone for the entire celebration of the Mass. The opening is often a song of praise to our God, upbeat and joyful. When our voices are silent during this song of praise, our children follow our lead and model our behavior. If our music ministries do not lead people in praise and worship of God, it is our responsibility to respectfully approach our pastoral leaders and voice our concerns. To make our case however, we must go with a solid foundation of information from Church documents and apostolic letters on the relationship between worship and Sunday Mass. Will we be deadwood or firewood at Mass, asking our children to follow in our footsteps? Only we can decide.

> *What can you do?* While waiting for Mass to start review the songs that will be used at Mass by looking them up with your child. When the song number is announced, turn to the song and sing out. Encourage your child to sing out as well.

> *What can your child do?* Browse the songbook while waiting for Mass to start. When the song number is announced turn to it and sing out.

Greet And Welcome

As the Mass begins "In the name of the Father...." the celebrant often invites the people to greet one another. This is an opportunity to get to know members of the parish by name and to grow together as "community."

> *What can you do?* Model and teach your child to greet others by saying, "Hi my name is .... What is your name?" Then responds, "Hello... (person's name). I am pleased to meet you." Model and teach the members of your family to remember at least one person's name that they meet so that you can greet the person again by name at the Sign of Peace.

> *What can your child do?* Greet at least one person saying, "Hi my name is.... What is your name?"

Forgive And Be Humble And Merciful

Jesus tells us that if we come to Church to worship the Lord and remember that our brother or sister has something against us, we must leave and make amends. Notice that Jesus does not say if we are holding anything against our brother or sister, but rather, if they are holding something against us. The Lord wants us to know that He is concerned about our sin for the simple reason that it will hinder us greatly from worshiping Him and drawing closer to Him. We must therefore strive to come before the Lord with a free conscience—a conscience that tells us the people we have hurt in the past have kind thoughts about us now in the present because we have made amends with them. Wow, most of us will have some work to do within our own families. However, we can invite our children into this work of making amends. We can teach them how to ask others for forgiveness and by teaching them how to forgive. In this way, when we arrive at this part of the Mass we are ready to seek God's forgiveness and mercy. We are ready to continue to pray the Mass, crying out, "Lord have mercy."

What can you do? Model and encourage your child to cry out to God for mercy saying, "Lord have mercy. Christ have mercy. Lord have mercy." Ask your child for forgiveness when you offend your child. Forgive your child when your child offends you. Teach your child to ask for forgiveness, make amends for offending others as soon as possible, and forgive others without conditions.

What can your child do? Ask God for mercy. Learn to ask forgiveness of others and forgive others without conditions.

Praise And Give God Glory

With an honest appraisal of our sins, a firm commitment to make amends, we are ready to praise God with a sincere heart and give Him glory. The Gloria is a powerful prayer and song of praise to God. Our children will only join us in singing this song if they see us singing out and giving glory to God ourselves. If the Gloria is recited, still we recite it with enthusiasm in our voices.

What can you do? Teach your child the words of ''The Gloria'' and practice saying it and/or singing it with enthusiasm. Sing it or recite it into an audio tape player and encourage your child to memorize it. Encourage your child to sing out or recite ''The Gloria'' with enthusiasm at Mass. Refer to your missal as needed.

What can your child do? Practice singing and/or reciting ''The Gloria'' at home with excitement and enthusiasm. Sing or recite ''The Gloria'' at Mass. Use a prayer book or missal as needed.

Listen And Get Wisdom

As the Liturgy of the Word is proclaimed, we have the privilege of hearing God speak directly to us. Listening to the Word has the power to transform us, no matter our age or vocation in life. If we wish for our children to value listening to the Word of God early in their lives, we, their parents and their teachers, must be prepared to present the Word to them in a vocabulary and format they are able to understand. In order for this to happen, the children at Mass should be invited to gather in a separate space, to listen and respond to the Word of God.

> *What can you do?* Review the readings before Mass. Talk with your child about the readings, putting them in your own words. Encourage your child to listen for one specific word when the readings are proclaimed at Mass. Model listening and being attentive to the Word yourself, by focusing on what is being said and by looking at the person proclaiming the Word. If there is no children's liturgy of the Word, present a proposal to your pastor and/or pastoral team to begin one in your parish.

> *What can your child do?* Talk about the readings of the day before leaving home for Mass. Listen especially for one word that has special meaning. When the readings are proclaimed at Mass, be attentive, focus, and listen.

Learn And Be Changed

The homily helps us to understand the meaning of the Word that was just proclaimed. The homily presents us with an opportunity to listen for what we most need to change in our lives. If there is a children's liturgy of the Word, it should be followed with a teaching and sharing time, relating the Word to their daily lives. If there is not a children's liturgy of the Word, parents will need to help their children understand the meaning of the Scriptures after Mass ends.

> *What can you do?* Model listening and responding with eye contact to the homilist. If there is children's liturgy, invite the children to draw what they heard and then let them know that

they can offer it to God at the Offertory procession. If there is no children's liturgy of the Word, ask your child to listen for one word that he or she hears repeated in the homily. Give your child pencil and paper to write down or draw a word he or she hears repeated in the Homily. Discuss the homily with your child after Mass.

What can your child do? Listen attentively to the homilist. Write down or draw pictures or write down words that are repeated or emphasized. Talk about the homily after Mass. If there is a Children's Liturgy of the Word, make a drawing and offer it to God. Carry it up in the offertory procession.

Present Your Petitions

Both adults and children have so many needs to present to the Lord. Yet, as a community, we rarely include petitions from the heart of our young children, pre-teens, teens, and young adults. At every Mass, the petitions presented to God should include the needs of all age groups and if possible be read by children and adults. Since children do not have a voice in the planning of the Mass, it is the responsibility of adults to invite children to present petitions. Adults must be the ones to advocate for this to happen for our children. However, when this does not happen, the least we should do is ask our children to pray their own petitions in the silence of their hearts.

What can you do? Respond to each of the petitions enthusiastically. If your parish does not involve children in the petitions, present a proposal to your pastor and/or pastoral team.

What can your child do? Respond to the petitions with enthusiasm. Pray his/her own petitions in the silence of his/her heart.

Give Your Offering

What does it mean to give a tithe to the Lord? A tithe is the portion of our treasure that we offer to God. Specifically, the word tithe signifies one tenth of our harvest or possessions. An acceptable tithe is the portion we give to God that is taken from the first fruit of our labor. This means that a true tithe is not our leftovers but rather is the best of our harvest or the best of all our possessions. For example if we harvested ten bushels of corn, an acceptable tithe is one single bushel of corn that contains the finest ears of all the corn we harvested.

Every family in the parish must be taught the meaning of tithing to the Lord. Likewise, children of all ages must be expected to tithe by putting forth their best effort in work around the house for a small stipend. They can be taught how to compute ten percent of their stipend and offer it as their tithe to the Lord. Once when our family attended Sunday Mass at a military chapel, the children were invited to come forward to present their tithe to the Lord. Children of all ages came forward from their pews to the very front of the altar. They were running up to place their offering to God in the basket on the altar. No doubt these children will grow up knowing that it is their duty to honor God with the first fruits, the best of their possessions. When we allow children to come forward with their tithe we give them an event to look forward to and we keep them actively engaged in the movements of the Mass.

What can you do? Give your child an allowance for doing excellent work around the house. Teach your child to tithe (give ten percent) his/her weekly earnings to the Lord, placing it in an envelope with his/her name on the outside. Present a proposal to your pastor and pastoral team to set up a children's offertory rite, inviting the children present at the Mass to come forward to place their tithes in a basket on the altar. Do this before the ushers pass the baskets for offertory collection. Be sure to include teachings for the adults and the children prior to implementing the children's tithing program in your parish.

What can your child do? Tithe ten percent of his or her allowance in an envelope with his or her name on it for every Sunday Mass.

Present The Gifts

The gifts we bring to the altar of sacrifice are only made possible through God's goodness in allowing us to harvest both the wheat and grapes to make bread and the wine. The gifts we bring also represent our tithe to God, our return to Him of a mere portion of all that in reality belongs to Him—our possessions and our finances. We must allow our children to participate in presenting our gifts and their gifts to God. For this to happen, the gift bearers must be representative of all members of the parish across age spans and vocations. For this reason, parishes must guard against using only ushers as gift bearers. All members of the parish, and most especially children, must be invited, throughout the year, to present gifts to God at the Presentation of the Gifts.

> *What can you do?* When you attend Mass, volunteer your family to carry up the offertory gifts. When your family is asked to carry the offertory gifts, be sure that your child has something to carry, even if you do not. If your child has made a gift for God during the children's liturgy, encourage your child to bring it up to the altar in the offertory procession.

> *What can your child do?* Carry the offertory gifts when invited. Ask an usher if you can carry the offertory gifts.

Thank God And Sing Hosanna

Before the Liturgy of Eucharist begins we are called to thank God with all the angels and saints for His goodness and mercy, the gift of life, for His Son Jesus, His gift of salvation and His Holy Spirit. We give God glory and honor as we sing, "Hosanna in the highest."

> *What can you do?* Model and teach your child that the "Preface" is a time to thank God for his/her own gift of life as well as for the gift of eternal life. Teach your child that after the preface we are asked to sing out, "Holy, Holy, Holy."

> *What can your child do?* Thank God and praise Him by singing Hosanna.

Make These Gifts Holy (Consecration)

As the celebrant calls upon the Holy Spirit to come and make the gifts of bread and wine holy, we pause in silence to realize that God has the power to transforming the gifts of bread and wine into His Precious Body and Blood.

What can you do? Model and teach your child to give total attention to the words and the movement of the celebrant's hands as he calls upon the Holy Spirit to make the bread and wine holy saying, "Let your Spirit come upon these gifts."

What can your child do? Keep his/her eyes fixed on the action and the words of the celebrant.

Adore Jesus (Elevation)

The miracle of changing the bread and wine into the Body and Blood of Jesus is far too awesome for us to truly appreciate, and so we respond with a hush—total silence, awe, and reverence. The moment the celebrant elevates the Body and Blood of Jesus we bow in reverence and humility.

What can you do? Teach your child how to raise his/her head in adoration as the Body and Blood of Jesus are elevated.
Then teach your child how to bow his/her head when the celebrant genuflects in adoration to the Precious Body and Blood of Jesus.

What can your child do? Keep his/her eyes fixed on the action on the altar. Raise his/her eyes at the elevation. When the celebrant genuflects, you child can bow.

Proclaim What Jesus Has Done And Will Do!

Immediately following the elevation we are asked to proclaim our salvation in Christ, remembering what Jesus did for us through His life, death, and resurrection and remembering His promise that He will come again. This is the time to respond with an enthusiastic acclamation, "Christ has died. Christ is risen. Christ will come again.

What can you do? Sing or recite the acclamation with enthusiasm. Teach your child to listen for "Let us proclaim the mystery of our faith" and then respond.

What can your child do? Listen for the proclamation by the priest and then sing out or recite the response.

Remember And Agree

At this time we recall the history of our Church and the saints who have gone before us. We pray for our present Church leaders, the faithful, and all who have died. The celebrant closes the memorial declaring that all honor and glory is given to God the Father forever, through Christ, with Him, and in Him, and in the unity of the Holy Spirit and we agree with a loud and thundering, "Amen."

What can you do? Teach your child to listen for the celebrant's pauses for those living and those who have died. When this happens, teach your child to remember your family members by name. Teach your child to shout "The Great Amen!"

What can your child do? Pray for specific family members, both living and dead. Shout Amen!

Pray Together To Our Father

Just before receiving the Body and Blood of Christ, we pause to pray to our Father in heaven using the same words Jesus taught us. This is a time to pay particular attention to giving glory to God, surrendering to His will, trusting in His Divine care, calling upon His mercy, acknowledging our need to forgive others, and petitioning God to deliver us from evil.

What can you do? Teach your child to memorize the Our Father. Use a tape recorder as an aid if necessary. Pray the prayer each evening at bedtime. Teach your child the meaning of each phrase of the prayer. Relate each phrase to his/her life and your own life. Model holding hands and praying the Our Father at Mass.

What can your child do? Learn to pray the Our Father. Hold hands and pray the Our Father at Mass.

Give The Sign of Peace

The sign of peace is the final step of reconciliation preparing us to receive the Body and Blood of Christ worthily.

What can you do? Give the sign of peace to those around you. Offer hugs and kisses to family members.

What can your child do? Give and receive the Sign of Peace with those nearby. Offer hugs and kisses to members of the family.

Honor The Lamb Of God

Jesus is presented to us as the Lamb of God on the altar. We declare in this moment that we are not worthy to receive Him but we also believe that in spite of our unworthiness, God will heal us, forgive us, and send us His mercy.

What can you do? Model and teach your child to respond, "Lord I am not worthy to receive you, but only say the word and I shall be healed."

What can your child do? Respond by saying, "Lord I am not worthy to receive you, but only say the word and I shall be healed."

Receive Jesus

We go forward. It is time for the ultimate "Altar Call." We go forward to receive Jesus Himself into our bodies, our minds, and our hearts. We must open up to receive Him. We must surrender to His healing touch.

What can you do? Let your child go forward with you to the altar to receive a blessing from the Eucharistic minister. AS your child approaches the Eucharistic minister, ask your child to fold his/her hands across the chest. If a blessing is not offered to your child, ask the Eucharistic minister to please give your child a blessing while you both stand there. Another alternative is for the celebrant to call children forth who have not yet made their first holy communion, in order to give them a blessing and lay hands on them, immediately following communion. This is a very powerful ministry of the community to pray with the celebrant for the children.

What can your child do? If old enough, receive Jesus. If not old enough, go to Communion with his/her parent to receive a blessing. Go forward with the young children to receive a blessing after Communion.

Be Graced And Blessed

So many graces flow from every action of the Mass. As we prepare to return home, a special blessing is given to release the graces needed to live out the Gospel message.

What can you do? Sign yourself with the Cross as the celebrant gives his blessing. Teach your child to do the same.

What can your child do? Bless him/herself when the celebrant says, "...in the name of the Father, and of the Son, and of the Holy Spirit. Amen."

Go Forth, You Are Sent

To signal the end of the Mass, the priest or deacon gives us a command. We are told to go forth into the world to love and serve the Lord. The Church intends for us to bring Christ to the world and to bring the world to Christ by our unconditional love of all those we meet. The Church takes this final opportunity to challenge us to respond in thought, word, and deed to what we heard proclaimed in the Scriptures and what we heard reinforced by the homily.

What can you do? Model for your child by responding, "Thanks be to God." with enthusiasm in your voice.

What can your child do? Respond "Thanks be to God." with excitement in his/her voice.

Love Others and Live In Christ

As we leave Mass, we have choices to make. We can choose to leave Mass in the exact same way we came in, with the exact same sinful thoughts, words, or actions, or we can choose to respond to the Gospel message by changing a sinful thought, word, or action that needs to be changed. The graces to be transformed have been given us in this great Sacrament. We must cooperate with these graces and take up holy thoughts, words, and actions in our lives.

What can you do? Model love and care for others the moment you leave Mass. Perform a kind deed or minister to another person after Mass. Ask your child to accompany you if you bring Communion to someone who is homebound, visit the sick, or make a meal for a family in need.

What can your child do? Choose one kind act to do for someone in the family.

Each time we attend Mass with our children and with children from the parish community, our words and actions dictate our expectations for children's behaviors. We say, in effect, "These are the behaviors I would like my children to exhibit during Mass. These are the virtues, the values, the dispositions, and the beliefs I would like my child to express in worshiping God and praying the Mass." If we wish for future generations to love the Lord, love worshiping the Lord, and treasure the true presence of Jesus in the Eucharist, we will need to change how we ourselves are praying the Mass and how we are teaching our children to pray the Mass.

Some of us have spent a good amount of time complaining about the lack of energy and enthusiasm present in our brothers and sisters who pray the Mass. However, we would spend our time better reflecting on how we ourselves pray the Mass. Once we begin to pray the Mass fully, under the anointing of the Holy Spirit, we will be the perfect ones to help others pray the Mass through the workshops or mini-missions. We must all take responsibility for how the Mass is prayed not only for ourselves but more importantly for our children and future generations of children.

Take Time To Reflect And Act

Form a discussion group to talk about the responsibility of every adult in your parish to teach and model for children how to pray the Mass.

Propose and design initiatives that enhance your parish's understanding of the Mass, increase adult and child participation in the Mass, and enhance the way liturgical ministers perform their ministries at Mass. Present the proposal to your pastor and pastoral leaders.

Integrate teachings into every ministry and organization in the parish. Focus on how to pray the Mass with fuller participation and greater understanding.

Nursing Homes and Rehabilitation Centers

The Nursing Home

Recently the Renewal office received a request from a local pastor to sponsor a Life in the Spirit Seminar for the residents of a local nursing home. The pastor contacted the Renewal office directly. Although not a Catholic, the pastor requested the support of the Catholic Charismatic Renewal because he himself, only recently, had been baptized in the Holy Spirit. The pastor communicated to our Renewal director that he wanted to have greater affect on the residents in terms of making Christ come alive in their lives. He didn't know how to do this but he did believe there were those who could help him. He often spoke with the Catholic priest who also ministered at the nursing home. As God would have it, the priest was charismatic and the one who referred the pastor to our Renewal office and thus, a collaborative ministry was taking shape.

The Renewal office contacted a local prayer group to see if they would be willing to present a Life in the Spirit Seminar at the nursing home. The prayer group agreed. In the process of setting up the seminar team, the prayer group leaders invited its own members to be on the team and the leaders reached out to other prayer groups to add team members. The pastor was part of the team, as was the Catholic priest who served as chaplain in the nursing home. In all, ten prayer group members accepted the challenge to put out into the deep.

The first team meeting was spent discussing the goals and objectives for the retreat. The team was keenly aware of the fact that the people they would be ministering to had physical as well as mental needs that needed to be met by the team. Once the goals and objectives were set forth, the retreat coordinator facilitated a discussion to discern the talks and assign various retreat roles and responsibilities to team members. At the first meeting a lengthy discussion took place as to how exactly to do a Life in the Spirit Seminar for nursing home residents representative of many faiths and having many and varied disabilities. The more input team members gave, the more they all realized this retreat would not be like a normal Life in the Spirit Seminar. If fact, all acknowledged that it was up to the Holy Spirit to determine what they would do and how they would do it.

As the discussion progressed, the team realized they would need to cut the time in half for each talk. They also realized that the language of the talks would need to be simplified and the content of the talks would need to be more repetitive. These adaptations would indeed be challenging. However, the team also knew God would anoint the weekend. The team had no idea just how abundantly God would anoint the retreat, not only the team, but also each of the participants.

Managing the schedule for the weekend proved to be the most challenging of all the adaptations that were made. First, the time allotted for the entire retreat was drastically cut due to the physical needs of the residents. The Friday evening session ended at 8:30 p.m. and the Saturday morning session did not start until 9:30 a.m. Due to the shortened schedule, chapel visits had to be eliminated. There was no time for confessions, although all were invited to talk with the pastor at any time throughout the weekend.

In preparation for the discussion that was to follow the first talk on Friday evening, the participants were assigned to small groups by a number on their nametags. This did not turn out as expected because after the first talk, nearly one fourth of the participants thought the evening session was over and went to their rooms for the night.

The next morning, not all of the people who came Friday evening returned but a good number of new participants came. Once again, the small groups had to be re-arranged at the last minute to ensure that the groups had a mixture of new participants and those who had attended the prior session. Community building was not possible during the small group sessions because each talk and sharing session had different participants. Some participants left to watch sports on Saturday. Others went to lunch and for some unknown reason, did not return. Some of the participants expected someone to come to their room and get them when it was time to go to a session, even though the sessions were announced over the loudspeaker system. Still others went off to take their afternoon nap and never returned. The coming and going of participants was a common occurrence throughout the entire retreat and yet the team adapted each session by simply surrendering to God's plan and the movement of His Spirit.

The physical needs of the residents also had to be considered throughout the weekend. Some had difficulty hearing. Those who had difficulty hearing were often the same ones who did not speak during sharing group for the simple reason that they could not hear. One person was coherent during one talk and sharing session and then completely incoherent during the next. Another person did not come to a session because she did not know the team was still on site giving another session. One did not have a hearing aid. This person could not hear the talks, and so did not attend any other sessions. The grace for the team was that God had them in training to learn how to become keenly aware of people's needs. This team found themselves becoming extremely sensitive to the needs of each individual in the small group—a grace that was not expected.

On Saturday evening, there would be no anointing prayer for the Baptism in the Holy Spirit. Instead, the charismatic priest chaplain, who had just arrived at the retreat to give the talk about the Holy Spirit, fell under God's anointing. He gave his talk in very simple language and then he went to each person and prayed over them. The group ministers remained with their respective groups and prayed in intercession as the priest prayed. When each participant had been anointed, the priest, under an anointing felt called to go around one more time to each person to pray for each person's need—what they wanted Jesus to do for them. He and team prayed for their need. The participants were deeply moved by this double personal prayer experience. On Sunday morning the last two talks were given and the pastor closed the retreat with a prayer service.

Lessons learned

The talks cannot be over ten minutes in length. Any longer and the residents begin to fall asleep. The New Life in the Spirit Seminars Team Manual (2000) is an excellent guidebook for the retreat. Since the talks could be no longer than ten minutes, the presenters found the outlines in the book to be extremely helpful. In fact the talks were delivered almost entirely to the points made in the book. As the witnesses were also given "in the Spirit" God used them to fill in and emphasize whatever needed to be reinforced in the talk. The team learned that they needed, above all, to be open to the Spirit and flow with whatever happens because the residents of a nursing home are so diverse in their attention span, ability to comprehend, and their physical needs.

In terms of the environment for the weekend, the team recognized that they could not ask the participants to move to another room for prayer and praise and then talk because changing rooms took a very long time due to slow movers, wheelchairs, and walkers. The team also realized that the next time they would have to communicate individually with each participant throughout the weekend to be sure they understood when the sessions would be. The team felt extremely blessed with the physical arrangement of the environment, which had a large gathering space and smaller private rooms for small sharing groups. They commented that not all nursing homes are as conducive as this one was for offering a weekend retreat.

Overall, the team reported that the retreat was a tremendous success. Weeks later, some residents commented to their pastor that they were feeling excited and blessed because of the retreat. The pastor himself was refreshed and renewed in his ministry, believing now that he could bring his people to new life in Christ. The retreat gave him new hope for all the residents of the nursing home. Word has it that the pastor has started a charismatic prayer group for residents of the nursing home.

The Rehabilitation Center

There is a rehabilitation center in our diocese that is filled with residents who are better described as God's living saints. These men and women are full of God's love and express it with every movement of their bodies. They are quadriplegics, paraplegics, severely brain injured, hearing or speech challenged, or extremely limited in small or large motor skills. Yet, no matter their disability, they are viewed by all who encounter them as having great ability—the ability to give and receive love, the ability to praise God, the ability to pray to God, the ability to thank God in all things, and most important of all, the ability to find meaning and even joy in their suffering.

The level of holiness in which these residents live out their lives seems unimaginable to us—even unattainable. Most of us have never been privileged enough to know such saints. Sadly too, most of us do not know that these saints are living in our own back yards—just a short car trip away. The prayer group whose story I am about to tell knows about such saints. This is because they have been ministering to them and they have been ministered to by them for the past four years.

It all started one evening when members of their prayer group were doing their usual task of helping to carry one of the rehab center's residents from the car into the meeting. The director of pastoral care at the center had been bringing one of her residents to the prayer meeting for some time. As the resident's condition began to worsen, it became more difficult to ensure her safety in traveling to and from the prayer meeting.

In one spontaneous moment, while carrying the woman into the prayer meeting, a prayer group leader happened to ask the pastoral director, "What else could we do to make it easier for both of you to be with us?" Without hesitating, the pastoral care director asked if there was any way the prayer group could meet once each month at the rehabilitation center. "Why not?" they responded. That night the prayer group agreed to try the new location for three months to see how God's plan would unfold. That was the start of prayer group ministry at the rehab center.

It was agreed that the meetings would be held at the center one weeknight out of the month. A few of the prayer group leaders were familiar with rehab centers and nursing homes through personal experiences with members of their own families. Their background knowledge, and that of the pastoral care director, was critical in setting down goals, creating a schedule, and developing the format for a prayer meeting at the center.

During the first planning meeting, the prayer group realized that several changes needed to take place in order to make the prayer meeting a good experience for the residents who would come. First, the meeting had to be moved up from 7:30 p.m. to 7:00 p.m. Secondly, the meeting time had to be shortened, keeping it to no more than one hour. Third, the nursing care staff had to be informed about the time and place of the prayer meeting so that they could prepare the residents to come to the meeting. Additionally, the nursing care staff would have to postpone bedtime preparations for those residents who wished to attend the prayer meeting. These changes were critical to the success of the meeting.

Some prayer group members said they felt a bit awkward in their new meeting place, especially those who were not familiar with nursing care facilities. The leaders were sensitive to both members and residents and decided to keep praise and worship as the focal point of the meeting. Almost the entire evening was spent in praise and worship. The leaders soon realized that music highlighted or emphasized the "abilities" of the residents. It was easy for the residents to praise because they used their bodies and their communication skills to their fullest capacity. There was much joy in this for each of them. Each resident was given a songbook and a "one-hand clapper" to use whenever they wished to express praise, worship, or simple joy throughout the meeting. Everyone felt a part of the celebration of God's love. Music turned out to be the winner the first night and every night thereafter.

Over the past four years, many powerful prayer meetings have taken place at the center. Should the nursing staff forget that it is prayer meeting night the residents will simply refuse to go to bed. As soon as this happens, one of the nursing staff will realize what day it is. Then their nurses get them ready and take them to their prayer meeting. Sometimes the nurses take their breaks and join in the praise and worship. Everyone who comes is invited into the circle of love that is made up of hearts, hands, and voices as well as wheelchairs, beds, walkers, canes, and ordinary chairs.

The format of the prayer meeting follows a typical prayer meeting schedule with less time given for each separate ministry. The music ministry leads praise and worship for thirty minutes. Prayer group members help the residents to find the song by opening their books and pointing to the song. Praise and worship is followed by ten to fifteen minutes of quiet time to listen for the word of God. It is amazing to be in the presence of these saints as they listen and proclaim the prophetic word. At times their utterances, unknown to those present, send down the power of the Holy Spirit on each one present in the meeting. At other times, the wisdom they proclaim is simply put—astounding.

Once the prophetic word is proclaimed, there is a five-minute teaching on a topic that has particular meaning for the residents. Those who teach have learned to speak very slowly and deliberately, choosing their words carefully. Their motto is, "keep it simple." The teaching that is given is a quick and helpful tidbit that will get the residents thinking about how they can improve their ministry to their nurses, families, and one another. The residents know that they are gifted and they take their call to ministry very seriously. They know too they are called to the ministries of teaching others through modeling, healing others through touch, smile, and intercessory prayer, and loving others through joy giving, love-giving, and sharing themselves.

Next, the residents offer up their prayer petitions. Everyone is given an opportunity to call out petitions. The music ministry wraps up the evening with a closing song. When the song is over, all gather with hands joined, to pray the Our Father. It is always amazing to watch as the residents struggle to find a hand to take hold of for this prayer to Abba. No one begins the prayer until the circle of love is complete with all hands, beds, wheelchairs, walkers, and canes touching. When the meeting ends, prayer group members push those in wheelchairs and beds back to their respective nurses' stations and say goodbye as they place the residents in the loving hands of their caregivers.

Though these saints may be physically or mentally challenged, they are immersed nonetheless in praising God with their whole being. They live for the moment. They do not seem to have the barriers of "control, self-consciousness, and fear" that most of us seem to have when it comes to spontaneous praise, thankful hearts, accepting their cross, and surrendering completely to God. Their prayer group leaders report that it is phenomenal to watch them and to be a part of their lives. They are honored to be with them.

Several times throughout the year, the prayer group conducts a healing service in place of the usual prayer meeting. The healing service ends with personal prayer for each one present. Blessed oil is used along with *The Simple Blessing Prayer.*

One prayer group leader tells the story of a resident who has no memory at all. This resident can only live in the now moment. Everything to him is always brand new—a first-time experience. He approaches every experience with the excitement of a child. Although he is unable to raise his left arm, he puts his right arm under his left and pushes it up in the air in praise of God. He gives new meaning to the phrase, "We bring a sacrifice of praise unto the house of the Lord."

There are as many as 60 and as few as 25 residents attending the prayer meetings each month. Prayer group members attending range from two to six. To help remind the parish and newcomers about the change of location, a sign is posted on the door to the meeting room, giving directions to the rehabilitation center.

This "Pentecost" prayer group wishes to declare to other prayer groups around the country that, "There is nothing that should stop you from this type of ministry. It does not take very many people to make it happen. You must go and minister to those who are hungry and longing to grow closer to God. If you have people who know how to lead a prayer meeting and lead praise and worship, or put a praise and worship tape into a tape player and turn it on, you can do this ministry." Their message to each of us is, "What is preventing you from putting out into the deep?"

Once each year the director of pastoral care of this same center calls the Renewal office to request a Mass and healing service for the residents. Our "On The Road Again" team responds. The chapel is filled with these precious saints of God. After the Mass and healing service we too go room to room asking residents if we might pray with them. Once again, we pray *The Simple Blessing Prayer.* There are so many ways to put out into the deep to create a firestorm of renewal in the mainstream Church.

Take Time To Reflect And Act

Form a discussion group and consider if, when, and how you might bring a Life in the Spirit Seminar to nursing home or rehabilitation residents. Write a plan of action for a nursing home or rehabilitation center ministry.

Invite members of your prayer group to consider offering a prayer meeting to a nursing home or rehabilitation center in your area. Set goals, develop plans, and implement your plans. Start out simple, perhaps even a few times a year, or take the plunge into the deep waters and commit to a prayer meeting in a rehabilitation center or nursing home one day each month.

The Passion of The Christ

I was not surprised to learn one of our local churches had a long-range plan in place for more than eight months prior to the release of Mel Gibson's movie, *The Passion of the Christ*. Their plan responded to Jesus' Pentecost mandate to "Go, proclaim the Kingdom of God, and heal" (Mt 10; 28; Lk 9).

As part of their strategy, the church developed logistical plans to situate members of their congregation in theater parking lots to minister to people as they exited *The Passion of the Christ*. They also developed tracts to reference and hand out to people as they talked to the moviegoers about sin and redemption. They conducted formation workshops to teach their people how to minister to the people as they exited the movie and headed for their cars. They specifically taught them how to approach people and begin a conversation with them about the movie—asking how the movie touched them and asking about the emotions the movie triggered in them. They taught their ministers how to pray with people to seek God's forgiveness of their sins and to accept Christ into their hearts.

Most important of all, they gave the moviegoers personal invitations to come to their churches that same night. They also welcomed them to come to their churches to join in a study or discussion group about movie. Their final gesture was to let the moviegoers know that they were invited to come to their church services on Sunday mornings. We can only imagine how many of these people who were ministered to were Catholics.

Would that we Catholics were so creative so as to think out of the box. Indeed, a handful of Catholic parishes did plan initiatives to offer discussion groups both before and after the movie. These have been a tremendous forum for Catholics to gather and share their faith. However, since we had organized plan to evangelize Catholics in parking lots or in their pews, we were forced to take a back seat as Catholics were ministered to by Christians from other churches. As a result of not thinking out of the box, some Catholics who attended Sunday Mass prior to viewing the movie may decide to attend a different church after viewing the movie.

Many Catholics who view *The Passion of the Christ* will surely be among those who come into a deeply personal relationship with Jesus, and there is no doubt that most will remain Catholic after viewing the movie. However, there may be some Catholics who view the movie and then join the ranks of ex-Catholics simply because another Christian had the energy, drive, and courage to show up at a movie theater parking lot to talk with them about their movie experience of God's love and mercy.

The evangelists who minister to our Catholic brothers and sisters will invite them to get on their knees and ask Jesus to come into their hearts and into their lives in a personal more deliberate way than they have ever done before. For some of them, this pseudo "altar call" will signal the start of a deep and on-going experience of inner conversion.

At first, many of our Catholics who are ministered to by other Christians may attend both Sunday Mass and another church's Sunday service. However, some Catholics who attend both churches soon become ex-Catholics as they find a home in a church that understands what they are experiencing and helps them to live their lives according to the Gospel of Jesus Christ and through the power of His Holy Spirit.

If parishes do not create opportunities for Catholics who have "conversion experiences" to grow in Christ, intellectually and spiritually, they will do what other Catholics have done—they will leave the Church for other Churches. These other churches will give them personal encouragement to grow in Christ, teaching them how to read Scripture, and how to pray, praise, worship, and adore God in community and in their families. They will give them teachings that help them grow holy in their everyday routines and experiences and finally, they will help them discern their gifts and place them in ministries where they can use their gifts.

Some will argue that parking lot evangelization is not the "Catholic way." Others will say it is not the Church's way. Still others may argue that regular Catholics simply do not go out into the streets to bring people to Christ. Those who argue and make these types of statements either have forgotten about, or are completely unaware of, the Pentecost mission of the early Church and the Church today. Going out into the streets is what the disciples did for a living. Throughout His years of ministry, Jesus reached the people by preaching and teaching in streets, from boats, on the tops of hills, in the valleys, and along the byways. The disciples did the same, when they left the upper room at Pentecost and went throughout the land spreading the Good News. If Jesus had stayed home, there would be no Gospel. If the disciples had stayed home, the Church would have died when they died.

Jesus tells us to go to the ends of the earth to proclaim the Good News. Yet, we seem to have missed the mark. We rarely go outside of our own church walls to bring the world to Christ. In fact, sometimes we do not even do a good job of bringing our own Catholics to Christ, and if we do, we often fail to follow-up or support them spiritually once we do. Sometimes it seems that the renewal programs that bring Catholics to Christ, (Cursillo, Marriage Encounter, Teens Encounter Christ, Life Teen, Alpha for Catholics, Christ Renews His Parish, Renew, and even Charismatic Renewal) are programs that awaken a spiritual hunger in Catholics. When the hunger is not satisfied these Catholics sometimes leave the Church. In effect, we brought them to Christ and then unknowingly delivered them up to other churches.

What do ex-Catholics experience in these other churches? First, these churches seem to be very skilled at discerning their gifts, forming them in their gifts, and involving them in a variety of ministries that invite them to use their gifts. Church ministers provide them with one contact person with whom they can relate, and who will support them in both their spiritual and personal needs. Ministers also refer them to smaller support communities with brothers and sisters who have similar interests and/or needs, referring them to one other couple or a group of people to journey with them. Finally, many of us know what it is that ex-Catholics experience in these churches because it was told to us first-hand by our own friends and family members who found Jesus and left the Catholic Church for other churches. Despite all our efforts, we could not convince them to stay in the Church.

It is time for us to go out to reach God's people, Catholic, and non-Catholic alike. We can no longer expect people to come to us. We must become known as the Church that introduces people to Christ—to His life, death, resurrection, ascension, and the anointing of His Holy Spirit. In fact, we must become a real threat to other churches when it comes to bringing souls to Christ. We will know we have succeeded in this task, when we become as much of a threat to other churches as they currently are us.

There is great hope! Everyday is a day to pray and reflect, asking God to show what new thing He want to do with us and through us. Even if we missed initial opportunities to evangelize using *The Passion of the Christ,* we ought not to miss the opportunity to enhance the spiritual growth and development of Catholics who have already seen the movie or of those who will see it at sometime in the future.

As we strive to become more fully the Church of Christ, we can be assured that we will have the same fire of the Holy Spirit sending us forth to gather in souls, as did the disciples in the early Church. We will be anointed by the Holy Spirit to think about ways to evangelize people—ways that are outside of the box. We will be able to take the world's inventions, technologies, and products, and use them for Christ. We will be able to use the events of everyday life to bring others to Christ, and Christ to others. We will find ways to minister to our people on an on-going basis, discerning their gifts and their needs and meeting both through innovative, out-of-the-box initiatives.

Let us learn from our mistakes! Let us begin to think out of the box when it comes to evangelizing Catholics, Christians, and non-Christians.

Take Time To Reflect And Act

Form a discussion group to talk about the opportunities that are present in everyday life to bring souls to Christ.

What ideas can be put into action plans in the future in response to movies that have a religious theme?

How can *The Passion of the Christ* be used as a tool to bring souls to Christ, today and in the future?

Develop initiatives that respond to the needs of those who personally experienced God's love and mercy for the first time in their lives.

Develop initiatives that respond to the needs of those who encountered Christ as their personal Lord and Savior for the first time.

Design study groups and discussion groups that help people to understand the content of *The Passion of the Christ* and relate it to the Gospels of Matthew, Mark, Luke, and John.

Mini–Missions: Bringing Catholics
To Christ Every Week

I suppose it is a good thing that most of us do not have to look at the people in the pews from the priest's vantage point. If we did, we might see what some of our priests see—a sampling of the living dead—fondly referred to by some as the "Frozen Chosen." Sometimes, when people think about their experiences at Mass, whether at an inner city, rural, or suburban parish, they simply want to cry out, "Our Church is dying!"

What is a pastor to do? What is the solution? There is only one solution—Jesus the Christ. We must wake up the people. Bring them to new life in Christ. We must call forth our dead Catholics to arise out of their sleep. We cannot simply leave them in their pews to rot. We have a responsibility to wake them up, shock them if we must. Of course, there will always be those who do not wish to be revived. However, among those who appear to be the living dead, are souls longing to be brought to life in Christ. They need clever creative invitations and prodding to come alive in Christ. We can do it, if we have the will to do so.

Mini-missions are one innovative way to bring Catholic souls back to life in Christ. A mini-mission is a one-hour single topic mission given immediately following the Sunday morning Mass. The mission topics address culturally relevant and exciting topics such as Disciplining Your Kids, Parenting, Preparing for Retirement, Bored in Retirement, Kids And Television Viewing, Teenage Parties, Body Piercing, Movies, Drug And Alcohol Abuse, Life After Divorce, Money Management, Bankruptcy, Caring For Elderly, The Terrible Teen Years, Strong-Willed Children, Elder Parents In Day Care, Grief, Step-Children, How To Succeed In A Second Marriage, Defending Your Faith Is Not As Easy As It Once Was, and so on.

The idea behind a mini-mission is to entice Catholics to come for spiritual nourishment with the least amount of inconvenience. Why present a mini-mission after Sunday Mass? People are already there, no parking hassles, no interference trying to get out of the house. They are already in a warm and cozy environment, and they usually don't have any place to rush off to on a Sunday morning. As the mission is preparing to start, the parish can provide coffee, tea, and juice along with donuts, bagels, and muffins—the right stuff to meet everyone's needs.

Mini-missions are designed to invite Catholics to remain in the Church or church hall to receive teachings that bring the Gospel of Jesus to life in ways that are relevant and meaningful to their own personal lives. Each topic is taught within the context of Christian principles, referencing Scripture, tradition, and the Catechism of the Catholic Church. The teaching is presented within a 30-minute time slot. The presentation is followed by a 25-minute small group sharing. To close the small group sharing session, the participants pray with one another using *The Simple Blessing Prayer.* To close the general session, the presenter prays a prayer of empowerment over the participants asking God to renew each one with an outpouring of His Holy Spirit and the gifts of His Holy Spirit that are most needed for each person to grow in love for Him and for one another.

Prayer group leaders are the perfect ones to propose mini-missions to pastors and pastoral leaders. Members of the prayer group who have teaching and preaching experience are excellent resources to use in proposing, planning, developing, and implementing mini-missions. Teachers for the mini-missions can be selected through a formal discernment process that focuses on each person's knowledge and experience of the mission topic, desire to minister, and ability to communicate effectively under the anointing of the Holy Spirit. Formation workshops can be offered to help form mini-mission teachers from among parishioners who feel called to the ministry. Once again, prayer group leaders are the perfect ones to help in the discernment and formation process.

Take Time To Reflect And Act

Form a discussion group to talk about the possibility of offering mini-missions in your parish community. Write a proposal to present to your pastor and pastoral council members. Once approval is given for the mini-missions, become actively involved in the planning and implementation phases of the project.

Develop a questionnaire that lists mini-mission topics and distribute the questionnaire to the parish ministries or to each parishioner. Design topics that meet the needs of the parishioners. Conduct a formation day for presenters and group facilitators. Set up a schedule of dates and topics for three months. Make announcements in bulletins and newsletters and at Mass. Be sure to give each participant an evaluation to complete.

For Renewal Leaders

Form a discernment team to determine if the Renewal has the resources to offer mini-mission formation to parishes wishing to implement the mini-mission concept. If so, develop a proposal and submit it to your diocesan offices for pastoral planning.

The Mission Field Is Closer Than You Think

Two years ago, the operating board of our diocesan charismatic Renewal ministry gave approval for the ministry to offer parish missions to local parishes throughout our diocese. It was decided that letters of introduction and mission brochures would be sent to every pastor and parish pastoral council. The letter of introduction was also an invitation to pastors and pastoral teams to prayerfully consider mission topics that would meet the needs of their people. Parishes were also asked to consider inviting one of our mission teams to meet with parish leaders to learn how the mission team could be of service to the parish. The cover letter emphasized the desire of the mission team to meet the spiritual growth needs of the parish. The brochure was titled "Missions for Parish and Community Renewal: Be Holy As I Am Holy."

Our ministry office mailed over 150 mission brochures. We were hopeful that at least one parish would respond to our mailing. First, because our "On The Road Again For the Lord" ministry (Charismatic Masses and Healing Services) had already introduced many of the Renewal ministers to parishes throughout the diocese. Second, as a ministry, we sensed that pastors and pastoral associates respected our efforts to bring renewal and new life to the mainstream Church since many current and former Charismatics served in leadership roles in their parishes. Third, we knew that many parishes could no longer afford to bring in expensive mission teams from around the country. It seemed to be the right time for the Renewal office to offer our services to parishes.

Our hope for launching mission teams into parish ministries was totally dependant upon finding one parish that would take a chance on us. We needed one big break so to speak—one parish to invite us to conduct a parish mission. That break came when one of the Renewal ministry board members decided to follow up our letter of introduction and mission brochure with a personal conversation with his pastor and pastoral team. This particular board member sat on his parish pastoral council and was respected by his pastor and colleagues. Since he was already in a leadership role in his parish he made a legitimate request to his pastoral council that they at least agree to an initial meeting with the mission team.

Sure enough, through the follow-up efforts of this one Renewal board member, his pastor and pastoral council members agreed to invite the mission team to meet with them and present them with a parish mission proposal. When the mission team met with the pastor and pastoral council members, they went with no pre-determined plan of action—no agenda. Rather, they prayed only for the Holy Spirit to anoint the time they would spend with the pastoral council and pastor.

The mission team's priority was to listen to pastoral council members to hear what they felt was their greatest need for parish renewal. We asked members of the council to introduce themselves to us by giving their name, parish ministry involvement, and what their hopes were with regards to the spiritual life of their parish. As each council member responded, a common theme seemed to emerge. Each member expressed a desire for spiritual renewal for all of their people. Council members wanted people to know about God the Father's love. They wanted people to know Jesus—what He had done for each one personally through His life, death, and resurrection. They wanted their people to know about the Holy Spirit—what it means to be empowered by the Holy Spirit. They also wanted people to know how to love one another unconditionally—to know what love looked like, sounded like, and acted like in families, in the parish, between friends, on the job, and in the community.

One member of the council was free enough to voice concerns about Charismatics ministering in her parish. She was particularly worried that the mission team might promote "charismatic stuff" such as contemporary Christian music and tongues. The team assured her that they would not teach about or sing and praise in tongues. However, they did say that they would be using charismatic music to support their teachings. The team commented further that they would like to bring their own music ministers so that everyone in the parish, including the parish music ministers, could experience the mission. This assurance and invitation seemed to allay her fears.

The team also assured pastoral council members that they did not have a "charismatic" agenda but rather a "Pentecost" agenda that calls each one to go, proclaim the Kingdom, and heal. The team recommended offering Benediction each evening of the Mission if the pastor was open to it. The team also suggested the sacrament of Reconciliation for one of the evenings, and the team committed to having a prayer workshop on the last evening of the mission in order to teach the people how to pray with one another in their families and parish ministries.

The pastor and pastoral council were given several options for the mission in terms of the days and times of day it would be presented. It is important to remember that mission teams must always defer to the pastor's or pastoral team's vision and sense of how their parishioners would best respond to a mission experience. The pastor and pastoral council members recommended that the mission be offered on four consecutive Sundays at 6:00 p.m. They further recommended that the parish provide a soup and bread supper each mission Sunday at 5:00 p.m.

Several weeks prior to the start of the mission, the mission team met with the pastor to work out the details of the mission schedule, the liturgical rites, and Reconciliation. The title of the mission and the titles of each mission Sunday were discerned at that meeting. The mission was titled, "Can You Hear Me Now? Love God." Each mission Sunday was titled as follows: From Subversion To Conversion; From Desolation to Restoration; From Personal Pleasure to Eternal Treasure; From Dead Wood to Firewood. The pastor informed us that he was very interested in the *Afterglow of the Eucharist* ministry for his parish.

Once everyone had an opportunity to share what they believed to be the spiritual growth needs of the parish, the mission team was ready to talk about how to best their needs for spiritual revival. To help with this task, we distributed the mission brochure to each member of the pastoral council.

We referenced the brochure to talk about the topics and the titles of possible missions. We talked specifically about how we would teach, preach, witness, and pray for the parishioners to grow in holiness, prayer, and communion. We gave specific reasons why people should come to a parish mission. We included a brief format for the mission, and we talked about the benefits of a parish mission. We also gave background information about the team members. Finally, we summarized our thoughts about what makes for a mission—a good spiritual growth experience for members of a parish.

What's In A Brochure?

The contents of any marketing brochure must be clear, concise, and filled with relevent information for the reader. The following text boxes contain sample texts of what our ministry used to market our mission teams to parishes throughout our diocese.

The Brochure Cover

The brochure cover needs to present an attactive graphic or photo—one that is dynamic enough to entice people to open the brochure and read it. The cover should not only announce the ministry that is sponsoring the missions, but it should contain the ministry's contact person, address, phone and email to make it as easy as possible for pastors to contact the ministy.

The Parish Mission Format, Titles, And Topics

Parish missions provide opportunities for spiritual growth and development in a format that affords both the time and the attention needed to address the critical issues facing families today in the context of Christian living. We explained to the pastor and pastoral council members that the mission team uses storytelling, witnessing, and the everyday experiences of family, parish, work, and community life to nurture and support the spiritual growth and development in the parishioners. The following text box provides an example of how we explained the mission format.

The Mission Team weaves together Scripture, story-telling, faith sharing, worship, and praise with emphasis on the healing power of Jesus in the Eucharist. There are prayers for physical, emotional, spiritual, and intergenerational healing. All of these things come together with a sufficient dose of humor mixed with good old-fashioned common sense! A parish mission can be presented in consecutive evening or weekly sessions or in a weekend retreat format. Adoration of the Blessed Sacrament and Benediction are offered nightly. The Sacrament of Reconciliation is offered on a designated evening.

The mission topics listed in the brochure were presented to pastors and pastoral leaders as possibilities. We explained that the mission topics or titles were designed specifically to entice as many parishioners as possible to come to the mission—the titles addressed issues related to parenting, family planning, financial planning, teens, strong-willed toddlers, family prayer, spiritual development, divorced and separated, and grief.

We assured parish council members that no matter which topics they chose, the team would focus the content of the mission on conversion and transformation through the creative love of the Father, the redeeming love of the Son, and the sanctifying love of the Holy Spirit. Additionally, if the parish so desired, the mission team offered to customize topics and/or titles. The following is a list of topics we offer to parishes in our Mission Brochure:

You may wish to customize your Parish Mission by requesting your own mission topics and titles, or you may select from one or several of the topics listed here:

Can You Hear Me Now? I'm Always Working For You! Love God

Wanted—Catholics Dead or Alive. I Prefer Alive, Love God

When You've Had Enough Cry Jesus. Then We'll Talk, Love God

When Living In the World Gives Way To Living In the Spirit

Eight Ways to Ensure That God Can't Heal You

The Afterglow of the Eucharist: Let's Pray

Pray For Me 'Cause I Can't Pray

The Road Less Disciplined: The Way to Heaven

How To Keep Your Children From Leaving The Church, When They're Old Enough To Drive or Can Anyone Tell Me Why My Children Left The Church?

The Seven R's of Spiritual Renewal

Low Fat-High Protein Recipes for Spiritual Growth

From Subversion to Conversion; Desolation to Restoration; Personal Pleasure to Heavenly Treasure

Catherine of Siena: The Climb, The Conversion, The Surrender, The Kiss

Defending Your Faith; Growing In Grace

Parenting Your Parents

Time Out For Moms

Dads On Duty

Why Should I Come To A Parish Mission?

When designing a marketing brochure it is important to talk about the value of a parish mission. At times, our pastoral leaders become frustrated and grow weary of offering spiritual growth experiences when so few people attend. We in the Renewal are in the unique position of bringing enthusiasm and a fresh hope to pastors and pastoral teams by the way we present ourselves—the excitement in our voices and the passion of our commitment to be a part of parish renewal. We can help parishes refocus on the notion that it is not about how many attend but rather what happens to those who do attend.

> *The Gift of a Parish Mission:* When we set aside time to be with Jesus our minds are renewed, our hearts are healed and our lives are never the same again. Time away with Jesus only happens when we intentionally step aside from our busy lives. A parish mission gives us the perfect opportunity to do this. Why not plan a mission for your parish that will open hearts to God's love and mercy?

It is possible that parishioners will not support a parish mission if they do not believe the parish mission to be a meaningful experience for them. There are many powerful missions being given throughout the country. However, there may have been times when Catholics have had less than personally meaningful mission experiences for a variety of reasons. Through years of experience in retreat work, many of us have learned that spiritual growth experiences uplift people during the experience. However, when there is little or no follow-up, the spiritual growth experiences seem to have a very limited impact on people lives.

The same is true for spiritual growth experiences such as retreats, days of renewal, or missions. Likewise, spiritual growth experiences that fail to give us concrete ways to change the direction of our lives tend to make us feel indifferent towards future experiences. For these reasons, those who sponsor parish missions must find the precise words that will encourage people to come to a parish mission. People must be encouraged to receive blessings for their lives, to have their spiritual and emotional needs met, and to find deeper meaning in their lives.

> Are you ready for a change in your life? Do you want to shed your sinful ways of living life? Do you desire to be transformed into the image and likeness of God? Are you ready for your life to be full of grace? Are you ready to be led by the Holy Spirit in all you say and do? Are you longing to know God and to let God know you? Are you willing to set aside time for God so that God has time to touch and heal your life and the lives of those you love? If you responded yes to even one of these questions, come set aside time to be with Jesus. Your mind will be renewed, your soul refreshed, your heart healed, and your life will never be the same again.

How Can A Parish Grow In Holiness, Prayer, And Communion?

When marketing parish missions to pastoral leaders it is critical to reference Scripture and the Church's teachings. Such references add emphasis and validity to the team, the mission topics, and the mission itself.

The Church continually invites us to give special consideration to the Holy Spirit whose mission it is to make us holy, draw us closer to God in prayer, and enable us to love one another. The mission of the Holy Spirit is to sanctify the Church and the renew the face of the earth, making us holy and pleasing to God and preparing our souls for an eternity with Him. Through the power of His Holy Spirit we come to know Christ and the One who sent Him. We are able to hear His voice for ourselves, our children, our families, our Church, and our world. Jesus is the Source of all life—the one sure investment for our future. He is the one true lasting inheritance we have to pass on to our children, to future generations (Apostolic Letter: Dominum et Vivicantem of His Holiness John Paul II—The Holy Spirit in the Life of the Church and the World, 1986). In order to help parish communities come to know the full power of the Holy Spirit at work in their lives, the Mission Team is offering a variety of parish missions. Please take a few moments to review the mission topics listed in this brochure and pray about whether or not your parish community is called to be renewed through one or more of these mission topics.

How Will My Parish Benefit From A Parish Mission?

It is important to include ways a parish might benefit from a mission. Dynamic missions have the potential to revive parish worship, revitalize ministries, and transform the entire parish communities.

During and after the mission your parish community will:
- Receive a fresh outpouring of the gifts of faith, hope, and love.
- Be re-empowered with the gifts given them at Baptism and Confirmation.
- Be refreshed and renewed physically, emotionally, and spiritually.
- Become more aware of God's healing presence in their family and work situations.
- Become more closely bonded as a Christian community.
- See relationships with spouses, family, friends, and community members be strengthened and healed.

Who Is The Mission Team?

Pastors and pastoral teams will definitely want to know the credentials and the Church agency that is sponsoring the mission teams. Therefore, we must have the endorsement of the Renewal leaders in our diocese since they are under the authority of our local bishop. Parish missions given by Catholic Charismatics who are mature in the Spirit are a powerful tool for putting out into the deep to catch souls for Christ. Be sure to include this information in a brochure.

> Parish Mission Teams serve under the authority of the Ministry to Catholic Charismatic Renewal, Diocese of _____, and under the spiritual direction of _____. Each team member is grounded in Scripture and in the teachings of the Catholic Church. They come with years of ministry experience and with their gifts having been discerned by the pastoral leaders of the Renewal.

One Pastor's Review

Until prayer groups and Renewal ministry leaders actually present their first mission, the mission team will need to depend upon the recommendations of Renewal leaders and priests who can vouch for their ministry gifts. Their recommendations should be in the mission brochure. However, once the first mission is presented, the mission team should ask for a recommendation from the pastor and the pastoral leaders. Their endorsement will have a profound influence on future mission assignments. The moment a parish recommendation is given to the mission team, the recommendation should be added to the brochure. The following is an example of a recommendation that was given to our mission team after their first parish mission was presented.

> *Thank you for a marvelous parish mission. I only wish more of our parishioners had been there. If you ever need a letter of recommendation from me, or if a pastor wants to speak to me on the phone, I will gladly tell them that you will be a great benefit to their parish community.*

Parish Mission Follow-Up

Follow-up is critical to the success of any parish mission. Since presenting the mission, "Can You Hear Me Now? Love God."

The parish has continued the ministry of praying with each other for healing. They began the "Afterglow of the Eucharist" ministry several months after the mission. The team has had follow-up conversations with members of the pastoral council and plans to continue to offer the services of the mission team for any spiritual needs the parish might have.

Since giving this first mission, the Renewal Mission Team has met with two other parishes to discuss the possibility of offering them parish missions. We are excited and hopeful as the Renewal puts out into the deep.

Take Time To Reflect And Act

For Prayer Group Leaders

Develop a list of mission topics that might be of interest to your parish. Discern prayer group members' gifts that can be used for planning and implementing parish missions: Develop a "Prayer Group Ministry Bureau" that includes dossiers on individual prayer group members listing their background and experiences as teachers, preachers, music ministers, spiritual directors, retreat coordinators, healing ministers, etc. (see The Renewal and Prayer Groups As Training and Formation Centers). Ask to have a meeting with your pastor and pastoral leaders. During the meeting, offer the Bureau binder to your pastor and pastoral leaders for their review and consideration of Renewal ministers for parish ministry work such as mini-missions, retreats, workshops, seminars, etc.

For Renewal Leaders

Form a discussion group to talk about developing a "Parish Mission Brochure" to send to your parish or to parishes in your diocese. Develop a brochure that includes your goals, objectives, formats, mission titles and topics, general overview of mission content, benefits to parishes, and benefits to God's people. Send the brochure to parishes in your diocese. Include a cover letter. Follow up by telephone.

Adopt A Parish Initiative
A Radical Approach to Keeping Catholics Catholic And Bringing Ex-Catholics Home

As experienced ministers in the Renewal, we are eager to bring our gifts and years of ministry experience into the mainstream Church. However, any ideas we propose will remain merely ideas without direct clergy advisement, support, and approval. For this reason, Renewal leaders must offer to sit with diocesan directors for evangelization, committees, pastors, and pastoral leaders to share their visions for evangelizing the Church and bringing ex-Catholics home. All must come together and pray for how God desires to renew His Church so that all who call themselves Catholic will be fully committed to Christ and to His Church. All must come together to pray and discern how God wishes to set His Church on fire so that all who have left the Church will be eager to come home, because there is now something great and wonderful to come home to.

While it is true that many join the Church each year through the powerful Rite of Christian Initiation, many also leave the Church each year for neighboring churches. For this reason we must be ready to collaborate, team up, join forces, work in partnership, pull resources, coordinate efforts, and do whatever it takes. That is to say, we must be ready to do whatever God asks us to do in order to reverse the flow of Catholics out of the Church and create a new grace for the Church—namely multitudes of Catholics staying home and coming home.

To this end, we do not need a program to keep Catholics from leaving the Church or bring ex-Catholics back to the Church. We already have a program. It is the Gospel of Jesus Christ. What we need, according to John Paul II (2001) are new and different initiatives that fulfill the deeply personal needs people have for spiritual growth. We need initiatives that enable parishes to become schools of prayer, schools of holiness, and schools of communion. We need new initiatives that enable the Gospel of Jesus Christ to be lived out in the thoughts, words, and actions of men, women, and children alike for there are so many Catholics longing for solid food on which to chew—specific ways to be and to live in a complicated and tempting world.

John Paul II (2001) challenged us to develop new initiatives that bring the Gospel of Jesus Christ to people in profound and life-changing ways. He challenged us to develop initiatives that enable people to contemplate the face of Christ and encounter Him frequently—in the Eucharist and in one-another, as we are sanctified and purified through the gifts and the power of His Holy Spirit.

Some might argue that the Sunday homily was designed to do this work. However, we must consider that the Holy Father is calling new initiatives. The Sunday homily is not new. Additionally, the time allotted for the Sunday homily makes it nearly impossible for the preacher to offer specific instructions and challenges for living in the Spirit and changing how we currently think, speak, and act in our lives. Homilies tend to be more like pep talks—a rallying of the faithful, an encouraging thought for the coming week. It is difficult in such a short amount of time to reach parents who are hungering to know how to raise their children according to God's principles and plan, workers who want to know how to engage in ethical practices in the workplace, married couples and those who live in community who want to know how to love unconditionally, Catholics wanting to know God's ways, how to pray, and how to grow in holiness.

Whether it be an ordained, religious, or layperson, if anyone believes he or she has a single initiative that could possibly respond to the personals spiritual needs of Catholics today, they are surely obligated to offer it to the Church for consideration. It is becoming far too painful to sit back and watch as good Catholics exit the Catholic Church for neighboring or distant churches. When they get there, they are pleased to remain for two-hour services, once or twice each week. They are proud to tithe and eager to give large pledges to support new church construction projects. If we are honest with ourselves, we must admit and be willing to talk about the fact that ex-Catholic prosperity is now prospering other churches. At the same time, Catholic churches are being clustered and even worse—some are being closed for lack of members and funding.

One well-known Catholic evangelist exclaims, "Why are we closing Catholic churches when we should be filling them?" This is the question every committed Catholic must ask of himself or herself. We must also ask, "What are other churches doing that we are not doing?" As we ask ourselves these questions, we must not be so haughty to proclaim, "We have tradition and the Eucharist on our side." If people knew Jesus' true presence in the Eucharist, Jesus would be enough to keep Catholics from leaving the Church. However, since this may not be the case, Catholics are able to leave the Church without looking back and without understanding what they are leaving behind. If Jesus in the Eucharist were enough for them, they would have never left.

Another critical point to be made is that it would be dangerous to think that Catholics will remain Catholic or want to become Catholic simply because our rich history and tradition date back to the time of Christ. History and tradition will not bring souls to Christ, nor will history and tradition bring people into the Church. As we have seen first hand among our friends and family members, history and tradition are also not good enough reasons for Catholics to remain Catholic.

Indeed, we do not need new programs. Rather, we need many unique initiatives that help people apply the Gospel to their everyday lives, discern their gifts for ministry, teach them about the healing power of God that is present in the Precious Body and Blood of Jesus, and open them up to the power and gifts of the Holy Spirit at work in their lives. We need many and unique initiatives that educate people on ways to pray, encourage and give them ways to grow in holiness, and teach them what it means to be in communion with one another.

We, who are in the Renewal, must be willing to propose such initiatives at whatever starting point, ministry level, and age needed, in order to be among those who put out into the deep to renew the Church in this new millennium. Most important of all, we ourselves must understand and respond to the endless possibilities of how God desires us to grow in holiness, prayer, and communion, and how He desires us to remain rooted in the Sacraments and the teachings of the Church.

There is one major initiative that has challenged the Renewal office to put out into the deep in a way that some may say is far too frightening and difficult. It is a plan to establish mission teams of four to six persons who agree to go out to a single parish and, in effect, "adopt the parish" for a period of three to five years in order to support and nurture the spiritual life of the parish in whatever ways the parish wishes to grow. The emphasis will be on helping parishes develop initiatives that lead Catholics to Christ and give them on-going spiritual growth experiences. Such experiences might include what it means to live in the Spirit; what holiness looks like in ordinary everyday life; how to receive and operate in the gifts of the Holy Spirit; how to pray vocal, meditative, contemplative, and healing prayer with others; and how to turn church music into worship and praise.

The mission team members would first serve as the spiritual growth coaches, mentors, teachers, and trainers of parish leaders, that is to say, members of parish council, lectors, Eucharistic ministers, music ministers, bible study leaders, RCIA and CCD directors and teachers, support group leaders, retreat directors and so on. Then, the goal of the mission team would be to assist the parish leaders and ministers in discerning, developing, and using their gifts to support the spiritual growth of their parishioners. Finally, the mission team would help the leaders to identify coaches and mentors for the parish, from among their own parishioners. The team would then mentor the mentors and coach the coaches until the parish felt it was fully equipped to support and nurture the on-going spiritual growth and development of its people forming and supporting its own coaches and mentors.

To be sure, not all parishes will need nor will they desire this type or degree of assistance from "outsiders." However, for those who are floundering or frustrated, on-site ministry and formation by outsiders may be exactly what some parishes need and want. These are radical ideas to be sure. However, the notion of coaching, mentoring, and providing training for continuous progress towards a common purpose, is a familiar practice to educators, those is sales, and other professionals who desire to grow, develop, and perform better on the job. This model would be a dynamic initiative for nurturing a parish's continuous progress on the path towards wholeness and holiness.

Preparations are underway in our diocese for launching this "Adopt A Parish" initiative. The following chapter describes how to set up a "speakers' bureau" or, as it is called, a "Renewal Ministry Bureau." This preparation work will give us information about the resources we have to offer our local Churches. We will be able to gather and organize specific information about our Renewal leaders and ministers. This information will, in turn, guide the decisions we make with regards to not only what we are able to offer our diocese and our parishes, but also how soon we are able to offer it.

Take Time To Reflect And Act

For Prayer Group Leaders

Form a discussion group to talk about the idea of forming a "mission team" for your parish that could support the parish in evangelizing Catholics. Talk about how the team might design and offer workshops, retreats, mini-missions, and missions that address a variety of relevant topics for all aspects of parish life. Talk about how you could incorporate "how to live the Gospel" as well praise and worship music, healing prayer over the people gathers, and praying with one another.

For Renewal Leaders

Establish an "ad hoc" committee to study the possibility of offering "mission teams" to your diocese that could support parishes in their evangelization mission. Read the following chapter, "The Renewal and Prayer Groups As Training and Formation Centers" to learn how the Renewal can tap into the gifts that are present within its active members. Set up a "Renewal Ministry Bureau" to identify resource people who are able to minister in the mainstream Church at parish and/or diocesan levels. Describe how mission teams might design and offer workshops, retreats, mini-missions, and missions that address a variety of relevant topics for all aspects of parish life. Talk about how you could incorporate messages on how to live the Gospel along with praise and worship music, healing prayer over the people gathered, and teaching families and friends how to pray with one another.

The Renewal and Prayer Groups
As Training and Formation Centers

The moment the Renewal accepts the challenge to be renewed, it will find itself on the doorstep of the mainstream Church, being invited to come in and share its gifts, its years of experience, and its life in the Spirit. Renewal leaders will be called upon to share their knowledge and their gifts with various ministries already present in the mainstream Church—ministries that are hungering to know how to better nurture and support the spiritual lives of children, pre-teens, teens, young adults, adults, and the elderly. Renewal leaders will also be called upon to share their energy, ideas, and wealth of experience in designing and implementing new ministries in the mainstream Church—ministries never before imagined.

As this begins to happen, the Renewal must to be ready to respond. Over the years, we have seen many leaders, preachers, teachers, healing ministers, and prophets come into the Renewal. Many are still active with us. Some are semi-active, and many more are inactive. If the Renewal is to put out into the deep, Renewal leaders must first be able to identify their available resources—that is to say, people who are willing to minister in the mainstream Church. They must identify their resources from among those who are active, semi-active, and even those who are currently inactive in the Renewal. In fact, a great place to start "calling people home" might just be with our ex-Charismatics who are in the mainstream Church. They would be great contact persons for us as we move into the mainstream of parish life.

As Renewal leaders make preparation to put out into the deep, it will be necessary to have a system in place for tracking potential ministers. All active members of the Renewal must be invited to put out into the deep. Inactive and semi-active members must be asked if they wish to be reactivated to put out into the deep with us. Once a tracking system is in place, Renewal leaders will always have easy access to their ministers and will be able to keep an objective record of their on-going formation activities, charisms, capabilities, gifts, and talents. A systematic approach to maintaining a list of available and qualified ministers enables leaders to objectively define, describe, organize, and assess its ministers. It also enables leaders to keep ministers' profiles up-to-date for future reference. With accurate and up-to-date information, Renewal leaders will be able to recommend ministers to parishes and diocesan offices with a certain degree of confidence.

Prior to setting up a bureau, Renewal leaders must gather, pray and discern if they are being called out into the deep—the mainstream Church. If so, developing a bureau is the starting point. Once the bureau is established, leaders will be able to determine the type and amount of ministry to offer parishes and the mainstream Church.

The Renewal Ministry Bureau

A good way to start tracking the gifts and availability of Renewal ministers is through a speakers' bureau or as will be called here, a Renewal Ministry Bureau. The Renewal Ministry Bureau consists of a three-ring binder with profiles of individuals in the Renewal who agree to be called upon for ministry work in the mainstream Church or in the Renewal. The binder contains a one-page profile, or summary, of each person including education and prior experience. Each profile contains detailed contact information as well as a listing of degrees, certificates, job experience, hobbies, talents, spiritual gifts, and ministry gifts. It also lists prior ministry experience including type of ministry, location, number of participants, topics presented, and role and responsibilities.

It takes but a few simple steps to set up a Renewal Ministry Bureau. The best entity to coordinate the set up of the bureau is the Renewal office. The following steps make it easy to do:

1. Option 1a
    Set up an "Information Days" (two-hour workshops on at least three different days and dates) for active, semi-active, and inactive Charismatics in your diocese. Use an enticing title for the day! "If You Are Or Ever Were A Catholic Charismatic, This Day Is For You!" Do not say much more. Let everyone wonder what it is and if they are curious enough they'll come. If not you can always reach them by mail. The

agenda will be simple. Renewal leaders will share their vision for renewing the mainstream Church, and then explain the need for a Renewal Ministry Bureau.

1. Option 1b
    Or send a cover letter to all active, inactive, and semi-active Charismatics in your diocese. You may need to resurrect old mailing lists. In the letter, describe the Renewal Ministry Bureau, explain the concept, and explain why you are setting up the bureau. Also include the goals of the Ministry Bureau. A sample letter follows:

Dear Brothers and Sisters In Christ:

Our renewal office is attempting to compile a listing of Catholic Charismatics along with their ministry experiences, gifts, and talents. The reason we are compiling such a listing is that we have been receiving calls from the diocesan office and parishes to offer retreats, workshops, and days of renewal. We recognize this as a new movement of God's Spirit and we want to prepare ourselves for what He is doing in us and through us. As part of this preparation, we realize we must have a more detailed and more current description of Charismatic Catholics who are willing to minister in the mainstream Church. To aid in this process, we are establishing a Renewal Ministry Bureau. A Renewal Ministry Bureau consists of a three-ring binder that contains listings of individuals who are available for ministry work both within the Renewal and within the mainstream Church. The binder contains a one-page summary of each person including education, qualifications, and prior experience. The questionnaire asks for contact information and degrees, certificates, job experience, hobbies, talents, spiritual gifts, and ministry gifts. Each entry also describes prior ministry experience including type, location, number of participant, topic, role, and responsibilities.

This Renewal Ministry Bureau is vital to our efforts to coordinate our resources and respond to ministry requests coming to us from parishes and from our diocese. For this reason, it is vital that you complete the questionnaire and return it to us at your earliest convenience. We need to hear back from you. If you have any questions please feel free to contact our office. Once we receive your questionnaire, we will be contacting you to determine the level of ministry commitment you are able to make. This will be noted on your Bureau entry.

May God bless you abundantly with His love and mercy.

---

2. Design a questionnaire to enclose with the cover letter. The questionnaire should ask for demographic information as well as information about education and prior ministry experience. A sample questionnaire follows:

Renewal Ministry Bureau

Name _____ DOB _____ M/F _____

Affiliation _____ Parish _____

Address _____ City, State, Zip _____

Home Telephone _____ Work Telephone _____

Fax _____ Cell/Mobile _____ Email _____

Degrees:

Certificates:

Holy Orders:

Parish Ministries:

Skills and Talents:

Hobbies:

Spiritual Gifts: Circle all that apply:

Tongues	Prophecy	Word of Knowledge
Preaching	Teaching	Healing
Administration	Leadership	Interpretation of Tongues
Discernment of Spirits	Other: Please explain: _____	

# of Years living in the Spirit (Baptized in the Holy Spirit)

From the following list, indicate the types of ministry work you have done and the frequency.

Role	Frequency	Role	Frequency
retreat presenter		workshop presenter	
seminar presenter		healing minister	
word gift minister		prayer team leader (core)	
prayer team intercessor		prayer group teacher	
group leader		group facilitator	
spiritual director		spiritual advisor	
praise and worship leader		hospitality or greeter	
conference session leader		keynote speaker	
leadership board member		lector	
Eucharistic minister		other	

Prior Ministry Experience

Date	Where	Topics	Role/ Responsibilities	# Attending
____	_____	_____	_____	_____
____	_____	_____	_____	_____
____	_____	_____	_____	_____
____	_____	_____	_____	_____
____	_____	_____	_____	_____

Are you willing to use your gifts in ministry work in other parishes throughout the diocese? Please feel free to comment below:

3. Mail the questionnaire and cover letter.

4. As the questionnaire forms are returned, summarize the responses by tallying the information onto a summary form. This form might be titled the "Renewal Ministry Bureau Summary." Across the top of this form, enter all of the ministry gifts that are listed on the questionnaire. Along the left side of the form, record the name of each person who returns a completed questionnaire. Transfer information from the person's questionnaire onto the summary form.

| **Renewal Ministry Bureau Summary** | | | | | | | | | | | | | | | | | | | |
Name	retreat presenter	workshop presenter	seminar presenter	healing minister	word gift ministry	prayer team leaders	prayer team intercessor	prayer group teacher	group leader	group facilitator	spiritual director	spiritual advisor	praise and worship leader	hospitality	conference session leader	keynote speaker	ministry board member	lector	Eucharistic minister	Other

5. Within one week of receiving a questionnaire, the ministry office must call the perspective minister and conduct a personal interview to determine his/her availability for ministry—months, days of the week, hours of the day, distance from home he/she is willing to travel, etc. This is also a good time for Renewal leaders and respondents to ask clarifying questions and review the responses that were recorded on the questionnaire in the event that he/she wishes to add or delete information. Use the back of the form to record the following information and additional responses:

Questionnaire sent: on												
Questionnaire returned on												
Months available for ministry	J	F	M	A	M	J	J	A	S	O	N	d
Weeks available for ministry	WEEK 1			WEEK 2			WEEK 3			WEEK 4		
Days available for ministry	M		T	W		T		F		S		S
Times available for ministry	AM				AFTERNOON			PM				
Are you willing to travel to parishes over 30 miles away?												
Additional comments:					Attendance at Formation Events:							

6. File the completed questionnaires in alphabetical order in the Ministry Bureau binder. Update the binder each time a new questionnaire is submitted to the office. Prior to filing the questionnaire in the binder, be sure to transfer ministry information onto the "Renewal Ministry Bureau Summary" form.

Once the Renewal office has sufficient information about its potential ministers, the office can schedule a series of formation days. Formation workshops should be on-going throughout the year and should focus on the topics most needed to further develop the bureau ministers. For example, if calls are coming in to the office for teen retreats, those individuals interested in working with teens should be formed in topics, formats, and methods that best meet the needs of teens. Topics for parish retreat workshops might include discernment of gifts, formation of preachers, teachers, healers, prophets, the training of group leaders, facilitators, and the role of praise and worship leaders, retreat spiritual directors, music ministers, and so on. Finally, the

Renewal office should keep a record of all who attend the formation workshops. The office can transfer the workshop event attended onto the back of the minister's profile.

Whenever requests are given to the Renewal office for ministers for diocesan or parish ministry, persons with profiles that match the needs of the caller can be recommended. The Renewal office in effect, becomes a clearinghouse of teachers, preachers, healing ministers, prayer ministers, musicians, praise and worship leaders, spiritual directors, retreat directors, and workshop presenters who are placing themselves at the service of the mainstream Church. Once the Renewal Ministry Bureau is in place and ministers are formed, the office is ready to present the Renewal Ministry Bureau to the diocese for a review of its ministers. In so doing, the Renewal ministry is submitting to the discernment and the authority of its bishop. Once the profiles are approved, the Renewal office is ready to send a letter to parishes announcing the Renewal Ministry Bureau.

In this regard, it is important to remember that if the Renewal office recommends one of its ministers to the diocese or a parish, the Renewal office accepts responsibility for the minister's work. As such, it is very important that the Renewal office take seriously its responsibility to train, coach, mentor, and supervise the ministers it sends out into diocesan and parish ministry. Prayer groups make are the most ideal settings in which current and potential preachers, teachers, and other ministers can practice ministering. This is because prayer groups are safe and caring environments whose leaders live in the Spirit and operate in the charisms of the Holy Spirit. Such gifted and experienced leaders are the perfect one to mentor, coach, teach, and train future ministers to be sent out into the mainstream Church. Renewal ministry events such as Life in the Spirit Seminars and Growth in the Spirit seminars are also ideal places to find Charismatics on fire for the Lord and eager to serve in His Church. Guiding them to prayer groups for ministry formation has great meaning for them and bears great fruit for the Renewal.

Take Time To Reflect And Act

For Prayer Group, Renewal, Diocesan, and Parish Leaders

Gather Renewal leaders together to discuss what you already know about Renewal members' credentials, experiences, talents, spiritual gifts, and availability to minister to parishes if called upon to do so by your diocese. If required, meet with the appropriate diocesan offices to get approval of any plan to offer mission teams to parishes.

Develop a Renewal Ministry Bureau that includes dossiers on individual prayer group members listing their background and experiences as teachers, preachers, music ministers, spiritual directors, retreat coordinators, healing ministers, etc.

Based upon the information filed in the Renewal Ministry Bureau, develop a brochure that summarizes the gifts and ministries that the Renewal could make available to your diocese. Form a "marketing team' to develop and market parish missions to your diocesan parishes.

Write a cover letter explaining the Renewal Ministry Bureau. Send the letter to diocesan offices and parishes. Follow up the letter with a personal phone call. Meet individually with pastors in your diocese to discuss the possibility of offering parish missions.

The Seven "R's" of Spiritual Renewal
Renewing The Church In The Third Millennium

Renewing the Renewal is a call to action that can be responded to by mainstream Catholics and Charismatic Catholics, whether active or inactive, whether in national, diocesan, or prayer group leadership, or whether attending prayer group or not. To understand what it means to renew the Church, it may be helpful to consider seven synonyms for the word renewal. In so doing, we can see how each word carries with it a different perspective on what renewal could mean for the Church. Using these synonyms, the Catholic Charismatic Renewal can be viewed as a movement that has the potential to revive, replenish, repair, revitalize, rekindle, rejuvenate, and regenerate the Church.

If the intent of the original Charismatic Renewal Movement was to renew the Church through the Baptism of the Holy Spirit, we can be assured that our primary mission has not changed over the last thirty years. Yet, by its very nature, the means and methods used by the Renewal to bring people into the Baptism in the Holy Spirit or life in the Spirit must be dynamic, open to change and ever changing in response to the needs of the Church. In essence, the Renewal Movement and the way it promotes life in the Spirit must be open to continual renewal lest the movement lose sight of God's original purpose for it—to renew the mainstream Church.

If the Renewal is to revive the Church, we must wake up from our dead sleep! Through the power of the Holy Spirit, we must awaken our minds to what is happening around us. There are Church issues and life issues that demand our response. We cannot afford to become drowsy nor complacent with a laissez-faire attitude towards the Church and the world. We must ask God to stimulate our senses with a love for the Church through prayer, spiritual reading, conversations with our priests, fellow Catholics, and others who love Christ and the Church. We must be knowledgeable enough to defend the Church, seek to understand her Doctrines and teachings. We must know how to defend purgatory, the priesthood, Eucharist, Reconciliation, Confirmation, and Baptism. We must study her early history and formation. We should know how to access information about the

Desert Fathers, and the doctors, mystics, saints, and martyrs of the Church.

If we study well we will be able to teach others, lead discussion groups, and present workshops for our parish and even for our Diocese. Once we are revived we will be able to revive others. Therefore, we must stir up excitement within ourselves for the beauty of the Church, the graces that flow from her, and the gift that she is to all who encounter her. We must look alive, act alive, and speak with a lively voice and tone. If the Renewal is to revive the Church, we must awaken ourselves and awaken the mainstream Church to life in the Spirit, the traditions of the Church, and Scripture.

If the Renewal is to <u>replenish</u> the Church, we must be ready to say "yes" to wherever we are needed in the Church, even if it is not where we wish to be. We must be willing to work for the Kingdom of God, no matter the cost, without reward and without notice. We must pray to know what else or what new thing God wishes us to do in our family, our work places, and our friendships, to make them and us more holy. We must pray to know what new thing God would have us do in our parish to make it more holy. We must ask God to show us how we can add to the spiritual life of our parish—what role, capacity, or service is currently lacking that we might perform so that our parish community might become more holy.

Our prayer groups must find out about the parish's greatest need for spiritual renewal. Once they have this information they must propose new initiatives in the form of activities, workshops, retreats, and seminars that meet those needs. Diocesan Renewal movements must have the courage to ask diocesan ministries what their greatest needs for renewal are, and then they must propose initiatives that can meet the needs. If the Renewal is to replenish the Church, we must be an instrument of "completeness" agreeing to fill in what is missing and what is most needed in the present-day life of the Church.

If the Renewal is to <u>repair</u> the Church, each one of us in the Renewal must first be teachable. We ourselves must be eager to learn, willing to receive correction, and be thankful when correction is given. We must continually present ourselves and our thinking to those in authority over us, whether at work, at home, or in our parish communities. We must invite others to challenge us in their thoughts, words, and actions so that we are able to recognize, acknowledge, and repent of our sins, and once we have repented, we must be prepared to repair the damage done, no matter the cost.

Prayer group, diocesan, and national leaders must be willing to ask others for an honest appraisal of the images and messages, they portray as well as the behaviors they model in the parish, the diocese, and at a national level. Leaders within the Renewal must be willing to sponsor "listening" sessions in which members of the Renewal can share their frustrations and their concerns. Renewal leaders must be humble servants, willing to accept honest criticism, and eager to change what needs to be changed. If the Renewal is to repair the Church, we must first ask forgiveness for the ways we have injured others—members of our prayer groups, parishes, and diocesan communities. We must receive God's mercy and forgiveness and resolve to speak and act in loving ways towards others.

If the Renewal is to <u>revitalize</u> the Church, our presence in the mainstream Church must be more vital, and more necessary than it has ever been before. We must be a critical resource for our parish, a resource that other ministries can tap into when, and as needed. We must continually grow in our knowledge of Scripture and Church tradition, as well as the teachings and doctrines of the Church. We ourselves must search out new avenues for proclaiming the Good News in our families, communities, and parishes.

Our prayer groups and Renewal movements must be so vital to the Church that others seek us out when they need ministers for retreats, missions, workshops, seminars, and days of renewal. We must be willing to sacrifice time, talent, and treasure to become a more vital part of our Catholic community. We must also be eager to propose concrete ways to revitalize our parish, diocese, and Church. Our presence in our parish must be noticed, not for who we are, but for who Christ is in us and for what God does through us. If the Renewal is to revitalize the Church, we as individuals, prayer groups, diocesan Renewal movements, and the National Charismatic Renewal Movement, must be more meaningful and indispensable to the Church than we have ever been before.

If the Renewal it is to <u>rekindle</u> the Church, our life in the Spirit must affect the parish like a firestorm. Such a fire of the Holy Spirit in us must be one that cannot be quenched or extinguished by setbacks, frustrations, resentments, jealousy, envy, anger, gossip, despair, nor any other out-of-control emotion that destroys unity in the Body of Christ. Nothing must keep us from spreading the love of God in our family, community, and our parish. The fire of the Holy Spirit must be a holy wild fire, one that conveys the Gospel of Jesus Christ with enthusiasm and excitement. It must be a fire that draws others to come, pray the Scriptures, and meditate on God's gift of salvation—Jesus Christ.

We must be willing to respectfully operate in the charisms of the Holy Spirit in our personal ministry in the Church—charisms such as tongues, prophecy, word of knowledge, discernment, preaching, teaching, and healing. We must not be afraid to talk about the charisms to those who are curious. We must be eager to explain the gifts to them and extol their great benefits in aiding growth in wholeness and holiness and in building up the whole Body of Christ. Renewal leaders must not be so limited in their thinking as to believe that the charisms of the Holy Spirit can only be received through Baptism in the Holy Spirit seminars. Renewal movements at all levels must challenge themselves to find new ways to introduce the charisms of the Holy Spirit into the mainstream Church. If the Renewal is to rekindle the Church, we must be more on fire with the power and the gifts of the Holy Spirit than we have ever been before—and our fire must spread to the mainstream Church.

If the Renewal is to <u>rejuvenate</u> the Church, we must be ready to step aside from our ministries in the Church in order to allow younger members to take our places. We must actively seek out younger persons and raise them up into leadership positions in Renewal Ministries and prayer groups as well as in every ministry in the mainstream Church. We must coach and mentor well enough that the young are easily able to replace us. We must be willing to become unknown to all except Christ Himself. In essence, we must agree to decrease so that Christ might increase in us and in others. If the Renewal is to rejuvenate the Church, we must be willing to raise up younger members of the Body of Christ who understand that they must both lead and develop leaders from among those they lead.

If the Renewal is to regenerate the Church, we must intentionally work to pass on our faith to our family, our community, and all those we encounter. We must pray for God to create opportunities for us to pass on our faith to the next generation, lest they inherit our wealth without our legacy of holiness. We must use every occasion in life—births, deaths, sickness, marriages, birthdays, joblessness, and even bankruptcy, to put a "Holy Spin" on every aspect of life. We must pass on to younger generations, a foundational way to grow in holiness—committing to both teach and model holy living so that they become more holy a generation than we are.

Prayer group, diocesan, and national leaders must be willing to design and propose initiatives that focus on bringing life in the Spirit to young adults, teens, pre-teens, and to parents of young children. Such initiatives must be proposed to diocesan ministries that serve pre-teens, teens, young adults, falling away Catholics, and fallen away Catholics. Such proposals must focus on initiatives that respond to the needs of Catholics once we have discovered from them what it will take to keep them Catholic. If the Renewal is to regenerate the Church, we must pass on a legacy of holiness to the next generation.

It is interesting to note that not one of the actions of renewing the Renewal is focused on increasing participation in Renewal activities or prayer groups. Not one of these initiatives is focused on increasing the finances of the Renewal. Rather, these renewal actions are concerned with renewing the whole Body of Christ, the mainstream Church.

A renewed Renewal, a new millennium Renewal must be one that is powerfully driven by the Holy Spirit, deeply rooted in Christ and the Church, and confident in its mission to renew the mainstream Church. If the Renewal is open to being renewed, it must continuously strive to be more holy today than it has ever been in the past. The hallmark of the Renewal must be its willingness, or rather, its eagerness to be continuously renewed.

Indeed, we must not long for the Renewal to be like it was twenty years ago. Instead, we must pray fervently for the Renewal to perceive the new things God is doing to renew His Church. If we can perceive it and flow with it, the Renewal will be vital and meaningful to the Church. It will rekindle the fire of the Holy Spirit in the Church. It will replenish and fill in the gaps of what is most needed in the daily life of the Church. It will rejuvenate the Church, inviting the young to receive the gifts of the Holy Spirit and use them in leadership in both the Renewal and the mainstream Church. It will challenge us to live daily in the Spirit so that our lives become a legacy—a gift to be passed on to future generations. If we can perceive it and flow with it, the Renewal will be an instrument to do God's work—repairing, mending, putting in right order, and correcting what He desires in order for His Church to fulfill her mission on earth—her Pentecost mission.

Each time we are disappointed in the present and tempted to reminisce about the past, we must ask ourselves, "What new thing is God doing here? What must I let go of from my past in order to perceive the new thing? What does God want me to know about renewing His Church in this time? In this place? In my life? What is God's now Word to me? What can I do in renewed service to my Lord that would bring His life, love, peace, and healing to those in my family, my parish community, at work, and at play?

Take Time To Reflect And Act

Take a few moments to ponder which of the seven "R's" God is asking you to embrace in order to experience a renewed "Baptism in the Holy Spirit." What specific actions is He asking you to take in order to live more fully in Him?

Take a few moments to ponder which of the seven "R's" God is asking you to embrace in order to bring the "Baptism in the Holy Spirit" to people in the mainstream Church. What specific actions might you take to bring renewal to the mainstream Church?

A Prayer for Renewing the Renewal

The 7 R's	What Must I Do?	Prayer for Renewal
Revive	Wake up	Revive us O Lord. **Awaken our minds and our hearts. More than this, Lord, help us wake up from our sleep. Revive our senses that we might feel Your constant touch, taste Your goodness, see Your beauty, and smell Your Sweet Presence.**
Replenish	Be an instrument of "completeness"	Replenish us O Lord. **Fill us up with Your Love. Satisfy our hunger and thirst. Nourish us with Your Divine Presence. Make us whole and complete in You. Heal in us whatever is unhealed. Cleanse in us whatever is impure. Transform us continually into Your image and likeness.**
Repair	Be willing to receive correction, and be eager to correct what needs to be corrected	Repair us O Lord. **Release your grace into our souls as a light of truth, convicting us of our sins and our failure to love. Make us willing to receive correction and eager to correct what needs to be corrected. Dispense your mercy Lord, that we might be restored to inner peace and joy. By Your Grace and mercy may we live our lives in Your Spirit.**
Rekindle	Be on fire	Rekindle us O Lord. **Set us on fire with love for You and for Your Church. Renew in us a passion for Your Church. Let it be as a burning flame in our souls, one that cannot be quenched. Place the gifts of Your Spirit deep within us and grace us to surrender to the fullness of their power each day of our lives.**
Revitalize	Be more vital	Revitalize us O Lord. **Teach us how we can be more vital to Your Church than we have ever been before. Give us your eyes to see, ears to hear, and hands to work for the vision You have for Your Church. Anoint us to be Your instruments that our work may be ever more meaningful to Your Church.**
Rejuvenate	Be ready to step aside	Rejuvenate us O Lord. **Show us the way to be humble. Grant us the courage and humility we need. May we never own or possess our ministries and positions of authority but rather continually mentor and raise up others to take our places.**
Regenerate	Become a legacy	Regenerate us O Lord. **May our lives become a legacy—a gift of holiness to pass on to future generations. May we grow so holy as Your Church that our lives would be lighted pathways to holiness, ways to be followed by our children and our children's children for generations to come.**

Picking Up Anchor—Putting Out Into The Deep

The challenge to renew the Renewal must be responded to with an honest appraisal of the current state of the local, diocesan, and national Renewal Movements. If in some areas of the country, the Renewal is alive and well, we must continue to follow the guidance of the Holy Spirit to keep it alive and well by doing the work of Pentecost. If, however, the fire of the Renewal appears to be dying out, we must discern which of these seven R's is most in need of renewal and then agree to be God's instrument to change what needs to be changed in order to re-ignite the fire of the Holy Spirit. We must be willing to propose new initiatives at national, diocesan, and local levels. We must also provide leadership for such initiatives, and actively support and encourage members to join us in implementing these initiatives.

We ourselves must agree to study, read, research, and share the Gospels, the teachings of the Church, and the writing of the saints and doctors of the Church. We must do this so that we keep our hearts and minds alert in a continuous process of on-going formation—spiritual growth and development. Such formation is not for a select few but it is for all of us. Each one of us is capable in some small way of studying Scripture, learning about our faith through the Catechism (1994) and learning about what the Church teaches in apostolic letters, documents, and encyclicals. If we cannot study on our own, we must study with others—a friend, a mentor, a spiritual director, our prayer groups, families, pastors, or pastoral leaders. If we do not know the answers, we are not exempt from finding them. If someone asks us a question about God, the Church, our faith, and we do not know the answer, we must respond, "Let's try to find the answer together."

Indeed, it may be very challenging for us to prepare ourselves to go out into the deep, but John Paul II tells us there is no time for complacency nor is there time to relax our commitment to Christ and His Church in this new millennium. John Paul II (2001) declares further that our experiences of the past [all of our years of living in Christ and through the power of His Holy Spirit] should compel and inspire in us, new energies for the Church.

We must only look ahead—not back. As we do, our steps must quicken for what awaits us is an exciting work of pastoral revitalization—a work involving all of us (John Paul II, 2001).

Finally, each one of us individually must discern if we are being called to renew our own life in the Spirit. If the answer is yes, we will be required to re-embrace the Pentecost mandate which bids us to go, proclaim, and heal, knowing that each of us has a critical role to play in renewing the Church. It is, in the end, up to each one of us, and all of us together, to renew our Renewal and thus renewal our Church. To do this, we must agree to be among those who revive, replenish, repair, rekindle, revitalize, rejuvenate, and regenerate the Church through the power of the Holy Spirit.

This much we know for sure—God's grace is sufficient to renew us individually and to renew His Church. The new millennium Pentecost question is, "Do you wish to be among those who set ablaze the firestorm of the Holy Spirit in the Catholic Church?" If so, are you willing to:

- Dispel one or more of the myths about the Catholic Charismatic Renewal?
- Assist parishes in developing themselves into schools of holiness, schools of prayer, and schools of communion?
- Rephrase some of the words you use to talk about your "life in the Spirit" in order that living in the Spirit will be more widely embraced by pastors, pastoral leaders, and ministers in the mainstream Church?
- Ponder the real Pentecost question?
- Design and implement the *Afterglow of the Eucharist* ministry at your parish?
- Teach one, several, or many persons how to pray *The Simple Blessing Prayer,* encouraging families and people at every level of parish life to pray with one another?
- Become involved with a traveling team that introduces life in the Spirit to parishes through Charismatic Masses and healing services?
- Become involved in the preparation of candidates for Confirmation and First Holy Communion through retreats that promote life in the Spirit?"

- Design and organize Mini-Missions after Sunday Mass that help Catholics connect the Gospel and teachings of the Church to their daily lives?

- Share with or teach others how to make the Mass more fulfilling and more grace-filled?

- Be a part of a mission team for your parish that promotes and supports people in living in the Spirit?

- Propose a plan to contact our brothers and sisters who have left the Catholic Church, interviewing them to find out why they left and designing remedies that "fix" the reasons they left and then invite them to come "home?"

- Go to any place you are called to proclaim the kingdom of God and heal?

- Be formed in your gifts for ministry and help form others in their ministry gifts?

- Consider which of the seven R's of spiritual renewal you most need to embrace in your life, your prayer group, and the Renewal?

- Pick up anchor and put out into the deep—the mainstream Catholic Church?

If you, your prayer group, the Renewal, or your parish community act on even one of these challenges, you will indeed be among those who renew the Renewal and thus renew the mainstream Church. You will become a vital gift and a part of the firestorm that is being set ablaze in the Catholic Church in this new millennium.

May we eagerly accept the challenges that lie ahead, calling us forth to renew the Church! May we perceive the new thing God is doing, listening just as the prophet Isaiah did. If we listen intently, we may just hear the Lord speaking the same words He spoke to Isaiah, and even more, "See I am doing a new thing. Do you not perceive it? I am sending my Spirit—as powerful and mighty as a firestorm—to renew my Church and the face of the earth! Will you allow me to use you? Will you go, proclaim my Father's kingdom as I did, and will you heal? Remember this— You are my disciples and I am with you always."

References

_____ (1994). *Catechism of the catholic church.* Liguori, MO: Liguori Publications.

The new life in the spirit seminars team manual (2000) (Rev. ed.), Locust Grove, VA: Chariscenter USA.

Jacobs, Rev Sam. (2000, January/February/March). *On the use of blessed oil.* Chariscenter USA Newsletter.

John Paul II. (2001). *Apostolic letter of the holy father pope john paul II: Novo millennio ineunte—On the arrival of the new millennium.* Boston: Pauline Books and Media.

John Paul II. (1986) *Encyclical letter of john paul II: The holy spirit in the life of the church and the world—Dominum et vivicante.* Boston: Pauline Books and Media.

John Paul II. (1998). *Apostolic letter of the holy father pope john paul II: Dies domini—On keeping the lord's day holy.* Boston: Pauline Books and Media.

Marazon, Renée A. (1998). *Deliverance prayer: A matter of wisdom, discernment, and obedience.* Perrysburg, OH: MAPS for life.

Marazon, Renée A. (2003). *The catholic handbook of child growth, development, and learning.* Perrysburg, OH: MAPS for life.

Marazon, Renée A. (1988). *The simple blessing prayer* [brochure]. Perrysburg, OH: MAPS for life.

Minutes from the Spiritual Leadership Council Meeting, Diocese of Toledo, Ohio, Ministry to Catholic Charismatic Renewal (2003, August).

Minutes from the Spiritual Leadership Council Meeting, Diocese of Toledo, Ohio, Ministry to Catholic Charismatic Renewal (2003, September).